I0434855

A Man's World

Other Books by Ellis Cose

The Press
A Nation of Strangers
The Rage of a Privileged Class

A Man's World

How Real Is Male Privilege—and How High Is Its Price?

Ellis Cose

HarperCollinsPublishers

A MAN'S WORLD. Copyright © 1995 by Ellis Cose. All rights reserved. Printed in the United States of America. No part of this book may be used or reproduced in any manner whatsoever without written permission except in the case of brief quotations embodied in critical articles and reviews. For information, address HarperCollins Publishers, Inc., 10 East 53rd Street, New York, NY 10022.

HarperCollins books may be purchased for educational, business, or sales promotional use. For information please write: Special Markets Department, HarperCollins Publishers, Inc., 10 East 53rd Street, New York, NY 10022.

FIRST EDITION

Designed by Nancy Singer

Library of Congress Cataloging-in-Publication Data

Cose, Ellis.
    A man's world : how real is male privilege—and how high is its price? / Ellis Cose.—1st ed.
      p. cm.
ISBN 0-06-017206-1
    1. Men—United States—Attitudes.   2. Men—United States—Psychology.   3. Sex role—United States.   I. Title.
HQ1090.3.C67   1995
305.32—dc20   95-14602

95 96 97 98 99 ❖/RRD 10 9 8 7 6 5 4 3 2 1

For and in memory of Tina Djedda,
who brightened every life she touched

CONTENTS

ACKNOWLEDGMENTS

To thank everyone who helped bring *A Man's World* to fruition would generate a list longer than any reader should be asked to wade through. I could not allow this book to be published, however, without acknowledging some huge outstanding debts. Keith Campbell was not only my researcher but a colleague in every sense of the word and a font of suggestions and ideas. Michael Congdon, my agent, served as sounding board, chief critic, and a valuable source of intellectual and emotional support. Wendy Wolf and Diane Reverand, my editors at HarperCollins, performed the heroic task of keeping me on track. The editors of *Newsweek*—in particular Maynard Parker, Mark Whitaker, Alexis Gelber, and Aric Press—were kind enough to accommodate my demanding book-writing schedule. Richard Steier helped to reduce the number of errors that made it into print. Lee Llambelis, my wife, brought not only a rare sensibility to her reading of the text, but, more important, an unwavering love that sustained its production.

Introduction

Stirrings of Discontent

More than three decades have passed since Betty Friedan discovered "the problem that has no name." *The Feminine Mystique* characterized the malady as "a strange stirring, a sense of dissatisfaction, a yearning that women suffered in the middle of the twentieth century in the United States." "There may be no psychological terms for the harm it is doing," wrote Friedan, but her words made clear that the damage was serious. The feminine mystique was "burying millions of American women alive" by keeping them from fully developing their capabilities.

In describing the affliction, Friedan pointed toward a cure: emancipation from electric waxers and washing machines, infiltration of the high-powered world of the mind (and men), construction of an independent identity. Women still have not arrived at that blessed state of equality—and disagreements over how to achieve it abound— but the fact that women had, and have, legitimate complaints has never been much in dispute.

Many men today also feel a sense of dissatisfaction. Yet the root of the problem is anything but clear. Men, as a group at least, are already on top. No one is denying them intellectual affirmation or demanding that they sacrifice their ambitions to a life of homebound drudgery. The most that is being asked (or so we are led to believe) is that they share what they already have. And why in the world shouldn't they be willing to divvy up the power and perquisites that men have hoarded so long?

Yet, as a growing chorus of male voices are making clear,

many men feel anything but powerful. Instead, they feel vulnerable, off balance, and in need of assistance to help them redefine their place in a newly confusing world. If their problem has a name, it is "bewilderment." Although in this gender-bending time of transition, most men are functioning just fine, they are also exceedingly confused. They are not at all clear what is expected of them—especially by women. Nor, even as they acknowledge the necessity for change, are they certain that they like the way things are headed.

If they are married, they feel trapped between work and their families. If they are divorced fathers, they fret about being lousy dads. If they are dating, they wrestle with bewildering new rules of romantic engagement. If they are working, they are haunted by the specter of sexual harassment charges. If they are unemployed, they face a crippling loss of identity. Whatever their situation, their rights and their roles are shifting—perhaps being downgraded—as demands and attacks on them increase.

In 1992, when pollsters Yankelovich Clancy Shulman asked men on behalf of *Time* and the Cable News Network whether they thought "the time has come for a men's movement to help men get in touch with their feelings and advance men's causes," 47 percent said yes, 42 percent said no, and 12 percent were not sure. That so many men feel in need of a champion and a guide may seem bizarre to those who believe that men have it made, yet it is obvious that many men don't feel they do.

Male insecurity and intergender conflict are as old as the story of Adam and Eve. Still, something new is coming through the complaints: a striking sense of despondency. If he is white, the American male is a prime target for male-bashing feminists, "diversity" trainers, and "equal opportunity" litigators. If he is black, he is considered a member of an endangered species. If he is Latino, he is told that his very culture is irredeemably sexist. Whatever his ethnicity, he is being held to a different standard—socially and even sexually—than were men of a generation ago. And whatever his class, he is being told that the age of male power, perquisites, and privilege has passed.

In 1994, following publication of *The Rage of a Privileged Class* (my previous book, focusing on the problems of black professionals), I received an avalanche of calls and letters from men and women of all races. Some of the most interesting correspondents were white men. Several complimented me on the book, many complained about it, but most eventually ended up making the point that, whatever problems racial minorities—or, for that matter, women or gays—might have, heterosexual white men also need sympathy. An especially poignant letter came from a Michigan resident, who said that he was "not sleeping well these days because of stress, fear, and depression." He went on to say that he had just turned fifty and was presently unemployed. "I used to have a family, two kids, a dog, 27 acres of land with a creek, two nice cars, insurance and self-respect," he wrote. "I don't have any of that any more." That he was a Vietnam veteran with a master's degree seemed not to count for much. The positions available in his field, he said, "are being swallowed up by women and minorities, with few exceptions." Though he had no grievance with minorities, he felt he had become one. "I've been treated like blacks probably were 35 years ago," like "garbage," he complained.

I didn't know quite what to make of his letter or how much credence to give his story, but clearly the man's sentiments were heartfelt. No less so were those of dozens of other white men who contacted me to say that their gripes were just as valid as those of the people in my book, that they, in short, felt like a persecuted class. My inclination to dismiss their arguments soon gave way to curiosity. And as I talked to a range of men—white, black, and other—and investigated subjects far afield of those explored in my previous book, I found I had stumbled onto a cornucopia of male befuddlement and discontent. Many of the men I encountered presented themselves not as the proud beneficiaries of the oft-assailed patriarchy, but as baffled innocents—vilified for sins they did not commit; victimized by discriminatory policies; and exasperated by mixed signals, double standards, and self-righteous hypocrisy.

One Queens (New York) resident claimed to have been brutally assaulted by his drug-abusing former wife. As he told the story, she cut him on the hand on two separate occasions, pummeled his head with a telephone, and threatened him with a gun (which he later found to be a fake). Yet when she absconded with their child, he realized how much the deck was stacked against him. Only after years of battle could he overcome the presumption that a child belonged with his or her mother. The experience has left him embittered. "It's like a man is hit by a car when this [custody] process begins," he said. "He's like dragged down the street with this child on his arm being dragged along with him."

New York-based journalist Michel Marriott attributes much of the increase in male anxiety to role disorientation. "There's no need for me to be a hunter," he noted. "There's no real need for me to be a provider. And I think what that sets up in men is very troubling. The way I deal with it is that I believe there are other things I can bring to the table; and I try to concentrate on some of those other things. Can I help the women in my life be better hunters? Can I pass along the tips that I've learned?" By the same token, Marriott said, he is trying to learn from the women around him, attempting to incorporate the way they view the world and to become less competitive and less "external" than he might normally be inclined to be. "I mean, I don't want to be Donahue, or Alan Alda—the all-sensitive male who cries at movies and stuff. . . . There're certain points [beyond which] I won't go, but there is definitely room for modification. And the only other model I have to look to for these other elements that are in me anyway are women."

Yet, says Marriott, he senses a conflict between the demands for an almost feminine softness and the expectation of a traditionally masculine toughness. "I think deep down inside all the liberation rhetoric, all the liberation literature, all the liberation philosophy . . . most women want to at least know that their man can be these things. That, if need be, he can be the protector. If need be, he can be the hunter. I think that's still important. I don't think they want it bandied around in their face all the time. So I think they want sort of more compassionate, more sensitive packaging; but deep down inside they want to know that coiled down in there somewhere is that old-fashioned guy that they can call on when they need him."

These clashing expectations, Marriott believes, account for many of the problems men and women currently experience. "I mean, that's a hell of a conflict for the man to carry around"—even if the man is "just by himself." "But then you [bring in] another person who may one day, or one moment, want this part of the man and one moment want the other part of the man without sending the right signals," and the potential for misunderstanding mounts. And to make matters more complicated, Marriott said, even in this era when many women make just as much as men, the pressure on men to be the providers is not substantially diminished. "Most of us are still convinced that we are looked to [to provide]. . . . If the family fails, if people are homeless, no one's going to point any fingers at Mrs. Marriott. They're going to say, 'What in the hell happened? What did Michel do?'" "Men," he stated, feel tremendous pressure "to have a certain sort of status and to maintain it. And no matter what anybody says, they feel responsible."

James Sniechowski, founder of the Menswork Center in Los Angeles, told me he has encountered scores of distressed men—"a broad spectrum of men who were basically saying, 'Something is going on here, and I'm not very contented with what's going on. I don't want to sound like a wuss and I don't know how to complain without either chastising myself for being a wimp or being chastised for being a wimp.'" Some of those men, Sniechowski noted, worried about how to raise sons or fretted over fathers they had never been able to get close to. Others resented what they perceived as overconcern for the hurts of women and minorities. They felt, "Nobody gives a shit about *me*. . . . They care about all these disadvantaged people, but they don't care about me." Sniechowski acknowledged the selfishness in that sentiment but added, "there's some real pain there."

The November 1994 election was widely read as something of a referendum on that pain. According to *Washington Post* exit polls, white men voted overwhelmingly for Republicans, whereas women voted primarily for Democrats. In normally Democratic Maryland, 63 percent of white men voted for a Republican for governor, while women divided their votes evenly between the two candidates; and in California, the Republican senatorial candidate won 59 percent of white males' votes even though he lost the race. Virtually every analyst who looked at the numbers attributed much of the lopsided white male support for Republicans to hostility to programs favoring women and blacks. Many white men "see the rights revolution in behalf of women and blacks moving beyond a level playing field to a system of exclusionary favoritism," wrote *Post* political reporter Thomas Edsall. Milton Viorst, writing in the *Los Angeles Times*, chalked up much of the white male vote to resentment at the loss of status. "A couple of decades ago, he was the sole breadwinner and the proud master of the household. Today, the two-income family has become the norm, and the wife often earns more than he does," he observed. Law professor and Democratic activist Susan Estrich evoked the image of her cousin Ben. "Ben is one of the angry white males who widened the gender gap in 1994 to the point of breaking records," she wrote in the *New York Times Magazine*. "He is not a sexist. He is happy to vote for female candidates. But he believes that the playing field is already level, that equality has been achieved and that women and minorities are now seeking special benefits at the expense of white men like him." Certainly, many politicians in California, including governor Pete Wilson, gave credence to that view with their support of efforts to eliminate programs favoring women and minorities. Thomas Wood, a leader of the fight to get the anti-affirmative-action measure on California's ballot, claimed he had personally suffered discrimination as a white man. He told me that a member of a search committee at a university once said to him, "Well, Tom, it seems, given your qualifications that you would just waltz into this job if you were the right gender, but you know, we have decided that we really do want to hire a woman."

That many white men feel particularly put upon is evident not only from reading the political tea leaves, but from listening to the rumbles of anger in the popular culture. "I'm like everybody in this room," West Coast comedian Jeff Wayne announced at one point during his performance. "I didn't get to pick the time period I was born in. I didn't get to pick my race or my gender." His advice to "all women and minorities: 'Don't blame me for the past. You want to

dig up my grandpa and kick his ass? You go right ahead.'"
Wayne planned to release highlights of his popular act as a
compact disk reassuringly titled *It's OK to Be a White Male.*

Obviously something profound is happening with
white American men, as a host of commentators have
noted. In a 1994 cover story titled, "White, Male and Worried," *BusinessWeek* concluded that many white men were
"feeling frustrated, resentful and most of all, afraid. There's
a sense that, be it on the job or at home, the rules are changing faster than they can keep up." "White Male Paranoia"
was *Newsweek's* name for the worrisome new syndrome
the magazine illustrated with a photograph of "D-Fens,"
the demented fed-up-with-the-world character played by
Michael Douglas in *Falling Down.* "Does Affirmative
Action Mean No White Men Need Apply?" was *U.S. News
& World Report's* take on the subject.

To see the rising discontent as something peculiar to
white men in America, however, would be to misread the
depth of male frustration. The same month that *Business-
Week* analyzed white American men's worries, the *Guardian*
(in an article titled, "Who's Afraid of the Big Bad
Women?") told its British readers of an International Men's
Day promoted by a "UK Men's Movement." Meanwhile
Maclean's told its Canadian readers of the difficulties that
men in Canadian society were having coping with changing gender roles. And in his 1994 book, *The Assassination of
the Black Male Image,* Earl Ofari Hutchinson argued that
black men are under siege, not only by white society but by
black female intellectuals.

In explaining why black men had not followed the lead
of their white brethren in 1994 and embraced the Republican party, Viorst theorized, "Maybe . . . a sense of insecurity is so natural to blacks that they take it for granted and
vote as they always have." A more likely reason, however,

is that black men, who have never felt fully accepted in the white man's world, are less than sympathetic to his gripes about policies favoring minority groups and females—especially when those gripes are championed by a political party whose rhetoric often crosses the line into the cesspool of racial demagoguery. Nor are black men as exorcised as white men about the decline of male power and privilege, since most don't believe they had very much of either to begin with. Moreover, many see their own situation as so much worse than that of whites—regardless of gender—that they dismiss white male worries as insufferably trivial. James Baldwin summed up the sentiment in *Nobody Knows My Name* when he admitted, "I am afraid that for a very long time the troubles of white people failed to impress me as being real trouble. They put me in mind of children crying because the breast has been taken away."

Yet what men of all races share is an investment in the notion of masculinity. Many also share a conviction that males are being unfairly assailed, that masculinity, whatever its color, has become (in the words of *Time* essayist Lance Morrow) "a bad smell in the room."

For the most part, this book focuses on issues that are common to men of all races. I generally do not attempt to categorize men—or their concerns and apprehensions—neatly by racial or ethnic groups. For although it is obvious that blacks, whites, Asians, and Latinos have different group experiences—and are burdened with different stereotypes—ethnicity is largely immaterial to much of what is happening to men today. Viewing the male experience primarily through a prism of ethnicity and race can obscure those issues that affect all men. In some respects, however, race remains relevant. White men as a group, as I suggested earlier, have traditionally occupied the preeminent rung on America's status ladder. African Americans have often been made to wonder whether black men had a place on the ladder at all. Any honest discussion of male privilege and power must at least take note of the racial disparity.

In fall 1994, New York's Whitney Museum of American Art presented an exhibition titled, "Black Male: Representations of Masculinity in Contemporary American Art." In the accompanying catalog, Thelma Golden, the curator responsible for the show, confessed: "In developing this project, I found myself faced with this thought: Since masculinity in general is about privilege as the internal force, is black masculinity a contradiction in terms?"

Certainly, not everyone would agree that masculinity is "about privilege as the internal force," but few would disagree that being a male, at least a white male, in American society has historically come with certain privileges. The right to vote, the right to inherit, the right to custody in the event of a divorce—all these rights and more were, at one time, conspicuously tilted in men's favor.

In our age, such rights have been more widely distributed, but certain male advantages clearly remain. A look at the leadership team of any *Fortune* 500 company provides sufficient evidence of that fact. More than 95 percent of top executives are male, according to a survey by Korn/Ferry International. Yet not only are woman excluded, in large measure, but so are certain types of men. Less than 1 percent of senior executives are black. Thus Golden raised (or implied) an interesting question: If being privileged is part of being male, are black males somehow exempt—if not from being considered male, at least from being considered privileged? If the answer is yes, the view that being male means being privileged quickly begins to unravel. For once black males are excluded, one is hard-pressed not also to exclude certain Latino men, poor men, blind men, gay men, uneducated men, and unemployed men. One eventually ends up concluding that privilege is not so much a male trait as it is a trait of males of a certain color, class, and rank.

Some people reject that line of reasoning. California psychologist Carl Faber, for instance, argues that even "disenfranchised" men still have power and privilege in relation to women. "From what I've read, the black women writing about how they feel black men abuse power with them and [white] men with white women, there's a whole pecking order of power and manipulation and hurt. . . . What I think I see is power being exerted by every group, and not just the high-powered white."

Sociologist Michael S. Kimmel makes a similar point. In an article published in *Society* in 1993, he contends, "The historical construction of masculinities, the reproduction of gendered power relations, involves two separate dimensions. . . . Masculinities are constructed in a field of power: 1) the power of men over women; 2) the power of some men over other men.

"Men's power over women is relatively straightforward. It is the aggregate power of men as a group to determine the distribution of rewards in society. Men's power over other men concerns the distribution of those rewards among men by differential access to class, race, ethnic privileges, or privileges based on sexual orientation—that is, the power of upper and middle class men over working class men; the power of white and native-born men over non-white and/or non-native born men; and the power of straight men over gay men. The constituent elements of 'hegemonic' masculinity, the stuff of the construction, are sexism, racism, and homophobia."

In real life, however, the power relationships do not always fit the mold. In other words, straight men don't necessarily have more power than gay men, whites don't always have more power than nonwhites, and men don't always have more power than women. What is one to make of the male-equals-power/female-equals-powerlessness equation when considering, say, the female chair of the executive committee of the Washington Post Company? It's difficult to argue that she has less power and privilege, in virtually any sense, than the man who drives the truck that delivers her newspaper. And even if we exempt from consideration the relative handful of women who are running large companies, what is the power-privilege relationship between a successful female attorney and a male homeless person? Or between a female banker and the man who takes away her garbage? Is the wife of a $500,000 a year corporate executive who has a college degree she never got around to using less privileged than the man who works at a job he hates for a salary that barely keeps a roof over his head? One could say, of course, that even those relatively powerless men have it better than some wretchedly powerless women, but that is not the same as saying that most women would care to be in those men's shoes or that the only relationship men have to women is one of the powerful to the powerless.

My point is not that men are less privileged than women. Clearly that is not the case. It is that to view the entire male-female interaction narrowly in terms of male privilege and female powerlessness is to miss all the complexity and subtlety of the real world.

Although it is true that American men have more of certain privileges than do American women, it is a small truth—or at least not a complete truth; it falls far short of illuminating the total relationship. It says little about what is happening with any individual man, or even with subgroups of men. It can't explain why so many men feel powerless—if not in relation to women, in relation to the institutions that dictate many of the rules of modern life. And it gives no insight into those prerogatives that women can exercise more easily than can men.

"The mythology still among women is that men have all the power; and if *you're* male, *you* must have all the power," said psychologist Judith Sherven. "I see it in my women clients. [There is] this sort of difficulty seeing men as singular individuals, who have singular lives separate and apart from *men,* and [a] willingness to just put blanket assumptions on any man."

There is something fundamentally sexist about an assumption that men, in a modern democracy, are the only ones empowered to act—that women are either naturally submissive to men, brainwashed by men, or afraid of men. To accept this assumption is to believe, in essence, that it is women's natural state to be dominated—that women have weaker wills or weaker brains or more fragile psyches. And that view seems at odds with everything that an enlightened feminism stands for. To reject this assumption, however, is to countenance the possibility that even in a society that systematically undervalues certain qualities in women, men can also feel undervalued and even abused.

Unfortunately, much of the discussion about gender these days proceeds from simplifying assumptions that deny people their individuality. Instead of being seen for who we are, we are divided into groups—those who are disenfranchised and those who are not, those who are oppressors and those who are oppressed, those who feel pain and those who cause it. And on the basis of such assumptions, many people conclude, for instance, that the plight of middle-class white women is similar to that of American blacks, since both groups are oppressed by white males.

The problem is that the groups seem to be "oppressed" in different ways. Blacks—and certainly black men—are not routinely invited to join the oppressor's family or to share the oppressor's wealth. And they certainly are not cherished by the oppressor in quite the same way. Nor is their political circumstance identical. Given their superior number, white women, theoretically, have the potential political power to take over just about every elective political body in America; blacks do not. Yet blacks tend to elect black representatives in areas where they are the majority, whereas women don't generally favor women. In fact, women seem to do the opposite. Despite the fact that both blacks and middle-class white women are discriminated against and that both have complex relationships with and feelings about white men, their situations are at least as different as they are alike. The relationship between the sexes is far more intimate and convoluted than is any conceivable relationship between the races.

If the sexes are at war, it is not a war that can be fought to the finish. We need each other too much for that. And yet, by assuming otherwise, some of our leading gender theoreticians have, in effect, established war colleges where we learn to assault each other verbally and to deny each other's distress. In such an exercise, members of officially disenfranchised groups have the obvious advantage of being able to claim the greater injury. So we have conversations in which one injured party essentially turns to another and says, "You can't be hurting from that little knife wound, since I, after all, have been shot." The obvious result is to dismiss the possibility that supposedly privileged and powerful men could have any possible cause for complaint.

Dr. Jean Bonhomme, president of the Atlanta-based National Black Men's Health Network, told me over breakfast one day how he had come to empathize with white men's pain. "[When I was in medical school], I met a white man who had been in Vietnam   He wasn't in medical school; he was in physician's assistant school. And he used to cry out in the middle of the night in the dormitory. I asked him what he was crying about, and he said he kept on seeing something that happened to him in Vietnam—which was he was talking to his friend, and the next thing he knew he was being wheeled into an operating room to remove shrapnel, the shrapnel being the skull bones of his friend. You know [an explosion] blew the guy's head up in front of him and the bone shards penetrated his neck. Now, I'm saying, 'They did *that* to a white man.' . . . There's a diversity of statuses in this society. Not everybody, just because they're white males, has had it good, you know. I think that stereotype is too rigid. And if that's what the white guys got, the black guys got it as bad or worse."

What struck me, as I researched this book, was how vulnerable many men—regardless of color—feel. One afternoon, for instance, I hopped into a taxi and soon found myself listening to a lengthy tale of woe. The cabbie revealed that he had been abused as a child in his parents' home. He did not specify how or by whom except to remark, "some of it was sexual." Shortly after his father's death, he had been sent away to live with relatives. Adjusting to his new life had been difficult. He was from a poor background, and his guardians' nice things and polite ways made him uncomfortable. Girls were even more bewildering. And they remained so.

I remained silent, unsure of the appropriate response, as he continued to tell his story. Though only in his early thirties, he was already in his fourth marriage. And he was not happy. Only recently he had accepted the possibility that his difficulty with relationships was connected to his childhood traumas. "No child should have to go through that," he mumbled, not specifying what *that* was. Whatever it was had been awful enough to persuade him not to have children. He was fearful, he said, of what might become of them, of what harm he might do to them. Then he added abruptly, as if anticipating a rebuke, "I *know* I'm not a pedophile." He dabbed at his eye, continuing to stare forward, making it impossible for me to see whether he was wiping away a tear. And as I stared at the longish brown hair at the back of his balding head, I realized that he had taken me to be a psychotherapist.

Given that he had picked me up at an institute dealing with psychological problems, the mistake made sense. Since I could think of no graceful way to correct his misperception, I tried to be supportive, telling him that he still had time to overcome his problems if he was willing to admit them and seek help.

He said that he was not very hopeful. His fourth marriage, though little more than a year old, was already in trouble. His wife had no interest in anything he had to say. There were few people, he confessed, to whom he could really talk. He was not comfortable entering into deep personal exchanges with his male buddies; if their chats became too intimate, he suspected they would drop him. He acknowledged that if he were in their place, he would probably act the same way.

He did have one male friend he could talk to, or at least whom he could talk at: "Whether or not he's an effective sounding board, as far as being able to relate or to understand what I tell him, I don't know. But if I buy him a couple of beers, at least he sits and looks interested, which might be all I need."

He laughed ruefully and said, "You know the thing was . . . I went through most of my adult life acting like nothing was wrong, just maybe chalking up the failed marriages to bad luck. The sad part about it is that I liked it better that way. I liked it better when I could just chalk this up to nothing but bad luck. I didn't like to see anybody get hurt in the situation, but if they did, well, jeez, I'm sorry. It just happened. But, now I'm finding more and more that maybe I wasn't all right. My last ex-wife put me in touch with a lot of that, although I didn't pursue it."

I asked him whether he had heard of men's groups, of people like him who got together to try to sort out their lives. "That would be a miraculous thing to be able to sit with them, with men, and be able to talk," he said softly, a hint of wonder in his voice. "'Cause I'm sure I'm not the only one who's having problems." We continued chatting until we arrived at my hotel, at which point he turned around and thanked me and added with a laugh, "Usually I just talk about the weather."

"Women make a lot of noise," Bonhomme told me at one point, "but it's not because more is happening to them. It's because the culture has given them more freedom to discuss it." Whenever a new member joins his discussion group, he said, "We have to give him a lot of time because it's like somebody who's been carrying around a hundred bricks and you tell him to put down one. That doesn't work. They all come crashing down."

Again and again, as I spoke with men (though not normally in taxis), I heard the sound of bricks falling from their shoulders. As I tried to understand what it all meant, I found myself reflecting on the voluble taxi driver, on his fear of opening up to his buddies and his comment that it would be a "miraculous thing" to be able to sit with men and talk. I am not prepared to call the exchanges "miraculous," but many of my discussions with men were, at the least, stereotype shattering.

Despite the obvious confusion among men and the apparent yearning for help in sorting it out, most men are about as likely to join a "men's movement" as they are to sign up for a knitting class. For one thing, men tend to be extremely wary of nurturing, touchy-feely males. In addition, the men's movement, as portrayed by the media, has generally come across as nothing more than an excuse for peculiar behavior: grown men prancing around the forest in very few clothes, beating drums and chanting Lord-knows-what, looking for all the world like actors in some exotic gay ritual, or maybe lunatics on holiday. Whatever they were up to, most "normal" men wanted no part of it. Even if the activity was not perverse, it did look awfully silly—making the men's movement a perfect subject for caricature. And, needless to say, the movement was skewered.

In a *GQ* article titled, "White Guys With Drums," Gerri Hirshey wrote: "In California forests, on arid Southwest mesas, on the industrial carpeting of urban therapy centers—boom-ba-BOOM!—men are beating tom-toms, their kids' toy drums, their BMW hubcaps. The men's movement is making more and more noise. Accountants, lawyers, mechanics, insurance adjusters are whomping away, hoping to summon the forgotten Wild Man within." "White guys with drums—that's some crazy rhythm," scoffed Hirshey. In the *New York Times Magazine* (in a piece called "White Men Can't Drum"), Sherman Alexie reported: "As a 'successful' Native American writer, I have been asked to lecture at various men's gatherings. The pay would have been good—just a little more reparation I figured—but I turned down the offers because I couldn't have kept a straight face." Author Alfred Gingold thought the men's movement so hilarious that he produced a book, *Fire in the John,* billed as a parody of movement texts, particularly Robert Bly's *Iron John* and Sam Keen's *Fire in the Belly.*

With television shows "doing these parodies of the men's movement, you know, white guys . . . going out and drumming and howling at the moon and dancing around the fire and this and that ... how could it not seem frivolous? How could it not seem like it was silly?," asked Stephen Johnson, a psychologist and executive director of the Men's Center of Los Angeles in Woodland Hills, California.

Even if the movement was not seen as wacky, many men and women would question its relevance. As Barbara Caplan, a director of the polling firm Yankelovich Partners Inc. (formerly Yankelovich Clancy Shulman), observed, women's goals since the onset of modern feminism have been so much clearer than men's. "Women begin with a real purpose, to change the establishment, to change the status quo," Caplan noted. "Men have reacted to the changes women have brought to the party." As more women have gone to work and the traditional breadwinner role has changed, men have been left asking, "If that doesn't define me, what does?" "Are [men] going to continue to react?" she wondered. "Or are they going to sit down and ask, 'Who are we? What do we want? What does it mean to be a man today?'"

Ron Henry, a Washington, D.C., lawyer and a volunteer at the Men's Health Network, believes that men face a task similar to the one that confronted women. "Our job is to recognize, as the women's movement has been doing for thirty years, that men are human beings, men are individuals, men have got inherent self worth, that there are things that a man wants to do in his life, for himself, for his family, and that's okay. . . . We've talked for thirty years about giving women choices, fine. But do men have choices? And to what extent have we lost sight of the fact that humanity is composed of two sexes, and if equality is what we're talking about, and if choice is an important thing, where's the choice for the guy?"

Men feel they must take all kinds of jobs simply to support their families, Henry said. And for that reason, he argued, society's most dangerous jobs, including the job of dying for one's country, are disproportionately relegated to men. "You find lots of people agitating for a woman's right to choose to go into combat, but you don't find anybody asking for an equal draft. Equality, if it's ever going to happen, has to be equality not just of rights but also of responsibilities.

"When guys talk to me, they say, 'Look, I could function in a society where the woman stays at home and it's the man's job to protect her; I can function in a society where the woman goes out and competes on equal terms with me. What I don't understand is this society that's neither, and it's a pick and choose smorgasbord of rights without responsibilities. That I have problems coping with,' they'll say."

In much of the public mind, as was noted, men's issues have become synonymous with a mythic quest for lost manhood, with beating tom-toms and baying at the moon and mouthing mumbo jumbo from ancient texts. In truth, as *A Man's World* makes clear, men have a much broader—and prosaic—range of concerns.

In the following pages, you will meet people from various walks of life trying to make sense of this second stage of the modern sexual revolution—a phase during which the demands and grievances of men increasingly compete with those of women as males and females alike struggle with the paradox of partial equality: with how to cope with a society that officially declares both genders to be equal and yet persists, in virtually every respect, in treating them differently.

How—many men ask—can they accept a notion of sexual equality that doesn't relieve them of the need to be the primary breadwinners or entitle them to a presumption of equal competence as custodial parents? Indeed, some of the most profound bitterness I encountered was among men who had been through divorces and thereafter concluded that society saw them as "wallets rather than nurturers," in the words of Dean Hughson of Braymar, Missouri. "I didn't know what it was to be a man until I was divorced," said Hughson, who is now working to try to make men realize "they can be fathers even in divorce." "I had the American dream," he told me, "but I lost my kids." And the reason for that loss, in his mind at least, is the society's blind assumption that women are better at parenting than are men.

Over the course of scores of numerous interviews with men like Hughson, I found myself concluding that the pain of fathers deprived of their children was singular and profound. Bonhomme told me, "I've found it easier to console people with cancer and AIDS than to console fathers who have lost all contact with their children. I mean, it is one of the most devastating things that can happen to anybody. We would think it was so cruel that a baby [would] be snatched out of her mother's arms and that she [would] not see it again. We would say, 'That woman will be so devastated. What a terrible thing to do to her. She's suffered so terribly. She will never get over the loss.' Well, exactly the same thing happens to fathers. They can't get over it. Their children mean more to them than anything else in the world. We think that men cannot love children. And I think that that's erroneous. I think that men have a huge capacity to love children. I think men love in a different way. I think they're protective. And they try to create a safe environment, but men can and have traded their lives to protect their children. They go to work in dangerous jobs. They'll face physical dangers and things of this nature. I mean, how can you say that a man can't love if he's willing to lay down his life for his child? He may not express it in the same way, but he loves very deeply. And a lot of the fathers that have lost their children, it's literally harder to console them than it is to console many people who are dying."

Bonhomme sees the area of custody as only one of many in which men's needs and potential contributions have largely been ignored. One of the results, he argues, is the difference in male and female life expectancies. "If you're going to create an environment that shelters women from the things that stress them," he said, "and fail to create an environment that shelters men from the things that stress them, of course you're going to have the disparity [in life expectancies]. It's like saying, 'We're going to take these people who have mild diabetes and give them low-sugar diets, but we're not going to take these people who have mild hypertension and give them a low-salt diet. Now, if you take that kind of intervention, you will erroneously conclude that hypertension is more dangerous than diabetes. The truth is that lack of treatment is more dangerous than treatment. . . . If you don't intervene in the things that are likely to kill people, of course they're going to die."

Much of Bonhomme's message, for the reasons discussed earlier, is anathema to certain theorizers. Men cannot be victims, they say in essence, since men are the victimizers. They see men's advocates as people whose primary purpose is to deflect attention from the legitimate grievances of women. Since the hostility between the opposing camps is often palpable, it's hardly remarkable that much of the dialogue about gender issues of late has degenerated into a dishonest debate in which opponents toss phony statistics and cooked numbers at one another to score victimization points.

In 1994, for instance, as the nation's attention focused on the O. J. Simpson case, male and female advocates for victims of domestic violence squared off against one another.

As men's groups issued statistics trying to make the point that battered men were just as common as battered women, Ronnie Weiss and Rita Smith of the National Coalition Against Domestic Violence released their own statistics, along with a statement by Weiss challenging the "tacit assumption that the same women who have been addressing the issue of violence" against women should solve the problem of violence against men. She went on to attack the numbers used to support the contention of husband battering as "highly biased and questionable" and "not backed up by hard data from criminal justice and health reports."

Weiss also pointed out that the shelter movement was started by women, who "got together, named the violence, spoke out and offered to help one another." She lambasted those who "still want to deny that violence against women is a problem." Finally, she declared, "I would like to issue a challenge to men in this country. If there is a problem—do something about it! Raise awareness. Raise money. . . . Do what women have done for years. Take real action against a real problem. Let's not stop asking questions about violence in the family. Let's just make sure we are asking the right ones." In the background sheet included with Weiss's commentary, Weiss and Smith provided some of the statistics their organization "believes most consistently and objectively document the realities of violence in the family." Prominent among them was the fact that, "according to the U.S. Department of Justice National Crime Survey, more than 2.5 million women experience violence annually." What they neglected to note was that most of these women were not victimized by family members—though most did know their attackers, as Weiss and Smith indicated. Only a fraction, just over a fourth, according to the Justice Department, constituted incidents of abuse by a husband, an ex-husband, or a mate—which was comparable to the number of women, just under one-fourth of the total, who were victimized by other women. Nor did they note that violence against men, who reported a total of 4 million assaults, was higher in every category except rape than it was for violence against women.

Such facts, of course, did not fit the particular political frame that Weiss was using. It is a frame that apparently only holds facts that indicate that women are victimized and men are persecutors. It has no place for, say, Susan Smith—the South Carolina mother charged in 1994 with killing her two young sons.

Yet, to illustrate just how pernicious political framing can be, let us imagine another political frame in which mothers are perpetrators and children are victimized. And let's apply that frame to the Smith case, setting aside whatever issues arise from her blaming a nonexistent black man for the crime. First, we would note that, according to Bureau of Justice statistics, women are more likely than are men to kill their children, and mothers are nearly twice as likely to kill their sons as their daughters. We would also note that though the number of children who are killed by their parents is relatively low, the number who are abused is much higher and grossly underreported. We might conjecture, on the basis of that underreporting, that literally millions of children are savagely battered by their mothers annually and that boys are at special risk.

We might therefore decide that the only remedy is to take to the streets and warn boys that the mother-son relationship is fundamentally rooted in hatred of or contempt for boys. Every mother, we would tell them, is a potential murderer. Such a statement would clearly be absurd, which, emphatically, is not to deny that the problem of child abuse exists and should be treated seriously. Yet, political framing leads to precisely these kinds of statements, which somehow, in certain quarters, seem a bit less ridiculous when made about men.

In a survey conducted by Yankelovich Partners Inc., nearly two-thirds of the women said they never thought men would understand them. Pollster Barbara Caplan did not interpret the responses as "male bashing," but as a simple acceptance of the probability that men may be fated to remain forever clueless about women. Interestingly enough, she saw that acceptance as a sign of hope, as an indication that women were exhibiting less angst about relationships, that "women are changing and saying, 'You don't have to understand me.'"

I'm not totally convinced that that's what the poll is saying. But I do accept the proposition that men and women, for the most part, are much less interested in bashing each other than in trying to figure out how to get along and how to navigate a world where gender roles are in flux. I don't expect this book to end the gender wars. Nor am I interested in making the case for yet another gender movement. Rather, I hope to help noncombatants step back and put into context the circumstances that have left many males befuddled and to provide some insights into the state of men as we approach the twenty-first century.

Chapter 1

MAN AS VICTIM

Despite the passage of laws making discrimination illegal and politicians of every stripe denouncing sexism as sin, most Americans are thoroughly convinced that gender still matters and that it matters quite a lot—that women, despite all the legal advances and consciousness-raising of the past few decades, are still not getting a fair shake. A Gallup poll taken in 1993 found that 71 percent of the women and 52 percent of the men believed that society favors men over women.

But though most men concede that women face special hardships, the sentiment is far from unanimous. Just over one-fourth of the men polled by Gallup believed that women "had a better life in this country" than men. Twenty-eight percent confessed to having felt resentment at the expectations society placed on them "as a man." And nearly half said that the women's movement had made men's lives harder over the past twenty years. (Sixty percent of the women agreed with that assessment.)

In short, the ranks of aggrieved men is large and apparently growing. "Whatever women have to put up with," they are saying in effect, "we don't have it so good either." To many ears, such a claim sounds ridiculous, grating, and whiny. Yet, an increasingly vocal group of activists are making that argument—and not all of them are feminist-bashing Rush Limbaugh clones.

The patron saint of disgruntled men is a former feminist named Warren Farrell, who counts among his accomplishments the fact that he was repeatedly reelected to the New

York board of the National Organization of Women. He became expert, he confesses in *The Myth of Male Power*, "at saying what women wanted to hear." But then one day Farrell began to question why women but not men were listening. "I reviewed some of the tapes from among the hundreds of women's and men's groups I had started. I heard myself. When women criticized men, I called it 'insight,' 'assertiveness,' 'women's liberation,' 'independence,' or 'high self-esteem.' When men criticized women, I called it 'sexism,' 'male chauvinism,' 'defensiveness,' 'rationalizing,' and 'backlash.' I did it politely—but the men got the point. Soon the men were no longer expressing their feelings. Then I criticized the men for not expressing their feelings!" So Farrell changed his tune and tried harder to incorporate men's experiences into his presentations. He found the transition unsettling. "Almost overnight my standing ovations disintegrated. After each speaking engagement, I was no longer receiving three or four new requests to speak. My financial security was drying up." When I encountered Farrell in late 1994, he said he was still paying the financial price for changing his perspective, but his fate has not deterred him or his like-minded brethren from continuing to voice their controversial views.

Mel Feit, executive director of the New York-based National Center for Men, admits that the proposition of male victimhood is not an easy sell. "Thinking about a men's rights movement is a little like thinking about a movement for the rights of wealthy people. . . . It doesn't make sense because the fact is that men do run the world. The president and vice president are men, always have been," and so, he notes, are most senators and governors—as well as the heads of most major companies. "Men make the rules, enforce the rules, and control the wealth," he concedes. So why in the world is he talking about men's rights?

Part of the answer, he said, is that the men who are running the world don't represent the men he cares about. "Now I would argue that for every man who is up there making an important business decision, there are probably twenty or thirty men who are in deep despair, who have no control over their lives. The fact of the matter is that to generalize about the condition of men and women based on one percent of men and women . . . creates a false impression of what's really going on. I don't have a Robin Leach mentality. I really don't care about the people on the top floors of the skyscrapers. I care about the people on the street who are suffering. And my view is that a lot of men are suffering. So it is accurate to say that some men run the world, but most men don't. I know a lot of men; I don't know a single one who's ever been president of the United States." When you put things in the proper perspective, he insisted, "a different picture, a different reality, emerges. And I see that in many cases men are really disadvantaged and victimized."

Feit, a bookish man of forty-three with long reddish hair, begged forbearance as he laid out his case. He compares himself to someone in, say, the fourteenth century who believed the world was round but was not believed because others were loath to change their perspective. He knows perfectly well, for instance, that women make less money on average than do men, but to him, that does not necessarily mean that men have the advantage. "Earning money means getting out of a warm bed when it's cold and snowing outside and going to a job you hate so you can pay the rent, so you can feed the kids. Earning money is not an empowering thing. It's spending money— that's where the power lies. And it turns out that women spend most of the money."

Several years ago, Feit said, he went to Macy's and painstakingly surveyed all the floor space devoted to men's and women's things. He concluded that women were apportioned more than four times as much space as were men. (A Macy's spokeswoman maintained that the ratio was much smaller. Of areas that could be classified by gender in the main

New York store, she said, 280,000 square feet were devoted to women and 150,000 were devoted to men. "Eighty-five percent of our customers are women," she explained.) In a department store in Chicago, Feit claimed, the ratio was even more lop-sided—roughly ten to one in favor of women. "These places are not museums," he snorted. "They are commercial establish-ments." They allocate floor space on the basis of what sells, and most of what they are selling seems, to him, to be for women. It is simplistic, he acknowledged, to conclude from such statistics that women are better off. But why, he asked, "is it any less valid to look at the statistics on spending than on earning?" Why, he wanted to know, "when we discuss economic privi-lege and power with respect to men and women" does no one raise such issues?

Feit is well practiced in this debate. Statistics roll off his tongue like rainwater. Some 90 percent of homeless adults are men, he insisted, as are 80 percent of suicides. "This society focuses excessively on the idea that young girls have self-esteem problems and we've got to take our daughters to work. But the boys are putting guns to their heads and blowing their brains out at a rate that is tremendous," he railed.

"Something like 70,000 Americans are seriously injured on the job every year. Nearly 60,000 of those are men. And we're talking about a hostile working environment for women?" (Feit's figures are different from those of the U.S. Bureau of Labor Statistics, which reports that roughly 2.3 million Ameri-cans suffer serious nonfatal work-related injuries and illnesses annually, of whom about two-thirds are men.) "For that man who is injured on the job and will never be whole, or that man who is driven to suicide . . . it's not a man's world," he added. But because of the public perception that men are in charge, "there is a lack of sensitivity to the ninety-nine percent of men who don't run the world."

The truth is that "men are sicker than women in almost

every category. The statistics are not good at all. . . . When you compare suicide rates, homelessness, disease, what you find is that men are doing really terrible," society's preoccupation with women's health notwithstanding, Feit said. And prisons are filled with men. "If you believe as I believe that men and women are inherently equal, that all people are created equal, if it turns out that any group of people wind up being incarcerated at any higher percentage, whether it's blacks who are being incarcerated more than whites or men being incarcerated more than women, you have to ask fundamental questions about how it got that way," he insisted.

Another obvious question is how did Feit get this way? How did he manage to come to the view that men are so victimized? It appears that he has felt this way forever. As a young man growing up in the New York area, he was frustrated "with the fact that no one else seemed to see what I saw." "I'm talking about when I was a kid eight or nine years old and discovered that I would be drafted because I was a boy and that girls wouldn't be," he adds. And as he grew older and found himself "going to school with women who were demanding their equal rights at a time when they had complete exemption from fighting a horrible war," his resentment grew.

As a college student, who, in the end, was not drafted, he had not yet discovered his life's work. "The thing about being a men's rights activist is that it's not the sort of thing that you think about doing when you're a kid." So he majored in physics, got a graduate degree in communications, and ended up working as the public relations director of a theater company. His sense of outrage did not go away. He felt a call to activism, and that was not altogether comforting.

"It's not the kind of thing that you can easily deal with in your twenties because it sort of says you're a little bit at odds with society," Feit said. "It complicates relationships with women. It's the sort of thing that you've just got to suppress.

You know, it's there, and you're not agreeing with what other people are saying, but it's not something you really want to have to deal with."

So throughout his twenties, he tried as best as he could to bury those feelings, but they "don't suppress well." The sense that "something is wrong" festers. "And with me, it just got to a point in my thirties when I said, 'I feel something; I want to talk about it. I want to educate people about my view.' And I simply decided maybe I could lecture on college campuses or do something else with it. And that's just the way it started."

After repeatedly offering himself up, he finally started getting invitations to speak at colleges. He also managed to get on television. By late 1987, with some small financial support from his family, he was ready to organize. He started with a small group of guys in his Brooklyn apartment and eventually was taking calls from people from around the world.

The organization is still small. Feit counts only 2,700 members, but he quickly adds, "We're in almost every state and have members in Canada, England, and Scotland. . . . And so, from a tiny office I have in my home and with a small staff, we're reaching far."

The message he is peddling is not only that men are victimized, but that many are hurting. And part of the reason, in his estimation, is that women have been less than honest. He has found it difficult, for instance, to maintain a serious romantic relationship with a woman ever since he took up his present line of work. "And the sense that I feel personally as a man, who is doing work that I like but does not make a lot of money doing it, is that most women will find me undesirable. They're not looking at my heart. They're not looking at the kind of companion that I would be over a lifetime. They're measuring my worth as a human being based on the size of my bank account. And I and a lot of other men are resentful of that." Men like himself have found that women are "just plain not interested." Hence, they "feel angry at being trapped in a role that values them for what they achieve externally and not for who they are."

Feit recalled reading a magazine article that featured very successful women—people, in many cases, making six-figure incomes. Despite their obvious prosperity, most of these women were unwilling to take financial responsibility for a man. "They said that when they [go] on a date, they expect a man to pay. And they expect to marry up. They expect that when they find a man to marry, he will be doing even better. It becomes almost impossible to do better financially when a woman is making six figures. I think that there is a sense among a lot of men that . . . women in society really do judge us based not on who we are, but on what we accomplish and what we've achieved. And . . . therefore if you're not success- ful, you're a failure as a man, as a person. And a lot of men are starting to ask questions about that. My sense of it is that it is the same women who are rightfully demanding equal pay and promotions in the workplace who refuse to take the responsi- bility of supporting families.

"When we take our daughters to work, one thing we should be educating them about is the responsibilities that go with making it in the world of work," Feit added. "And that means the responsibility of supporting a family. It may mean the responsibility of supporting a man, or at least paying the majority of the household expenses, because if you are doing very well, maybe there's a man who's a struggling artist who lives in a small studio apartment who women seem not to be attracted to."

He and men like him, Feit noted, "learned from the women's movement. We paid attention and we learned, and we changed." And now, he said, they feel abused. He acknowl- edged that many men's activists are basically conservative and wish nothing more than to keep women at home, but he thought most are "progressive men who wanted social change that would lead to a much greater equality and freedom for all human beings, and somewhere along the line felt that we were betrayed.

"The sense of betrayal I think men feel is that feminists didn't mean it," Feit stated. *They didn't mean it.* I mean, we learned, we listened. The rhetoric is wonderful. It's about human beings not trapped by an accident of birth, not limited because of that. It's about real equality. It's about intimacy in relationships. It was such a wonderfully uplifting message. What happened was that several of us men said, 'This is good. Now let's try to apply these concepts to our lives and see how we change.' And in the course of doing that, what we found was that the same women didn't want us to change. They wanted the man to be the provider and the breadwinner and the soldier. . . . We felt we were, in a sense, deceived. When we wanted to participate, we found that 'free to be you and me' meant 'free to be whatever I wanted to be if I happened to be a woman.' But the same concepts didn't necessarily apply to men."

Feit is certainly not a typical man, but neither is he alone in his outrage. A small but quickly growing body of literature has sprung up from men who aren't at all shy about trotting out their victim credentials.

Herb Goldberg's *The Hazards of Being Male*, first published in 1976, is one long lament of the male's condition. In the foreword to his tenth-anniversary edition, Goldberg summed up the problem he identified: "Specifically, men lived about eight years less than women, died from almost all major diseases at significantly higher rates, and as young boys suffered from autism, hyperkinesis, schizophrenia, stuttering, and behavior disturbances, leading to hospitalization at vastly higher rates. Indeed, there was nary a survival or health statistic that didn't show a disproportionately negative rate for men, not to mention the impoverished quality of most men's personal lives.

Most men were effective work machines and performers, and everything else in their lives suffered."

Many of the complaints, Goldberg believed, stemmed from man's estrangement from his emotions, his body, and even his sexuality as he struggled to exemplify a self-destructive male ideal. That role required, among other things, that man face danger fearlessly, that he maintain control even if it killed him, and that he sacrifice virtually everything for success. To do anything else was to be less than manly. So he was trapped in the role of a "cardboard Goliath," fearless except when it came to expressing his feelings, fated, if he was not careful, to a life of wretched loneliness and perhaps overdependence on a potentially treacherous woman. Even as man destroyed himself and watched the gap between female and male life expectancy widen, woman was increasingly free to be whatever she desired, from homemaker to executive, with no threat of social disapproval.

"By what perverse logic," asked Goldberg, "can the male continue to imagine himself 'top dog'? Emotionally repressed, out of touch with his body, alienated and isolated from other men, terrorized by the fear of failure, afraid to ask for help, thrown out at a moment's notice on the occupational junkpile when all he ever knew was how to work, it is perhaps surprising that the suicide statistics are only what they are."

Warren Farrell made many of the same points in his 1993 book, *The Myth of Male Power,* and his tone is even more indignant. He is angry at the psychological, rhetorical, and physical abuse that modern-day society heaps upon men; at the way it makes men fodder for war and calls it glory; at the fact that men are put through such hell that they kill themselves at rates several times higher than women. He is especially angry at feminists who scorn men as molesters but don't acknowledge men's role as heroes or who complain about job discrimination without admitting that men have always done such work as logging, construction, and mining that is more likely to kill them. If anyone is favored in society, he suggested, it is women, who, by his account, spend more money for their pleasure, have more spent on them for their health, and are coddled and protected to such a degree that they can get away with murder simply by saying they "felt helpless." Such solicitude for women, at virtually any cost, he fumed, "leaves us with a Battered Women Syndrome but no Battered Men Syndrome—as if women were the only victims of learned helplessness."

Aaron Kipnis, author of *Knights Without Armor,* likewise argued that "the conventional notion that men are somehow more privileged than women is starting to look like a bad joke." The fact is, he claimed, "many of us have, at various times, felt victimized, scapegoated, manipulated, dominated or abused by women." Indeed, in Kipnis's estimation men are so beleaguered and beaten down that they are in need of what he calls a "New Male Manifesto," which he dutifully wrote. That manifesto contains such aphorisms as "Men are beautiful. Masculinity is life-affirming and life-supporting."

A visit to any major library or large bookstore could yield a hefty stack of books that essentially make the point that the male bashers got it all wrong: that men are not powerful, but consumed with feelings of powerlessness, that their identity is fragile, their options are limited, their contributions are discounted, and their very essence is reviled.

To what extent such sentiments reflect the feelings of men in general is impossible to say. As all the authors point out, men are ashamed of owning up to such feelings. Most would rather die a thousand horrible deaths than admit that they are in pain. Yet, behind the macho mask, we are told, lies the face of frustration and, in some cases, despair.

"It's a whole new ball game for men," says Stephen Johnson, of the Men's Center of Los Angeles in Woodland Hills, California, "and there's a certain amount of confusion and bewilderment, if not beleaguerment, among men [who] are feeling that 'We're still being asked to be the primary breadwinners or to be men in a certain kind of traditional role structure, but at the same time, we're being elbowed and pushed aside and being told that we're supposed to be much more considerate and conscientious and compassionate about women and their issues—and as the victims of men. *And what about us?*'" Consequently, he says, all these men-as-victim books have cropped up, written out of the realization that if one is going to talk about victims, then "men are victims, too. . . . They're victims of the system where basically they're supposed to live up to a particular role structure but at the same time they're being told to act in other ways that are in opposition to that."

Alvin Baraff, founder of MenCenter in Washington, D.C., acknowledged that many people may see such a lament as bizarre, especially given the widespread perception that "men have everything already." Yet, he asks, "if they have everything already, why is their suicide rate so much higher than women's? Why do they get so many more heart attacks than women? Why do they die so many years earlier than women? I mean there has to be a reason. Why do they become alcoholics and drug addicts more than women?—though women are catching up. There are reasons."

Life for men, he added, "looks good on the outside, but men are not walking around that happy. And here's the result of it: suicide [and] huge numbers of car accidents, half of which can be unconscious suicides or self-destructive attempts. We don't have a happy bunch of men." Moreover, he stated, men are being constantly criticized, so much so that it seems that "everything a man does is bad. He's the abuser. He's the control freak. He's the rapist. *Nothing good!* [There's] nothing good being said." The result, said Baraff, is "anger and confusion."

Ellen McGrath, a clinical psychologist who heads the Psychology Center in Laguna Beach, California, and is the author of *When Feeling Bad Is Good,* finds that more men than ever are coming to her with problems. Though generally successful in their careers, they are floundering in their personal lives and are seeking female therapists as "relationship coaches." They want to understand women and how to cope with pressure. Some of the tension comes from corporate downsizing and the concomitant job insecurity; some of it is a result of the workplace opening up to women and minorities. Men are telling her, McGrath noted, that they "can't handle it." Company presidents, for instance, will say, "I know it's changing. Goddamn it, I don't want to." And then they will compare their situations to war and talk of their dreams of early retirement—even if they can't afford it. Their problems are often aggravated, McGrath believes, by women's insensitivity. "Women don't want to acknowledge that men are vulnerable," she observed.

The sense of bewilderment is not limited to those men who want to go back to the 1950s. In many cases, as Feit makes clear, it is felt most keenly by those who fancied themselves on the cutting edge of change. It is just such avant-garde types who are disappointed, as Feit put it, that new lifestyle choices for women have "not been accompanied by any similar freedom or change for men." They, in essence, want the same options they believe women already have: the option to drop out of work for a while, maybe even several years, and to spend time with their children or otherwise search for self-fulfillment without being made to feel as if they have somehow stopped being men.

Dr. Jean Bonhomme, president of the National Black Men's Health Network, notes that society has spent a great deal of time accommodating women's changing needs. "And I think the doors have got to open both ways," he says. Just as women are assuming traditionally male roles, "men have to be allowed to come more into women's traditional roles."

Feit contends not only that men must be allowed to be the

primary caretakers, but that they must be permitted to be as passive and as conventionally unambitious as are many women. He also believes that women must be as willing as men to accept the risk of sexual rejection.

"There is a feeling among many of the men in our group that in this culture it's the man who asks and it's the woman who decides," Feit said. "And sexuality is kind of warped by it." And because it's always "still up to men to risk the rejection," he observed, "it's very difficult to know what to do now. If you're not aggressive enough, you sleep alone. If you're too aggressive, you're going to be in serious trouble. You can lose your job."

So why, if men's lot is as rotten as Feit lets on, aren't more men making their unhappiness known? Why aren't the streets filled with tormented men giving voice to their pain? Why, when the Gallup Organization asks the question directly, do more men say that society favors men than say it favors women? The reason, in Feit's estimation, has a lot to do with pride.

"'Thou shalt not complain' essentially is a credo of masculinity," Feit said. "What we're asking men to do is to whine, is to complain, is to admit that in some respects women may have it better. Maybe that makes a man feel vulnerable, disadvantaged."

Most men, Feit believes, "are still raised to be chivalrous of women, to want to protect them. And to start to criticize the feminist movement is seen by many men as being critical of women." He senses a change, however. He is moved, for instance, by the reaction he gets when he appears on talk radio. Men "get on the line and just let it rip. I mean there are things that are really bothering them."

Obviously, some of Feit's complaints are frivolous. It's true that stores allocate a substantial amount of space to women's garments. It's also true that women spend considerably more for clothes than men do. According to the U.S. Bureau of Labor Statistics, even single women, who earn less than men on average, invest more in apparel. And the typical household or "consumer unit," in Bureau of Labor Statistics lingo, shells out over 60 percent more on women's clothes than on men's. The entire "apparel and services" category, however, accounts for less than 6 percent of the typical household budget. The bulk of spending, roughly two-thirds, goes to housing, transportation, and food—expenditures from which both genders obviously benefit. Given that fact, it's difficult to imagine many men getting exercised over the clothes-shopping gap—unless they happen to disapprove of the particular attire their women choose to wear.

Some of Feit's complaints—and he is not the first or only one to make them—cannot be so easily dismissed. Neither American culture, nor any Western culture, for that matter, is particularly reverential of male life. Men are significantly more likely than are women to work in the so-called death professions. They are three times more likely to be murdered. And they are more than four times more likely to kill themselves.

In 1993, for instance, men accounted for 92 percent (5,790 out of 6,271) of the deaths from work injuries in the United States. They constituted 90 percent of the work-related highway fatalities; 82 percent of the homicides; and virtually all the deaths in the mining, logging, construction labor, and forestry industries. Men's advocates believe that it is no coincidence that men predominate in such high-risk professions.

Warren Farrell, author of *The Myth of Male Power*, cites the phenomenon as evidence of a pernicious double standard that makes men the "disposable sex." He wonders why men get so little credit for literally putting their lives at risk to feed and clothe their loved ones. The lack of empathy, he suggests, has made "generations of men feel a bit unappreciated." That lack of appreciation, in the eyes of many men, extends far beyond the relatively small number of men in highly hazardous work.

Many see no more blatant sign of male neglect than the widening of the male-female life expectancy gap. "Are men really more privileged than women when their life expectancy is as much as nine years less than women's?" asked Aaron Kipnis in *Knights Without Armor.* Farrell made much the same point: "In 1920 women in the United States lived ONE year longer then men. Today women live SEVEN years longer. . . . Is the seven-year gap biological? If it is, it wouldn't have been just a one-year gap in 1920.

"If men lived seven years LONGER than women, feminists would have helped us understand that life expectancy was the best measure of who had the power. And they would be right. Power is the ability to control one's life. Death tends to reduce control. Life expectancy is the bottom line—the ratio of life's stresses to life's rewards," writes Farrell.

Reality, however, is more complicated than Farrell would lead one to believe. In 1920, the gender gap did favor women a good deal less than it does now. Men were then expected to live to the ripe age of 53.6 years and women to the age of 54.6 years. (Life expectancy is defined as the average number of years that newborns would live if they experienced the same age-specific death rates as the present population.) Even those projections were considerably higher than at the turn of the century, when neither men nor women were expected to reach the age of 50. By 1992, life expectancy for all groups had risen significantly. It stood at 79.1 years for women and 72.2 for men—a gap of 6.9 years. (The largest gain in life expectancy during the 1980s occurred among white men.) In short, simply pointing to the magnitude of the gap, when life expectancy for both men and women has greatly increased since the early part of the century, provides little insight into why it has grown.

Women in primitive times apparently also outlived men. Dennis Van Gerven, an anthropology professor at the University of Colorado, told the 1994 meeting of the American Association of Physical Anthropology that an analysis of mummified human remains showed that between A.D. 500 and A.D. 1500, women in the Sudanese Nubia were the healthier sex. An account of the findings by a Reuters correspondent reported: "Life expectancy in those days was about age 15, but women lucky enough to survive until age 20 could be expected to live another 22 years, while 20-year-old males averaged only another 20 years." Van Gerven called the findings "a nice counter to a culture that views strength as masculine."

Some of the reasons for the modern gap are obvious. Women are much less likely than previously to die in childbirth, whereas men are more likely to be murdered. Men are also more likely to drink and smoke to excess. A Canadian study suggested that simply by not smoking, a typical thirty-five-year-old man gained a life expectancy advantage of 5.8 years over his smoking counterpart. Young men disproportionately die in traffic accidents, and older men are more vulnerable to heart disease and lung cancer. Men are also exposed to more carcinogens in the workplace. In Western societies, AIDS—a relatively small but increasingly important factor—is more likely to strike men than women.

A number of studies have found that men and women handle sickness differently. Women seem to have more but less serious illnesses. They also are more likely to complain and to seek treatment. The more stoic men suffer silently and die.

Genetic differences also play a role. It is well established, for instance, that estrogen provides some measure of protection, that between puberty and menopause, women have a significantly lower risk of heart disease than do men. On the other hand, male sex hormones seem to increase the risk.

The difference between male and female life expectancy in the United States is roughly equal to the gap in anticipated life spans between blacks and whites. Although there is a consensus that the racial gap could be wiped out with changes in lifestyles and living conditions, there is less agreement on how to eliminate the gender discrepancy.

In 1987, the National Institute on Aging called a conference to sort out the state of knowledge on the issue. At that time, the size of the male-female life-expectancy gap in industrialized countries ranged from four to ten years. The multidisciplinary group reached no agreement on how to eliminate it, though several researchers remarked on the fact that it was evident even in the womb. Whereas 115 males were believed to be conceived for every 100 females, only 105 actually were born.

In 1994, when I asked Kenneth Manton, a Duke University demographer who specializes in morbidity calculations, whether he thought the gap could be erased, he replied, "Even if you balance up things on the social scale fairly carefully, I think you would still see some of the difference." For the moment, that seems to be as close to a consensus as the experts are likely to get.

Certainly, if the world could figure out a way to get men to stop smoking, stop drinking, and stop driving recklessly, the gap would close substantially. The gap would decrease even more if we could figure out a way to stop homicide and suicide, and it would narrow more still if we could make work environments safer and persuade men that it is all right to seek relief from physical and emotional pain.

To the extent that a reluctance or inability to do any of these things reflects an acceptance of male "disposability," Feit and company are justified in asking men to "whine" and even in portraying men as victims. The truth is that men are not so much victims of feminism, female anger, or female hypocrisy as of the inability to stop self-destructing. The solution to that problem seems to lie less in figuring out why many women are bashing men than in finding out why so many men seem determined to kill themselves.

*   *   *

But what of one group of self-described victims who are less and less reluctant to grouse in public—who argue, at length and in increasingly strident tones, that the problem is not with them but with a society that has abandoned any pretense of operating as a meritocracy? What, in short, of the storied and suffering angry white man? How much truth is there to the notion, prevalent in political debate, that white men constitute a persecuted class; that affirmative action and politically correct rhetoric have left them—as insinuated by my correspondent from Michigan—not much better off than blacks were thirty-five years ago?

It is a notion that, as James Baldwin suggested, evokes in many people a contemptuous disbelief. If it does not exactly put one "in mind of children crying because the breast has been taken away," it may induce thoughts of self-centered brats who can't stand to share their toys with anyone else. It certainly doesn't elicit a lot of empathy—at least not among those who are not white males. As one female executive put it, "I have a hard time taking this white male victim stuff seriously." Yet, as the exit polls and the myriad magazine covers devoted to white male angst attest, a number of white men are fuming. They reject the suggestion that they are trying to turn back the clock. All they want, they say, is to be treated fairly—which, for starters, would mean eliminating policies that favor women and minorities over white men.

Bruce Fein, a former general counsel of the Federal Communications Commission, told a congressional subcommittee in early 1995 that a program encouraging minority ownership of broadcast stations amounted to state-sanctioned racism. "It rewards sellers of broadcast properties with lavish tax savings if the purchaser satisfies racial or ethnic criteria reminiscent of apartheid. In other words, the FCC bribes sellers to discriminate against buyers whose only sin is to have been born white," he declared. Thomas Wood, a leader of the California anti-affirmative-action initiative, told a reporter for the *New York Times* to count him "among those angry men," and added, "The worm has turned."

In *The Rage of a Privileged Class*, I wrote: "When the talk turns to affirmative action, I often recall a conversation from years ago. A young white man, a Harvard student and the brother of a close friend, happened to be in Washington when the Supreme Court ruled on an affirmative action question. I have long since forgotten the question and the Court's decision, but I remember with absolute clarity the young man's reaction.

"He was not only troubled but absolutely choleric at the very notion that 'unqualified minorities' would dare to demand preferential treatment. Why, he wanted to know, couldn't they compete like everyone else? Why should hard working whites like himself be pushed aside for second-rate affirmative action hires? Why should he be discriminated against in order to accommodate *them*? His tirade went on for quite a while; and he became more indignant by the second, as he conjured up one injustice after another.

"When the young man paused to catch his breath, I took the occasion to observe that it seemed more than a bit hypocritical of him to rage on about preferential treatment. A person of modest intellect, he had gotten into Harvard largely on the basis of family connections. His first summer internship, with the White House, had been arranged by a family member. His second, with the World Bank, had similarly been arranged. Thanks to his nice internships and Harvard degree, he had been promised a coveted slot in a major company's executive training program. In short, he was already well on his way to a distinguished career—a career that, for him, was made possible by preferential treatment."

My point, of course, was that many of the arguments made against affirmative action are more than a little disingenuous; and I proceeded to explain in *The Rage of a Privileged Class* why

I believe that those who claim that huge numbers of white men are being displaced by affirmative action programs are out of touch with mathematical reality. Blacks and Hispanics make up 10 percent of the total employees in managerial and professional positions and white males make up 46 percent, I noted; so if one assumed that, say, 10 percent of white males had lost promotions because of affirmative action, it followed that "nearly half of those blacks and Hispanics had received promotions they didn't deserve at the expense of white men. Yet, if so many minorities are being promoted ahead of whites, why do black and Hispanic professionals, on average, earn less and hold lower positions than whites? It could be that despite being promoted unfairly, minority professionals are so incompetent that whites still manage to get ahead of them on merit. Or it could be that those white males who assume that minorities are zooming ahead of them are way off the mark."

Corporate consultant Ted Jones has an explanation for the perception that minorities and women are taking most of the good jobs. "Looking at the facts of what's really going on you find out they [white males] are getting the majority of everything. Then, why would they believe [they are not]?" All people, he concluded, "need a certain amount of illusion to face reality."

Even if the numbers don't support the outrage, the outrage cannot be denied. Lawrence Baytos, president of Diversity Implementation Group, has discovered that focus groups for white males can summon forth tirades against minority privilege. In *Designing and Implementing Successful Diversity Programs*, he catalogued their complaints. One man was angry at "seeing a lot of white males let go and then replaced with minorities." Another charged that more work was "being placed on fewer and fewer people and when the minorities can't handle it, it's thrown on us." Yet another observed that women were "making life difficult for white males. . . . They [women] had a bad deal, but it wasn't our fault. Now we have to pay for it."

A 1993 *Newsweek* poll found that 15 percent of white males claimed to have been a "victim of discrimination or reverse discrimination in getting a promotion." The same percentage reported having been discriminated against in getting a job. Forty-eight percent thought that "whites males are losing influence in American society today." Over half said that white males were "losing an advantage in terms of jobs and income." And just under half agreed that white males "should fight against affirmative action programs."

Many white men also felt misunderstood and under siege. Sixty percent told *Newsweek*'s pollsters that whites males were "more frequently the targets of antagonism from women and non-whites" than was the case five years ago. Fifty-nine percent said they thought "most women and non-whites view white males today as insensitive to the problems of women and non-whites." The majority of white males, however, disagreed with that assessment. Fifty-seven percent said most white males were not insensitive at all.

Anyone who has listened to talk radio, or just to talk on the street, knows that deep disappointment and corrosive anger have sprouted in the bosoms of white men—not all white men, of course, but many. That discontent has multiple roots, including simple misinformation.

Some of that misinformation is spread through the kindness of prospective employers. A women involved in hiring with a large corporation told me that certain officials in her company had taken to lying to white male candidates about the reason for their rejection. Instead of frankly telling them they were unqualified, managers told them that they could not be hired because the next slot had to go to a minority or a woman. The intent was to assuage white male egos. The executives accomplished that goal; but, in the process, they stoked white male anger.

When I invited anti-affirmative-action activist Tom Wood

to talk about his personal experience with discrimination, he acknowledged that he could not be certain that his gender had cost him a job. Nonetheless, a university search committee member had left him with that unmistakable impression. If only he were a woman, he recalled the man saying, he would "waltz into this job."

If the man lied in order to "let me down easy," he seriously misjudged the impact of his words, said Wood. "He couldn't have said anything to me that would have had a worse effect than that. I mean, if you think that I'm not as qualified as somebody else, just tell me. Don't tell me that I'm not going to be given serious consideration because I'm a white guy."

For Wood, the man's comments drove home a larger point—that while "it's absolutely forbidden and prohibited to discriminate against women and underrepresented racial minorities," it's okay to discriminate against white males. "So when a remark like that is made to me, it has a very different legal standing from a similar remark made to a woman or a racial minority. And, you know, I think that that needs to be changed. I don't think it's right."

Lying employers, of course, are not the only reason white men frequently end up feeling victimized by affirmative action. White male hostility is often aggravated by the backlash multiplier effect of minority promotions and hires. By that I mean that when a black or Hispanic person is hired for a job for which scores of white men applied, it is not just one white man, but potentially hundreds who feel they were unfairly denied work. By the same token, when a black or Hispanic person is promoted over, say, twenty white men, it is not just one white man who feels he has lost a job because of affirmative action but perhaps as many as twenty. The higher a minority person rises in the hierarchy, the greater the number of ostensible white male victims; and the ill will is magnified by gender and ethnic insularity—by the tendency of people to see their own group's injuries much more clearly than they see injustices committed against others. Just as minority group members and women are often unsympathetic to the complaints of white males, white men, by and large, are blind to much of the discrimination faced by women, blacks, and Latinos. Many see no acceptable rationale—whatever wrongs were perpetrated in the distant past, and however much various persons whine about being disadvantaged—for programs that coddle minorities while penalizing white males.

The rancor bred by affirmative action, insularity, employer disinformation, minority promotions, and self-delusion is compounded by a simple reality. When over half of white men say that they are "losing an advantage in terms of jobs and income," they are merely acknowledging the truth. As Sylvia Wagonheim, an attorney and workplace expert, pointed out, many white males are trapped in "second-class" jobs with little opportunity of improving their conditions. And that is "very uncomfortable." At least in the past, she added, they "had their skin color to hold on to." They could unashamedly feel superior to somebody. Now, "this white guy looks at the black guy . . . and the barriers are not there."

Much of the discontent is an emotional reaction to a perceived loss—of status, of opportunity, of stability. But at its core is a palpable sense of injustice. I have talked to enough aggrieved white men to believe they are sincere when they say that they want one standard of fairness for everybody, that they are less troubled by the decline of white male privilege than by the rise of favoritism toward women and minorities. What is wrong, they ask, with one standard for everybody? Why contribute to balkanization and polarization if the objective is to eliminate them? How can giving unearned advantages to minorities and women atone for the sins of the past? When, they want to know, can state-sanctioned discrimination end?

None of the questions have satisfactory answers—in part

because the supposed beneficiaries of the white male's decline (specifically, blacks, other minorities, and women) also harbor a deep sense of injustice. They may concede that white men's burdens have increased, but they don't, for the most part, accept the proposition that the tables have turned, that white men are somehow being wronged. Nor do they agree with the white male's assessment of his own evolution—in particular of his sensitivity to the concerns and distress of those who consider themselves less privileged than he. They also doubt the white male's sincerity when he talks of his desire and capacity to be color-blind and gender-neutral. Why, they ask, given so much evidence to the contrary, should anyone be convinced that sexism and racism can be relieved by believing in the virtue of white men?

Nonetheless, faced with an avalanche of evidence showing that white male anger is real, many people who are not especially sympathetic to the white man's plight are acknowledging the power of his outrage; and some are rethinking not only the efficacy of affirmative action, but the wisdom of trying to browbeat him into giving up a privilege that he either believes is vanishing anyway or is unwilling to admit that he has.

Chapter 2

BLACK, BRUISED, AND VILIFIED

Although some white men feel abused, as the testimony of Mel Feit, Tom Wood, and Warren Farrell makes clear, they do not generally consider themselves to be society's outcasts. They don't, for the most part, presume that the world has "prepared no place" for them—as James Baldwin said in *Nobody Knows My Name* in reference to black men.

Baldwin's point, of course, was that black men never had the luxury of assuming the world's congeniality. More than any other group of males in America, black men have kindled society's contempt. When Jean Bonhomme observes that whatever problems white guys may have, "the black guys got it as bad or worse," he is clearly alluding to that fact and to the ongoing effects of America's racial history.

In researching this book, I spoke with many people who had strong opinions about the effects of that legacy—on black men's self-image, on black men's aspirations, and on black male-female relationships. Among my informants was a black woman with a thriving career and a Ph.D. whose complicated and conflicted thoughts about black men were both provocative and revealing.

"I never ran across a lot of black men who liked women, who really liked women and appreciated women," she said. Perhaps, she speculated, "because of upbringing, because of society, black men haven't been allowed to, or just don't know how to like women and how to value them." She recalled something a physician friend of hers had said: "'Black men punish you for the ills of society. *They punish women.*' And I've felt that way with black men."

Well-educated women of accomplishment seemed to be particularly threatening to the black male ego. "I think part of the problem is that there are a lot of black men who feel intellectually inferior," she said. "And I think it's difficult for them to be with black women who they feel might be superior." She recalled a business meeting she had attended with some black senior executives. "After the meeting, we were walking out of this conference room, and one of them turned and said, 'Excuse me.' He was going to the men's room. And he turned and looked at me and this other black woman who was with me and he grabbed his crotch and said, 'This is one place that you can't follow me.'"

She had "dealt with a lot of that," she said, and had concluded that such men felt threatened by her very existence. Yet, she said, her unpleasant experiences had nothing to do with her decision to marry a white man. "I mean I didn't get up and go and decide that I'm not going to marry somebody black. It wasn't a conscious decision. It's also sort of who you have access to in the course of work every day—who it is that you interact with. And it sort of happened. I think the impression sometimes, especially for black women married to white men, is that we made a decision to do that. You know that, 'based on my experience, I'm not going to marry a black man.' And that just isn't true. It isn't a conscious decision at all."

She was not sure, she confessed, whether white men, in general, were less sexist than their black counterparts. "I think that's so individual. I don't think all men are sexist. Some are, of course. But white men are different [from blacks] in so far [as] it is their world. And that makes a big difference. My husband walks out of the door, and he knows the taxi is going to stop for him. It isn't a thing that he thinks about. I think it's their world."

If there is one thing black men are sure of, it is that this is not *their* world. Whether they punish women for the "ills of society" is debatable, but certainly those ills seem to find black men in grossly disproportionate numbers.

The statistics are compelling. Black men are less likely than either black women or white women to go to college and are twice as likely as white men to be unemployed. They are roughly nine times more likely than white men to kill and seven times more likely to be killed. Though they are less inclined to commit suicide than are white men, the gap is narrowing—particularly for young black males aged fifteen to twenty-four, whose suicide rate has quadrupled since 1960. In 1991, young black men were ten times as likely to kill themselves as were young black women.

"Every forty-six seconds of the school day, a black child drops out of school, every ninety-five seconds a black baby is born into poverty, and every four hours of every day in the year a black young adult, age twenty to twenty-four, is murdered," wrote Henry Louis Gates in the catalog for the Whitney Museum's "Black Male" exhibit. Such facts, he said, make it clear that "the much discussed crisis of the black male is no idle fiction."

In a widely disseminated 1990 monograph, The Sentencing Project reported that nearly one in four black males in their twenties was in prison or jail or on probation or parole. The comparable figure for whites was one in sixteen. "We risk the possibility of writing off an entire generation of Black men from having the opportunity to lead productive lives in our society," wrote Marc Mauer, the study's author and assistant director of the nonprofit research and antiprison advocacy organization.

"Between the ages of 20 and 24, when most young people are shaping their lifetime commitments toward the workforce, black males are less than two-thirds as likely to have jobs as are white males," wrote Margaret Simms, of the Joint Center for Political and Economic Studies, in a report entitled *Young Black Males in Jeopardy.*

The dreary statistics have led pundits to label black males "in crisis," "imperiled," "endangered"—perhaps doomed. Black men, like some long-suffering *Australopithecus* stranded in the modern world, seem to be wreaking havoc on everyone around them. For every statistic just cited, there are scores every bit as depressing. Be it drug arrests, HIV, average earnings, or fatherlessness, black men, especially young ones, are on the wrong side of the numbers.

"The perception is that black males are going to fail, and they are going to be emotionally disturbed," Vanella Crawford, project director of the Congress of National Black Churches, told attendees at a conference of the Carnegie Corporation of New York that examined the plight of young black men. Black women, she said, benefit from a more benign set of expectations.

Dr. Bonhomme recalls a meeting with a group of black male professionals during which they shared their boyhood experiences. "We were astounded at how many of us had been told, 'Black men ain't garbage. Your father was never garbage. You'll never be garbage.' They used a much harsher word than garbage. But the point is, we're a group of professionals, and this is what we've been told all our lives—negative expectations being pounded into our heads like this. We were shocked. I could understand it if I had been meeting with a group in a prison . . . but I was meeting with a group of black professionals, guys who drove Mercedes, guys who had houses out in the country, guys who had all of these kinds of things, who were lawyers, doctors. . . . My mother's line, 'You're just like your father' was the biggest put-down. So the point is . . . [that] the majority of us have been told these types of things. And we were shocked. We said, 'we're the ones who made it, and they've been telling us this.' You begin to see why so few of us make it."

Another man, dark brown complected, talked of growing up and seeing lighter boys getting much more attention—especially from girls. "It hurt," he said, and worse, "I bought into the shit." Though handsome by any reasonable standard, he didn't like the way he looked. And when he began to date, he found himself attracted primarily to women who weren't black—white, Asian, Hispanic, it didn't much matter. They all seemed to treat him better than black women did. Whereas black women "call you all kinds of shit; don't respect you," other women seemed to value him. Generally when he was with a black woman, he said, emotion creeping into his voice, "I felt a void." He had been living for several years with a women he referred to as a "white" Latina. "We aren't the way we are because we're vindictive toward black women," he said. "You go where the water flows easier."

"From age one, black women are taught that black men are nothing. Black men are taught to take their frustrations out on black women," filmmaker John Singleton observed.

The black woman who senses insecurity and resentment among black men is probably not imagining the feeling. Many black men feel worthless or unappreciated. Others feel powerless or under siege.

Joshua Solomon, a white student at the University of Maryland, set out in 1994 to explore how difficult living as a black man might be. The twenty-year-old had long been intrigued with John Howard Griffin's book, *Black Like Me*, which documented Griffin's experiences in the 1950s disguised as a black man in the South. Solomon underwent drug treatments similar to those Griffin had endured and struck out for Georgia. He quickly became tense and generally uncomfortable. He discov-

ered that he was treated rudely by a hotel desk clerk, shad-
owed as he walked through a store, warned not to go to
Forsyth County ("Some folks just don't like living with you
people"), interrogated by a cop, and generally treated like dirt.
After two days living as a black man in the Deep South, he
abandoned the experiment.

"I was sick of being black. I couldn't take it anymore. I
wanted to throw up. Enough is enough, I thought. I didn't
need to be hit over the head with a baseball bat to understand
what was going on here. Usually, I'd made friends pretty easily.
I was nice to them and they were nice to me. Now people acted
like they hated me. Nothing had changed but the color of my
skin. . . . I called my mother and told her I was finished with
my journey. All the hurt, all the anger, all the inhumanity. I
started to cry," wrote Solomon in the *Washington Post.*

A nationwide survey in 1993–94 found that 40 percent of
blacks rejected the idea that the problems of black men and
women deserved equivalent consideration; instead, they
believed that "black men are endangered and their problems
deserve special attention." Sixty-two percent of the respondents thought that black boys should be able to attend special
all-male schools. Twenty percent believed that black women
should eschew positions of political leadership so as not to
"undermine" black men. And whereas 65 percent supported
black feminists, 29 percent thought that "feminist groups just
divide the black community." Michael Dawson, the University
of Chicago political scientist who codirected the survey,
thought the findings gave insight into "why such events as the
Clarence Thomas/Anita Hill hearings are capable of starting a
firestorm in the black community."

The poll certainly underscores the deep conflict many
blacks feel over gender issues. Mindful of the civil rights movement and grounded in its emphasis on equality for all, most
blacks reflexively support mainstream feminist goals of eco-

nomic and political parity. Many also believe, however, that black men have been so battered by society that they desperately need shoring up—even at women's expense. Among black men, the hunger for support is palpable—as *Washington Post* writer Donna Britt demonstrated with her "valentine" to black men. The article, published February 14, 1990, in the *Post*, was titled: "Loves Won and Lost; For Black Men, One from the Heart."

"Statistics suggest they are 'endangered,'" Britt wrote. "Oprah, Geraldo and endless TV specials describe them as 'at risk.' Movies that deal with them portray them as afterthoughts and background music; the rest say they're thieves and abusers, the architects and victims of the drug culture. Their own women, it seems, have turned on them, shouting their failings from the rooftops and the pages of bestsellers."

Nonetheless, Britt stated, "black men manage to amaze." She rhapsodized over Michael Jordan's athleticism and Nelson Mandela's grace. And she praised black men everywhere for "surviving so much" and being so splendid. "I've been crazy about black men since the days when I jumped into my father's arms as he arrived home after laying bricks across town. I've loved black boys since my brothers teased and tortured and then took up for me. Since my high school freshman year, when Ricky Jenkins, emboldened by the darkness at a blue-lights-in-the-basement party, sneaked up and gave me my first real kiss." The prose-poem went on for nearly a thousand words. And the reaction was phenomenal.

In an article the following month, Britt wrote about the avalanche of appreciation that had come her way, along with her doubts about writing the piece. "Surely a country where a recent national survey of young people revealed the three most-admired people to be Bill Cosby, Eddie Murphy and Michael Jordan didn't really need an essay explaining black men's appeal," she reasoned. She had considered the article a challenge to conventional wisdom but otherwise "No big deal."

"Today—264 phone calls, 85 letters and three bouquets of roses later—it seems this nugget of appreciation was a much bigger deal than I ever imagined," Britt wrote. "And though it's mostly thrilling—I'm still getting calls and letters five weeks after the fact—something about the reactions makes me genuinely sad."

Her callers and correspondents ran the gamut, from a ten-year-old boy to prisoners, but the responses that particularly touched her were those from middle-class, seemingly secure black men. As successful as they were, they "sounded almost depressingly grateful" for her article of appreciation: "Several businessmen who called said that they read the piece at their desks, tears rolling down their cheeks." And gratified as she was that the people had reached out to her, "I felt undone by the depth of their feeling. It hurt, knowing that any group of men—and particularly this one, whose members had overcome the odds to distinguish themselves—could on some level feel so battered, so needy, that reading a purely positive essay about themselves would elicit a flood of gratitude.

"Frankly, I'd steeled myself for the opprobrium of black women who have been hurt and embittered by black men, women whose anger was articulated by 'The Women of Brewster Place' and 'The Color Purple.' It never materialized," Britt wrote. That so many black men would so desperately crave recognition of the fact that they could be decent, ordinary people says much about the pain of being a black man in America. And that pain, insist some observers, continues to get worse.

In his 1994 book, *The Assassination of the Black Male Image,* Earl Ofari Hutchinson argued that America has made the black male into a "universal bogeyman." "I'm a black man. I hear, see and feel the pain daily," he wrote. Black women, he acknowledged, were suffering, too. "But they're still women. Most white men don't need to wage the same ego war against her as they do against black men. They tell her that she wouldn't be in the mess she's in if HE would just get a job, stay out of jail, stop shooting or snorting, get married, stop making babies and quit dropping dead."

Not only are white men out to "assassinate" the black male's image, said Hutchinson, but so are many black women. Beginning with Michelle Wallace and her *Black Macho and the Myth of the Superwoman,* an array of female authors, from Ntozake Shange to Alice Walker, he said, had made careers writing about black males who were less than men.

"By the 1990s, the attack on black men had turned into a rout. Black women complained bitterly on TV talk shows, in books and magazine articles, that they couldn't find 'Mr. Right.' They were getting more frustrated by the day. Many black women longed for someone to tell the world once and for all about the misery and heartache these louses were causing them. . . . Terry McMillan did."

Novelist and essayist Ishmael Reed has similarly written about what he calls "a steady buildup of animosity towards black men." And he has commented with disdain on black women writers "who've peddled" and been rewarded for "black-male-bashing." He has reserved special contempt, however, for white "gender-first" feminists whom he accuses of singling out black misogyny "as if it were the only misogyny that exists." "Since the leadership of this faction of the feminist movement has singled out black men as the meta-enemy of women, these women represent one of the most serious threats to black male well-being since the Klan," writes Reed in *Airing Dirty Laundry.*

In a recent edition of her *Black Macho and the Myth of the Superwoman* (first published in 1979), Wallace recants some of her earlier views on black men. In a typical passage from the original book, Wallace wrote: "[The black woman] made it quite clear that she has no intention of starting a black woman's liberation movement. One would think she was satisfied, yet she is not. The black man has not really kept his part of the bargain they made when she agreed to keep her mouth shut in the sixties. When she stood by silently as he became a 'man,' she assumed that he would subsequently grant her her long overdue 'womanhood,' that he would finally glorify and dignify black womanhood just as the white man had done for the white woman. But he did not. He refused her. His involvement with white women was only the most dramatic form that refusal took. He refused her across the board."

Wallace now concedes that "there are many black men who love black women, and vice versa, although I didn't know it at the time I wrote *Black Macho*." She goes on to report, "When I began to date as a teenager in Harlem, I expected and found no better men than my father and stepfather had been. I expected and found hostility, anger, competition, violence, dishonesty, misogyny and ignorance. These experiences had a lot to do with my 'theories' about black men and black male/female relationships as a black feminist. . . . I am not saying that there aren't some black men out there who are mean to women and, indeed, I see this meanness as a political issue in our community. What I am saying is that I was not actually aware that there was any other kind of man."

Though Wallace apparently has called a truce, many women have not. They continue to believe that black men—as Bonhomme delicately put it—"ain't garbage." To some extent that view merely reflects what certain women feel about men in general. It no doubt also reflects individual women's experiences with specific black men. As A. L. Reynolds wrote in his provocatively titled *Do Black Women Hate Black Men?*, "too many black women have been hurt, abused, abandoned, left pregnant, helpless, and homeless by black men who refuse to accept responsibility for their marriages or their relationships;

hence, the reason for this anger by black women." Many women have also become fed up with what one woman described as the desire of black men to be "treated like kings."

The woman, a lawyer who now dates a blue-collar white man, recalls that in college, black guys were "high on themselves, legitimately, because in many cases they've pulled themselves up; and without a doubt they deserve some praise for all their accomplishments. But they also expected to be treated . . . like royalty, like they had done something that no one else could do. And the only people who would really put up with that and treat them like that were white women."

She believes that black women who date desirable black men "have to put up with a lot of shit. . . . You have to change your attitude when you're around them. You can't be as pleased with yourself. You can't be as proud of your own achievement because you're constantly boosting their egos, telling them, 'Oh. You're so wonderful.' And they make you feel like you have to be thankful that you're with them. I have too many things going on in my life to deal with that."

Obviously, not all black men insist on royal treatment, but some do demand delicate handling. I once was in the company of two black professionals who had been unofficially "fixed up." The conversation, during this first meeting, turned to male and female behavior. The man, who had recently exited a relationship-turned-sour, began to bemoan the difficulty finding a "good" woman. Most black women, he said, were incapable of subordinating their own egos to a man's; they were unwilling to give a man the kind of support he needed. At that remark, his intended date, turning colder by the second, demanded to know exactly what kind of support he required. He wanted a woman to cherish him, he essentially said, and to harbor him from the blows of a brutally hostile world. She wanted a man, she said, who would do the same thing but who also didn't expect her to defer to his overblown ego. After a few such thrusts and rapid ripostes, she all but dismissed her companion with the observation that he didn't need an educated woman but maybe a secretary or "a teller." Her tone left little doubt that she could just as easily have told him to go find himself a whore.

That encounter, the woman said later, was only one in a series of bad experiences with black male professionals. "This is a broad, sweeping generalization," she admitted, "but I think that any black man that has finished undergraduate school considers himself to be an endangered species. And that gives him this aura of, 'I can have anybody or any woman that I want.' And they tend not to want to settle down into an exclusive relationship with a woman. I think that they see themselves as a hot commodity."

She had dated black men from the Caribbean, she said, "and they don't have that attitude. It's kind of like an expectation that they would have done well, so that the fact that they are professionals is no big deal because they were never expected to be less than that. . . . Even though they might be arrogant in their own right, they don't [feel], 'I'm a black man who made it against the odds and so therefore I should have five women on a string.'"

For black female professionals in search of black male professionals, the odds alone can be daunting. More black women than black men graduate from college. For whites, the reverse is true. And more black women than black men work as professionals. An analysis of data from the Equal Employment Opportunity Commission by the *Wall Street Journal* in 1992 put the ratio at 1.8 to 1. It is because of such numbers that black college-educated women are much more likely than are white college-educated women to marry men without college degrees—that is, assuming that they get married at all. According to the U.S. Labor Department, roughly half the husbands of college-educated black women have college degrees compared with close to three-fourths of the husbands of college-educated white women. Black women are also more likely to be in the job market than are their college-educated white counterparts. Their educational achievements and work experience are doubtless likely to threaten some insecure men. By the same token, many are loath to settle for men they deem professionally beneath them.

Many women who are searching for love among black nonprofessionals find the pickings no better. Not only are black men without a college education at high risk for unemployment, but many (particularly young city dwellers) have adopted what sociologist Elijah Anderson calls the "code of the streets." That code is not particularly sensitive to women, for it requires the appearance of ruthlessness as a means of compelling respect.

Social scientists Richard Majors and Janet Mancini Billson have termed the attitude "cool pose." In their 1992 book named for the syndrome, they describe the posture as a "coping mechanism that serves to counter, at least in part, the dangers that black males encounter on a daily basis. As a performance, cool pose is designed to render the black male visible and to empower him; it eases the worry and pain of blocked opportunities. Being cool is an ego booster for black males comparable to the kind white males more easily find through attending good schools, landing prestigious jobs, and bringing home decent wages."

That pose, they noted, can take a toll on relationships, for it may "condition the black man to suppress and lose touch with all his feelings, including those that might facilitate nurturant relationships with others." In short, it may prevent black men from achieving any semblance of intimacy.

"If he feels rejected," Majors and Billson observe, "the black male may reject a woman rather than admit his hurt feelings. If he is frightened about sinking into the quagmire of unemployment and welfare checks, he may instead put on a bravado that dispels all appearances of fear. If he is sad about the fighting and deaths of his compatriots on the streets, he may mock her expressions of sadness. If she complains about his inadequacy in providing for her and their children, he may strike out in anger to cover his anguish. It may appear that he is emotionally drained, or dead. . . . He has become obsessed with being cool in order to obtain the rewards of courtship (sexual intimacy), but he fails to win genuine closeness and companionship because he has not allowed his deeper feelings to surface."

As a result, black men may be more inclined than white men to consider sex an act that is not attached to commitment or even to emotion. And that view can create a huge problem for black women, who see sex in a much more traditional light. The most comprehensive survey of American sexual practices yet conducted, the National Health and Social Life Survey, found that 42 percent of black men, compared to 32 percent of white men, held a primarily "recreational" view of sex. In contrast, the team of investigators based at the University of Chicago's National Opinion Research Center discovered that fewer than 9 percent of black women, compared to more than 21 percent of white women, saw pleasure as the primary purpose of sex.

Journalist Michel Marriott thinks that older black men are somewhat to blame for the attitudes displayed by many of their younger counterparts. "I think we, my generation of black men, have done a very poor job of passing on the lessons we have learned; so they've literally had to recreate themselves . . . from almost nothing. . . . The guys will talk about 'hos,' 'bitches' wanting to steal their money, take their manhood; so they overcompensate by trying to look very hard. To show emotions, to show that a woman could even touch them is a sign of weakness. So women are expendable. Women are tissues. You just run through them."

One young man, a former drug dealer who says his hustling days are behind him, looks back with a sense of wonder at how he once was: "I was ruthless. Cool cut and everything. Couldn't even tick me off." He had no interest in any meaningful relationships with men, and as for women, "I just wanted to go out and bump the girl and keep on stepping."

Samuel Sanchez, a social worker who directs a program providing educational opportunities to young poor people (mostly Latino and black) in New York, sees little evidence that many of his charges realize that a sexual revolution has occurred. "They're very isolated . . . in terms of awareness and consciousness, for the most part," he says. Consequently, the young men often refer to a woman as a "bitch or whore" and believe that men should "reign supreme in all decisions." "It's very macho," says Sanchez.

Samuel Betances, a sociologist at Northeastern Illinois University, thinks that such outsize machismo once served a real and productive purpose. Certainly for Latinos and others from areas where security was problematic and predators were plentiful, machismo was a source of safety for children and spouses. The "code of machismo" said that if you harmed a man's child, "you'll have to deal with that man." That code also demanded that "you had to work, you had to meet your obligations, you had to be a provider."

But in today's urban environment, the provider role can be difficult and the show of manliness can become exaggerated— "where the man is looking for a macho job and not having the job, having to be dependent, having to be in the streets. That [can] sometimes lead to a kind of boasting . . . and ultimately, when you [don't] have anything else to point to, you point to the size of your fists or other organs in your body to show how big of a man you are," Betances noted.

Whatever its origins, and whatever it is called—the code of the streets, machismo, or cool pose—the attitude can make life difficult for a woman who is interested in being anything other than an accessory to a man. Yet, to portray black men as belonging essentially to one of two groups—strutting macho men or self-absorbed professionals—would be grossly misleading.

Certainly these types exist, but so do many others. Millions of black men are neither endangered nor in crisis but are hardworking contributors to society. In 1991, according to the U.S. Census, 70 percent of black males aged sixteen and older were in the labor force. The majority of those over age twenty-four were married. Two-thirds of all black men over age twenty-four had completed high school, nearly 30 percent had attended college, and 11 percent had earned at least a bachelor's degree.

As Oliver Cromwell, a black college-educated Washingtonian, put it: "There are plenty of decent black men out there who are looking for genuine relationships just like their female counterparts." Many—as the reaction to Donna Britt's valentine attests—hunger for recognition of the fact that the term "decent black man" is not an oxymoron. Yet in this culture, as Betances noted, black and Latino men "are constantly defined by what we would consider our worst element."

Even some of those black men who are considered most at risk of self-destructing are managing to resist the stereotype. When I spoke with him in early 1994, twenty-one-year-old Michael Lockett was discussing how he had learned to accept his responsibilities through participating in the Philadelphia Children's Network's Responsive Fathers Program. He credited the counselors at the program with giving him the confidence to marry the mother of his three-year-old daughter. "We worked out our problems, got together, and decided we could make it," he said. He was currently working at a job packing hamburgers for shipping to a fast-food restaurant and was looking into colleges. "I want to be there for my children," he said. "So if they have any problems or anything, they can come to me. I want them to feel free to come to me and I want them to, well, go further in life than I did. I didn't go to college, but I'm going back now. And I want them to have the things that I didn't."

Twenty-year-old Brian Thompson, another participant in the program, was also trying to refocus his life. He was touched by the fact that others like him were making the same effort. "When I came here, I thought it was going to be like a bunch of nerdy-type guys sitting up in here," he said. "But it wasn't. It really shocked me because it was like a lot of guys that you see out in the street, that, if you ride by, you would consider them a drug dealer or probably a stick-up [man]. But it was them type guys sitting up in here, really wanting to do something. I said, 'It takes effort to get off of the corner and to come down here and sit up in here for about two or three hours talking, sharing your feelings.' You know, it was strange because I was seeing guys like me, street-type guys. 'Cause, when you see guys out there you don't think they got feelings at all. Like, you don't think they got no remorse for nothing. And these are the same guys who are sitting up in here trying to get themselves together."

Certain black men will never "get off of the corner." They have been convinced that the strictures of race and class leave them with nowhere else to go. And some who never succumbed to the streets nonetheless find life as a black man in America to be so confidence-sapping that they require more nurturing than many black women (or women of any color) are willing to give.

It would be a mistake, however, to assume that such problems define or are peculiar to black men, that they are racial traits. Men of all races have fragile egos, blinkered vision, and assorted other problems that get in the way of mutually fulfilling relationships. For a variety of well-documented reasons, black men face extraordinary pressures, and many react to those pressures in unappealing—and sometimes misogynistic—ways.

Kent Amos, founder of the Urban Family Institute, argues that looking at black men's difficulties primarily through a racial lens blinds us to a larger reality. "We're only looking at the tip of the iceberg when you talk about the black male," insists Amos, who contends that the entire society—not just the black man—is "endangered."

America, he says, is wrestling with "some very fundamental questions about what we value and who we value and how we value our society today." The answers offered so far, he believes, "portend a future of doom." The basic issue, as he defines it, is "a weakened society" whose moral fabric is fraying: "And as long as we make it a black male issue, we get the wrong answers."

In at least one sense, Amos is indisputably correct. The statistics that are worsening for black men are worsening for white men as well. Fatherlessness among whites has more than doubled in the past two decades. The number of whites, overwhelmingly males, arrested for violent crimes has roughly tripled since 1965, and the number arrested for aggravated assault has quadrupled. The fact that the problems are so much worse among black men makes it harder to see that they are bad among American men of all races.

Milton Morris, vice president for research of the Washington, D.C.-based Joint Center for Political and Economic Studies, observed, "Black men are having a great deal of difficulty coping with society in a way that allows them to be confident actors." That difficulty, he argues, is distressing because the problems it engenders "kind of go to the heart of black life."

Yet, isolated as many blacks are from much of mainstream America, black life does not develop in a racial vacuum. The ideal of manhood that is prevalent in many black inner-city communities reflects, if in a sometimes inflated manner, ideals loosed upon the culture generally. Eloise Anderson, director of California's Department of Social Services, compared urban gangsters who take part in drive-by shootings to cowboys who rode in and shot up a town. The young man who kills someone for showing disrespect has an analogue, she believes, in the gunslinger who brooked no insult. The model of the black male as gangster, she suggests, was spawned by his white predecessor, as celebrated and glamorized in popular culture.

When first-time father Brian Thompson talks of his need to "be around men and see how men think . . . cause I grew up with my mom and sister," he is voicing a craving for a more appropriate and more accessible role model than either neighborhood culture or popular culture has provided. Only in the most narrow sense is his a black male problem. It is, more accurately, a problem of a society that has divorced fatherhood from fathering and provided many boys with little guidance in understanding what it means to be a man.

Figuring out what it means to be a black man, of course, has not necessarily been easy in any age. After repeatedly hearing "black men ain't shit" from loved ones and its equivalent, or worse, from the larger society, many black men clearly gave up—and became what they were presumed to be. Even as we chastise or condemn those who have accepted defeat, we should take note of those who have not.

The vast majority of black men, as was noted earlier, are not out pillaging and plundering or standing on the corner getting high or abusing black women or living on the dole. They are working, despite the fact that many employers deem them undesirable, and often are struggling—against a society that frequently finds them threatening and worthless; against expectations of failure on every side; and often against their own intense anger at a world that, in large measure, despises them, even as it insists that they put on a happy face.

One woman, when asked what she thought of the bad rep-

Chapter 3

WHATEVER HAPPENED TO THE MEN'S MOVEMENT?

Though most Americans are willing to concede that some groups of men—blacks, the uneducated, and the unemployed, for instance—have it tough, many are perplexed and perturbed by the increasingly common spectacle of men with no apparent disadvantage claiming victim status. Some see the proliferation of male whiners as an inevitable offshoot of the "culture of complaint"—as proof that when people are encouraged to bellyache to gain advantage or sympathy, even those who have suffered no misfortune will find a reason to gripe. Others write off the male grumbling as little more than backlash, veiled resentment of women who are finally getting some of the respect they deserve.

Without doubt, many men—and women—find the injured-party role liberating. Victimhood not only frees you from accepting responsibility for your own fate, but it inoculates you against the whining of others. It is also true that some men are openly hostile to women's advancement—though probably not as many men as people tend to assume. Ninety-nine percent of the men polled by the Gallup Organization in 1993, for instance, said they approved of women receiving the same pay as men for the same work, and 88 percent favored women working outside the home, even if their husbands were able to support them. (In both cases, the percentage of men endorsing economic equality and independence was slightly—and statistically insignificantly—higher than the percentage of women.)

The most visible backlash is not against women's expanding role, but against what some men see as the excesses, hypocrisy, inconsistency, and mixed signals of the women's rights movement—at the proliferation of programs they believe unfairly favor women and at the type of rhetoric that philosopher and political scientist Ellen Frankel Paul calls "a quarter-century of flagellation of men by radical feminists."

Many men agree with Washington, D.C., psychologist and MenCenter founder Alvin Baraff's observation that "the role of the man these days is in absolute chaos as far as his knowing what his role is. . . . I don't think it's just white. I think that it's men in general, right now. All of your TV shows are bashing men. Every time something occurs that gives some of the leaders of the women's movement a chance to make some statement, it's always a statement that separates men and women further and further. And it's always anger against men." Lawyer Ron Henry made a similar point more succinctly when he asked in bewilderment, "How have we gone in one generation from, 'Father knows best' to, 'All men are rapists'?"

It is such men—baffled and often angry—whom many representatives of the men's movement claim to represent. And such men exist in droves. Yet to ask most men about the "men's movement" is to invite an amused or quizzical expression. For although nearly half of American men tell pollsters that the "time has come for a men's movement to help men get in touch with their feelings and advance men's causes" and though male frustrations are on parade for all to see, the men's movement—to the extent that one exists—has not been eagerly received.

Certain men, clearly, have become involved in gender issues. Some are trying to promote a new masculine ideal. Others are trying to heal male "wounds" or relieve male pain. But those in the forefront of the gender debate generally acknowledge that they are not typical men. Many are singularly sensitive souls who are searching for fulfillment or resentful men with an axe to grind or therapists who have passed through a midlife crisis and emerged with wisdom they are eager to share. John Q. Public, however, is skeptical. As Baraff observed, "You go and try to start a men's movement and it's very, very difficult."

In explaining why so many submissions to the *New York Times* "About Men" column fell flat, Eric Copage, the column's editor, observed, "Asians, blacks, Hispanics, gay people have something to push against." For white men, things were different. "If you're a white male," he said, "you're basically okay."

Being "basically okay" can make not only for less interesting prose, but for a certain amount of confusion about whether one has any business complaining—or claiming eligibility for a movement. Graphic artist William Croxton, for instance, believes that white men sometimes are unfairly assailed by women and minorities. Yet, he adds, "I do feel a certain amount of guilt. I do think there's a certain amount of guilt that goes along with being a white male—where you are, kind of, societally, the high person on the totem pole."

He seems uncertain why men would want a movement. "I think the femin[ist] movement has a basis in . . . deficiencies in [the] political structure and social structure." A men's movement, on the other hand, seems "pretty ridiculous. . . . I'm not saying it's not valid, because there's probably a lot of good that can come of it—getting men more in touch with themselves, which probably would translate into making the femin[ist] movement stronger. I don't particularly subscribe to it."

A New York lawyer was even less convinced that men need a movement. The very idea struck him as laughable. "This back-to-nature bonding bullshit where men go out into the woods and hug each other and rub dirt on their faces, I think it's bullshit," he said. "If you're the sort of person who can talk, you don't need that. I just think it's kind of a faddy little bullshit chichi—like the primal scream. It's just not for me and I think most men will wholeheartedly reject it."

He would also think it absurd, he added, "if women were doing the same shit in the woods. . . . I'm just very suspect of any activity where the conscious aim is to communicate in kind of what I would view as a very unnatural way. Like the people who go to this sort of rustic, woody setting to try to get in touch with their sort of feminine selves. . . . I don't think I'm very macho, but I think that's like bullshit. I haven't focused on why I think it's so ludicrous; but I think it's ludicrous."

The lawyer's reaction was not unusual, particularly among those who think of the men's movement as "men in the woods groping for their masculinity," as law student Charles Reeves described it. *Iron John,* Robert Bly's runaway bestseller, is largely responsible for that image—along with Bill Moyers's "A Gathering of Men," the ninety-minute PBS special on Bly that aired in January 1990.

Iron John is an inventive exegesis of the Grimm fairy tale that gives the book its name. Its publication marked the public launching of the so-called mythopoetic men's movement, for Bly treats *Iron John* not merely as a myth but as a guide to the male rites of passage that may be the salvation of modern men.

Bly fears that man has gone soft. Having explored his gentle, feminine side during the 1960s, man remains emotionally blocked and filled with anguish. He is too restrained to say what he really feels or to pursue what he truly desires. This "soft male," who hoped to find himself in femininity, has become separated from his male self. "If his wife or girlfriend, furious, shouts that he is a 'chauvinist,' a 'sexist,' a 'man,' he doesn't fight back but just takes it," wrote Bly. He is so naive, Bly believes, that he is oblivious to his own suffering. To discover his true self, he must leave his mother's house and go on a journey with the "Wild Man." *Iron John* is the mysterious and metaphor-filled description of that journey.

The adventure begins with an anonymous hunter who appears in a kingdom near a mysterious forest. Hunters who previously went into the forest vanished. Nonetheless, the stranger ventures into the wilderness against the king's wishes. Eventually he discovers the source of the trouble. At the bottom of a pond is a man with rusty iron-colored skin who apparently was responsible for the disappearance of those who had come before.

This Wild Man, who may be the "deep male" inside all men, is captured and locked up in an iron cage in the castle, but one day a golden ball belonging to the king's son falls into the cage. To retrieve the ball, the boy must free the Wild Man, and to do so he must steal the key from under his mother's pillow. He is, in short, moving beyond the realm of the feminine—of "conventional tameness and niceness"—and taking charge of his fate. Having done so, the boy realizes that he cannot stay at home without being punished. There is also a larger reason why he must depart: Since "only men can initiate men" and provide the male "hardness" he will need, he must leave the house of his mother to begin his initiation. Off into the forest he goes, on the shoulders of the Wild Man.

The Wild Man, of course, is not a barbarian but more like a mystical priest or, in Bly's words, a "meditation instructor," who provides his novitiate with the guidance he had heretofore lacked. The youth's first task is to guard a spring. Though the Wild Man warns him not to touch the water, he accidentally wets the finger that he injured freeing Iron John. To the boy's astonishment, the wounded fingertip becomes golden—an acknowledgment apparently of the wounds of the past. The next day a hair from his head falls into the spring and also becomes golden—which seemingly signifies something important about the recognition of fantasies, resentments, and sexuality. On the third day, while the boy gazes into the water—fixated on his "psychic twin"—the rest of his hair gets wet and also turns to gold. The Wild Man then puts the boy out of the forest—to experience poverty and other harsh realities of the world—but promises to help him if he is ever in need.

His golden hair covered with a kerchief, the lad comes upon a kingdom where he eventually obtains work as an assistant to the palace cook. Later, he is called upon to deliver food to the royal table. Fearful of revealing his glowing golden hair, the boy refuses the king's command to uncover his head. The king, obviously a father figure, orders that the boy be fired. The cook takes pity on the boy and finds him work in the garden. The boy is subsequently ordered to deliver flowers to the king's daughter, who also demands that he remove his headdress. When he refuses, she snatches it off, and his dazzling hair is revealed. She pushes coins into his hands, which he gives away. On later visits, he manages to keep his head covered—setting boundaries in the relationship that she has neither the will nor the judgment to set.

Eventually the kingdom goes to war. Though our hero wants to fight, his offers of assistance are scorned. He is given a broken-down nag with three good legs and derisively dismissed. But, he will not be denied his chance to shine in battle and revive the warrior within, so he calls upon Iron John and requests a suitable steed. The Wild Man furnishes him with a noble and majestic creature, as well as with warriors attired in iron. The young man arrives just in time to save the kingdom but vanishes before anyone can discover his identity and returns the borrowed horse and troops to his mentor in the forest.

Intent on unmasking the mysterious and heroic knight, the king and his daughter arrange a great festival to which all knights are invited. On three days in succession, our hero appears (each day on a horse and in armor of a different color), and on every occasion he catches the golden apple tossed by the king's daughter. On the third day, as he tries to escape, the king's men give chase. They do not catch him, but one wounds him in the leg. Also, his helmet falls off, revealing his extraordinary hair.

Shortly thereafter, the gardener's assistant is summoned before the king and unmasked. He admits that he is not only the mysterious knight but the son of a king, and he asks the king for his daughter's hand in marriage.

The young man's masculine quest has ended; the time has come for him to join with the feminine. At the wedding feast, we get yet another surprise. Iron John, our link to spontaneity and nature, is revealed to be a baronial king. The young man has freed him from the enchantment that turned him into the Wild Man. "All the treasure that I own will from now on belong to you," he tells our hero.

In Bly's hands the myth becomes a road map to self-discovery, whereby man learns, among other things, that he cannot find himself in women's homes or women's roles, but must—if he is to be fulfilled—engage the power and wisdom of man.

Many men, to put it mildly, are skeptical of Bly's prescription. Psychologist Carl Faber questions the wisdom of "retribalizing" with other men. A number of other men who were interviewed for this book saw Bly's ideas as "kinda nutso," in the words of graphic artist William Croxton. Graduate student Tim Benjamin thought that the notion of modern men congregating in the woods was "amusing." He acknowledged that he was less than well informed on just what it was that they did, "but I guess they're trying to recapture some kind of primitive masculinity and, well, I'm not convinced that there is such a thing that can be recaptured. And, if there is, I'm not sure it's something that should be recaptured." Another graduate student, Kevin Bruyneel, said much the same thing: "It seems they've reinforced sort of old gender stereotypes, which I have a very negative reaction to. . . . It's almost a regressive view of masculinity in terms of some kind of call to primal urges."

A twenty-six-year-old Ph.D. candidate in philosophy said that he had come upon *Iron John* shortly after its publication in 1990. "It hit me as something that I should look at and maybe think about [in terms of my] relationship with my father," he recalled. "For five or six months, I was really captivated and [felt] sort of like, 'Wow, this is interesting. [Bly] hits some insights, mainly about my father and my relationship to him more than anything else.' But this lasted, like I said, for five or six months, and then I became very skeptical, and I saw a lot of New Age appropriation of Carl Jung in it that I'm really suspicious of and not really impressed with. And then, actually as I read more feminism, I became less and less impressed with it. So then eventually I removed [*Iron John*] from my shelf and packed it away." Bly, he concluded, was "stuck in this tired old theme of rigid gender roles [and] incredibly traditional."

In 1991, *Washington Post* writer Phil McCombs attended one of Bly's "soul talk" sessions in the District of Columbia at which fifteen hundred men paid seventy-five dollars apiece to bond with other men, "beat drums, share intimate self-revelations and listen" as Bly provided answers.

"The mythopoetic movement," McCombs reported, "seems more than anything a highly intellectualized personal enrichment program for upper-middle-class whites, who are seeking to solve their problems through mythology and poetry just as they might otherwise do in a psychiatrist's office or a 12-step program. While leaders say that blue-collar men are involved, that wasn't evident in visits to council meetings here or in interviews with dozens of observers nationwide." McCombs also quoted sociologist Michael Kimmel, who called the movement "a retreat from strong, powerful, assertive women."

Some of Bly's assumptions are questionable. There is little evidence that the soft, timid men Bly worries about exist in huge numbers. Nor is it clear that those who do exist got that way from too much female influence. Nor is there much reason to believe that some belated participation in male rituals will fundamentally change what they are. And certainly, the number of men of any color or class who are willing to immerse themselves in poetry and myth in search of manhood is relatively small.

Journalists, who quickly realized the limited appeal of treks into the woods, have not been particularly kind to the men's movement. Indeed, they have generally viewed it as something of a joke. Stephen Randall, writing in *Playboy* in 1992, dismissed it as a media creation. The movement, as he described it, "is based on the notion that men are suffering. We tried so hard to please the women in our lives that we've forgotten the good aspects of being male. . . . So in order to regain the upper hand, to define ourselves, we go off on so-called wild-man weekends—no girls allowed, of course. Once there, we rage at our fathers for neglecting us, confess our innermost feelings to total strangers and co-opt the rituals of trendy cultures—African drum beating, native American chants and sweat lodges—to bring us closer to our Anglo-Saxon roots. Three days later, we go home as new men."

Fortune magazine weighed in with this observation: "The men's movement is dumber than the women's movement. The latter at least has coherent grievances and an ideology purporting to explain their source. . . . But the mainstream men's movement . . . is programmatically hollow. It is all New Age pop psychology and self-expression, targeted at men who are lonely and fearful and looking for something more meaningful than Monday Night Football. Instead of trying *Masterpiece Theatre*, many of them are joining groups that go off into the woods and beat drums to help them regain a sense of masculinity. In other groups, the men stand around in circles tearfully telling stories about their invariably inadequate relationships with their fathers. There seems to be a lot of crying in the men's movement."

Without question, one of the stupidest public relations moves the mythopoetic gurus made was to march into the woods and start beating drums. The image provided the media with a perfect target for ridicule. But are guys in the forest making feral noises really what the men's movement is all about? Stephen Johnson, director of the Men's Center of Los Angeles, thinks not.

Johnson, leader of the Men's Center, points out that a host of other activities are taking place far away from the woods. Through something called "gender reconciliation," movement figures are "creating forums for men and women to come together." Others, he insists, are dealing with issues of men's health and of racial division. "The men's movement . . . cannot just be . . . white guys that are going out and learning to dance, or to drum." Even issues of spirituality, he contends, are now on the men's movement plate. "People moved out of churches and synagogues during the sixties and the seventies and the 'God is dead movement' and that created an awful lot of problems for the community." It was important that groups such as his, said Johnson, help people return to their faith.

Yet, for all the endeavors Johnson describes, he seems unsure that there is even such a thing as a "men's movement." It is "different than the women's movement," he acknowledges. "It's probably more clearly characterized as a movement within men. Or maybe movements, men's movements, because it doesn't have the kind of political structure that the women's movement has. It doesn't have that political base."

"The first ten years at least of what's called [the] men's movement was about repairing the wounds to the soul . . . created by the kind of dysfunctional relationship between fathers and sons," says Johnson. He believes that men are now realizing that they also must work on their ties to their mothers—and on relations between men and women in general.

At one point, a few years ago, Johnson noted, men's issues "had started to really catch on, especially when the media had turned its attention prior to the elections, for that whole year, on the men's movement, prior to Robert Bly's book coming out." The media attention, however, quickly turned to parody.

"But the truth of it is that the reason why men needed to go out [into the woods] . . . is that they needed to get away from the urban environment . . . and they needed to sit down and take the time to ask some questions, questions that weren't being asked, that they hadn't particularly taken the time to ask before." Among activists, Johnson believes, the result has been salutary, that a growing consensus now holds that "the real work is in the trenches."

"We've done enough of our [personal] work," he says. "We've healed enough that we need to have something to do. We need to come and be of service to our communities. We need to create many more mentor relationships for fatherless boys that are at high risk, that are about to drop out of school, that are about to get involved with a gang, or that are about to get involved with drugs. . . . We need to be working with men who are about to get caught up in the prison system, or who are coming out of prison and work with them in terms of rehabilitation and re-entry back into society. We need to be working more with men who are sexual violators, and who have a lot of questions and issues having to do with sexual addiction, or inappropriate sexual behavior. . . . It's creating a man's social justice network, of men working together in a hands-on way to stabilize their communities. And that's what I think is most significant now."

Johnson also insists that, contrary to many people's perceptions, most men's advocates are not antifeminist. "They don't have the problem with the feminists, because a lot of the men that I know that are very involved with the men's movement were the ones that were the feminists years ago. All of these guys were men that were part of the feminist movement. The difficulty that I think men, and probably people in general, have is with the angry element of society—be it men or women—that have axes to grind. The feminists, for instance, men and women, are working to create this sense of understanding and mutuality—whereas the radical feminists, the ones that say that all sex with men is rape, they're the ones that are creating the backlash to the women's movement, because they're not healed. They may have been victimized by a man or men at some point in life and they're not resolved or healed."

Fathers' rights advocate H. W. "Sonny" Burmeister, president of the Children's Rights Council of Georgia, sees a men's movement much broader than the enterprise spawned by Bly. "There's definitely a fathers' movement," he says. "There's the gay men's movement. There's a men's movement in backlash to the National Organization of Women." Most men in such activities, Burmeister acknowledges, are "affected men—gay men, divorced men, men who have had their children taken away from them. It's been a reaction." But that, he believes, is beginning to change.

"I think that men in general are starting to say, 'Wait a minute. What's happening to our society? What's happening to our kids?'" And as a result, he says, men are starting to take an interest in social issues. "I think that there's a real uprise, a real core movement of men, not for somebody's ego, not for somebody's revenge, not for somebody's dysfunctional, pathological depression over a divorce, or losing their kids or something, but [stemming from] real caring."

James Sniechowski, founder of the Menswork Center in Los Angeles, dismisses the very concept of a men's movement: "In my opinion, there never was a men's movement. If we are going to use, for instance, the feminist movement for a model of what a movement is, the suffragette movement or whatever, there was no men's movement. There was a media flash for a short period of time that really brought the problem to the surface. One of the problems that occurred in the so-called men's movement was that some of the men who were doing the work rushed to the media and that's why the caricaturing occurred; but there is a movement occurring. It is what I call a movement in the psyche of men. And I communicate with men in Australia, in Rio de Janeiro, in London and Czechoslovakia; and I communicate with guys in South Africa, and in Ireland, and in Canada. And there is something going on in the psyche of Western men, and it's happening in all of those countries. There are 'men's movements' in every one of those countries. There are men's groups all over the world."

Sniechowski is uncertain whether the result of the activity will be political action. "It may have political fruits down the line. But what is happening is that men are going through a period of profound self-assessment. They're confused. They're without direction. They're scared. And part of what they want to reconnect with is whatever masculinity may mean, whatever manhood may mean. . . .

"Across the board, men are saying the same thing, that they're lonely, that they feel a sense of hunger that they can't get satisfied, that when they allow themselves to sink into their bodies and not just reside in their cerebral cortex, they feel a sense of emptiness; and that the emptiness has a lot to do with a connectedness, a disconnection is what the men are talking about."

Much of that talk is taking place quietly, in men's groups and other forums somewhat out of the media's distorting glare. "There are not a lot of major events going on," said Sniechowski. "And I think one of the reasons for it is that this is not something that is terribly public. Men did not like the [media] flash, they wanted to move into a corner and say, 'We need to do this work quietly first.' Nobody said those statements [but] once the flash became intense, men began to back away. Once the flash subsided, they began to come back . . . because it's not ready to be public; because men are having to change something that is fundamental, in my opinion, to the meaning of masculinity for centuries. And nobody is ready to start making statements about what the hell that change really, really is."

David Blankenhorn, author of *Fatherless America* and chairman of the National Fatherhood Initiative, is reluctant to call the recent surge of activity around fatherhood a movement "because we haven't succeeded yet in mobilizing men and women at the grass roots. What we have succeeded at doing in these early stages is gaining attention for the problem among opinion leaders—in the media, and politics and the private sector. . . . And whether or not we're going to get people to actually call an eight-hundred number and join a movement, we just don't know that. A movement to me means that there's a level of spontaneous activity at the local level. I mean populism was a movement, the civil rights movement was a movement."

Psychologist Alvin Baraff is indifferent to what all the men-centered activity is called: "I don't care whether there's a movement or not. I don't consider that I'm part of a movement. I consider that I just put my focus on trying to work in a therapy setting with men."

One group that is not at all coy about announcing its intention to be a major movement is Promise Keepers, an evangelical men's ministry founded by former Colorado University football coach Bill McCartney. The Promise Keepers' mission statement asserts the belief that God will use Promise Keepers "as a spark in His hand to ignite a nationwide movement calling men from all denominational, ethnic, and cultural backgrounds to reconciliation, discipleship, and godliness."

In 1994, Promise Keepers, according to its own figures, drew over 50,000 men to its revival in Anaheim, California, over 60,000 to Hoosier Dome in Indianapolis, and a capacity crowd of 52,000 to Folsom Field in Boulder, Colorado. The organization projected a total attendance at 600,000 for its fourteen scheduled mass meetings in 1995. Randy Phillips, president of the ministry, believes that the numbers indicate that the nation is "on the threshold of an awakening."

One point that several of these men make is irrefutably true. Men are not instigating anything remotely comparable to the political and social uproar that defined the women's movement. Men's gurus are not, by and large, trying to shake up "the system" or undermine the "matriarchy." With the exception of advocates for divorced fathers or some of the loopier characters-at-large, they are not demanding any broad array of new legal rights. Even the more politically sophisticated organizations, such as the Washington, D.C.–based Men's Health Network, are not trying fundamentally to change the political system. The network spent much of its energies in 1993 and early 1994 securing Congressional approval for the notably noncontroversial National Men's Health Week in June 1994.

Yet something noteworthy is going on—and not merely in the imaginations of middle-aged mythologists and therapists, though they sometimes show a tendency to make the enterprise into something grander than it is. Many ordinary men are indeed feeling a need to ask, "What does it mean today to be a man?" or, at the least, to have their own feelings and uncertainties confirmed through those of other men. All the guffawing over the men in the woods has made it easy to dismiss the fact that masculinity has come upon troubled times and that many men are still searching for answers and reassurance.

The taxi driver who mistook me for a therapist and remarked on what a "miraculous thing" it would be "to be able to sit with . . . men and be able to talk" was only one of several ordinary men I encountered who evidenced an intense interest in exploring masculinity. A television technician, upon hearing that I was writing this book, gave me his card and made me promise to call him and chat about what was happening with men. Even the lawyer who thought that the idea of a men's movement is "ludicrous" acknowledged that men need to get better at reaching out to one another.

"Some men . . . either don't have an outlet or have an inability to communicate, though they want to," he said. "And I've seen that and I do believe that it's a difference between men and women, that women are not really afraid to speak about things that are very intimate. . . . They don't view [that] as weakness, they don't view feelings and sadness and doubt as signs of weakness where I think men do. It's very difficult to talk about certain things. You're expressing these sorts of . . . feelings and things that have a tendency to depress you or to make you feel bad. . . . I think I have the ability to [express myself]. I just don't think I kind of need to do it, and I think if I needed to do it I probably could. But I think that there are many people, and I think that even myself on occasion, you want to speak about things, but . . . you just don't."

James Levine, of the Fatherhood Project at the New York-based Families and Work Institute, says that his experience running seminars and focus groups for men in corporations confirms the need that many men have to put their issues on the table. "I was amazed at the number of guys who showed up for these focus groups," he says. At one company, he recalls, "they had so many guys showing up that we had to stay on an extra day to run more focus groups." He takes their intense interest as an indication that, given a sanctioned area of safety, men will allow their concerns to surface.

Thomas Henry, of the Responsive Fathers Program in Philadelphia, has had a similar experience in working with young, inner-city unwed fathers. Originally, he said, he had planned to reduce the number of scheduled roundtable meetings of the men's group from once a week to biweekly or maybe monthly. Whenever he tried to cut back, however, the young fathers would outvote him. The support they received from the other men around the table was something they were simply unwilling to give up or see diminished.

Vincent Aires, one of the men enrolled in the program, recalled that his first reaction to the discussions had not been so positive. Two of his friends had told him about the group and he had responded, "I didn't want to hear about that shit. Go, and surround the table with a whole bunch of guys and we're going to talk about *my* problems. No, it ain't gonna work like that." When he discovered that the process was helpful, his attitude changed accordingly. "You can see how emotional everybody is about this program. If this program was to leave today, I think all of us would try to get money up to keep this going. Without this, some of us guys ain't nothing," he said.

Journalist Michel Marriott recalls that his initial participation in a men's group also felt a bit strange. "We had music going on in the background. We figured we had to have some kind of activity. We couldn't just sit around and all look at each other and start. So the activity was that we would all chip in and make a meal, which we thought was sort of symbolic of putting down our arrows and bows; and we're going to do, in a sense, women's work. So we're all making salads. And we did make a few macho concessions—I mean, like a lot of red meat. But we made this meal." But awkward as things were in the beginning, once the conversation began, it went on for hours.

Sexual fidelity, says Marriott, was a major issue, as was sexuality in general. There was also much talk of fathers and watching them deteriorate. One man's father, a proud man, had died of cancer, "and the son had to carry him up the steps to bathe him." And they talked about "how he dealt with that; how it made him feel; whether that is what awaits all men." They also discussed physical toughness—and why certain men felt compelled to flaunt it. He recalled being in a nightclub with a close friend, a man of small stature, who was accidentally touched by another man and responded by trying to humiliate him. "He got in the other guy's face and called him names, even called him a bitch—[as if to say], 'You're not even a man, but the lowest form of a woman.'" His group also talked, recalls Marriott, "about the pressure almost all of us with women feel ... of having the societal role of being a provider."

The discussions were worthwhile for Marriott, who believes that he is not alone in needing the support of other men. "There are things that are common that I think bother lots and lots of men. I think some of the stuff, too, is particular to black men; but I think there's a lot of universality here. I think men are troubled—many are troubled on a conscious level, but many are troubled on a subconscious level about their place in the society, about our usefulness. It used to be fairly blatant. You could look at a man and know his purpose. He was a protector. He was a hunter. He was a procreator, because he was always sort of a sexual predator. Those things were very, very obvious, in his behaviors and just in the physical makeup of *The Man.* Today, all of those things almost mock men because we have all of this mechanism that really doesn't plug in anywhere in society."

Group discussions in which men delve into the meaning of manhood are not new. What is new is society's willingness to think seriously about the fate and mission of men. Much of that concern is driven not by touchy-feely men's groups but by signs of crises in the world—crises that are interconnected because they derive, at least in part, from the changes taking place in the role of men.

The skyrocketing crime rate, as the National Fatherhood Initiative's David Blankenhorn acknowledges, has a lot to do with the recent flurry of interest in fatherhood, for violent crime is committed, for the most part, by young males—largely, he notes, from fatherless households. Promise Keepers has similarly linked its ministry to real-world problems—crime, drug abuse, rising suicide rates—and to confusion in men's roles. According to the organization's literature, the world of "negotiable values, confused identities, and distorted priorities" has provided Christian men with "an unprecedented opportunity to seize this moment." Rising concern over the well-being of children has allowed advocates for divorced men to link their cause to that of the growing number of children who are dealing with their fathers' absence.

The shifting nature of the economy and the fact that more and more able-bodied men are unable to find decent jobs raise difficult questions about the purpose of men (particularly those who are uneducated) in a society that has nothing for them to do. And even as men endeavor to redefine their place in society, their sons are increasingly endangered. In 1993, boys aged fifteen to nineteen were more than six times as likely to be murdered as were girls of the same age, and they were twenty times more likely to kill someone else. Boys aged ten to fourteen were also at a much higher risk of homicide than were girls in that age group. In their analysis of the 1993 figures for murder, FBI statisticians noted that the "most striking change in murder victimization since the 1980s is the youthfulness of the victims." Between 1975 and 1993, the number of murder victims aged ten to fourteen increased by 71 percent, with boys making up two-thirds of those killed.

Those boys who do not end up dead or in jail are much more likely than are girls to be judged emotionally disturbed or learning disabled. "Altogether, the research suggests that today's boys—deeply distressed and tragically misunderstood—may be victims of their own biology and society's confusion about masculinity. . . . While they may disagree about the cause and treatment, none of the various schools of research would argue with the notion that boys are in a kind of crisis, and that their educational disabilities burden families and communities," observed author Michael D'Antonio in a *Los Angeles Times Magazine* article titled "The Fragile Sex."

Men's issues, in short, are not all as frivolous as they would appear from men self-indulgently beating tom-toms or exchanging insults with hostile feminists. And Dr. Jean Bonhomme, of the Atlanta-based National Black Men's Health Network, senses that more and more people are involving themselves in an emerging men's agenda. "That perception may be real, or it may be that I'm getting into a network of people who are doing things all over the country," he allows. "But I will say one thing: I think that men are becoming a lot more vocal, and I think that's a healthy thing. I think there are things men would have taken on the chin five years ago. Guys are saying 'Look, this isn't right.'"

Men's health advocates, taking a cue from women, for instance, have focused on problems that disproportionately affect men—prostate cancer, testicular cancer, alcoholism, and lung disease. Other men are speaking out on issues far afield of those the public generally associates with the men's movement—black and Latino men are championing stronger roles for male leaders in inner-city communities, and Asian American men are decrying their limited portrayal in movies and other forms of mass media.

Many of the voices contradict or conflict with one another. The Promise Keepers, for instance, believe that homosexuality is a sin. The leaders of the Fatherhood Initiative think that divorced men, regardless of their intentions, will almost always be lousy fathers. These various voices are certainly not coherent or congruous enough to add up to a movement—and probably never will be. But they do add up to something more than a few guys howling in the wilderness.

"Awakening" is probably as good a term as any to describe what is happening—although used not primarily in a religious or mystical sense but as in awakening to the fact that "men's" and "women's" issues are not only equally important but inextricably linked—both to each other and to many of the pressing social problems in our society.

Chapter 4

THE RISE AND DEMISE
OF THE SENSITIVE MAN

In 1994, I attended a conference in Nashville held to explore the status of fathers in America. Vice President Al Gore moderated the meeting, and his wife, Elizabeth "Tipper" Gore, presided over one all-female panel. The women had clearly been selected, in part, for their enlightened attitudes, but it soon became clear that their perspectives varied. Patricia Torres Ray, Minnesota's ombudsperson for families, spoke of people's resistance to accepting her husband in his caretaker role. When he told people he stayed home and took care of the baby, they would ask, "Yeah, but what do you do?" Her husband felt compelled to respond, "Well I'm working on my doctorate degree at the university." "I think he feels that he has to excuse himself for taking care of our baby at home," Ray observed.

Beverly Wolliver, an educator from Williamsburg, Kentucky, empathized with her. "If you have an opportunity to get a job, what is wrong with the man staying at home if that's what he wants to do?" she asked. "If I choose to go out and work, why should he not choose to stay with the kids for a while?"

Elizabeth Cross, a plain-spoken office manager from Memphis, Tennessee, weighed in with a decidedly different perspective. "Men should be the ones out front," she said. "The men are the leaders, or should be the leaders. Society has turned around somewhat and a lot of females find ourselves—and sometimes I'm in that predicament—where we have to step out front and take the lead and do what we have to do; but hopefully the time always comes back around where that man will come in and say, 'Okay, dear, it's time for me to step up here and be the man, and it's time for me to do what I have to do.'" At that point Mrs. Gore interjected, rather timidly, "Well, do you think men are getting mixed messages?"

The truth is, of course, that society is constantly sending mixed messages—and has been for quite some time. And although men may not be fixated on the men's movement, many are extremely confused by the conflicting signals they are receiving—especially from women, who, as journalist Michel Marriott observed earlier, "may one day, or one moment, want this part of the man and one moment want the other part." In addition, a growing number of men seem to be at sea. As Darnell Whitten, a New Yorker in his early thirties, put it: "I think that in general men, young men, feel hopeless. They feel like things are falling apart."

In the distant past, things were much clearer—or at least most of us believe that they were. Somewhere along the line things began to change. Many pundits place the historical point of demarcation around the time of the Industrial Revolution.

That revolution not only reshaped modern society, but it was a seminal event in the shaping of modern man. It pulled him further away from home and deeper into the world of commerce, weakening his ties to the family, and particularly to his sons. In previous generations, sons were likely to follow in their fathers' footsteps. As most men went from being artisans, farmers, and small-time entrepreneurs to generic employees, they were rendered less capable of leaving a livelihood to their descendants. Man's shrinking role left him with something of an identity crisis, which recent events—notably the decrease in employment opportunities and security and the rise of the modern woman's movement—exacerbated. For a brief time, however, some men thought they saw a way out of their role confusion as a chorus of female voices told them precisely what the modern man should be: a paragon of sensitivity with the aura of Alan Alda.

Writer Harry Stein apparently was one of those earnest fellows who went to extraordinary lengths to remake himself into the stereotypical Sensitive Man. But Stein ultimately concluded that he had made a mistake, that, in fact, the entire group of men who transformed themselves at women's insistence were sold a bogus bill of goods.

In a May 1994 *Esquire* cover story, Stein denounced "the fabrication of a more sensitive, tolerant, giving, pliable species of male" as a "screwy bit of social engineering." Even women ultimately saw the pathetically timid creature ("basically a woman with a penis," is Stein's description) as not worthy of their attentions and snickered at "the too-sensitive man, sniveling about his feelings." Finally, Stein suggested, men were coming to their senses. The Alan Alda wanna-bes were giving way to Rush Limbaugh types. Men were realizing "that this business of allowing women to dictate the terms in the ongoing exchange between the sexes has been a disaster."

This is not the first time that men have rejected this particular ideal. In 1982, Bruce Feirstein's runaway bestseller *Real Men Don't Eat Quiche* drolly lamented the rise of the "wimp": "Alan Alda types who cook and clean and relate to their wives. Phil Donahue clones who are sensitive and vulnerable and understanding of their children."

Nearly ten years later, Aaron Kipnis observed in *Knights Without Armor* that "women's attempts to modify or control men's thinking and behavior" had led to a more "sensitive, receptive, gentle, conscientious, and socially responsible male." Yet, he added, "many of the so-called new, changing men are often powerless and ineffective in the world. As a result, women today are asking, 'Where are all the real men?'"

In 1990, four years before Stein pronounced the Sensitive Man passé, *Time* magazine declared a changing of the zeitgeist: "Now the sensitive male is a wimp and an object of derision to boot. . . . Now it's goodbye, Alan Alda; hello, Mel Gibson, with your sensitive eyes and your lethal weapon. Hi there, Arnold Schwarzenegger, the devoted family man with terrific triceps. The new surge of tempered macho is everywhere. Even the male dummies in store windows are getting tougher. Pucci Manikins is producing a more muscular model for the new decade that stands 6 ft. 2 in. instead of 6 ft. and has a 42-in. chest instead of its previous 40." Men, according to one macho man quoted in the article, were rising up against the feminists who had been "busy castrating American males" and pouring "this country's testosterone out the window."

More than a decade before *Time* rang down the curtain on the Sensitive Man, author Peter Stearns, in *Be a Man*, set down the basic argument. Just because men must and should accept equality, he said, "it does not follow that they owe women, society, or themselves a basic redefinition of manhood or the male personality. We are not compelled to become androgynous, and there are good social as well as gender reasons to resist androgyny." Most men, he declared, "believe themselves masculine, which means they can at best be bewildered, at worst repelled, by a thorough attack on an identification they cannot escape."

In reality, the so-called new sensitive guy was always more fiction than fact. A fantasy plucked from the minds of trendy intellectuals, he existed mostly in a gossamer world of chitchat—where perception and reality are presumed to be the same. Much of the male population saw him as something of a joke. And men were not convinced that women thought much of him either. Many men thought, as Columbia graduate student Ken Siedler indelicately put it, that women claimed they want "one thing and then sleep with another." Or, as Charles

Reeves, a twenty-six-year-old law student concluded, they wanted sensitivity with no loss of manliness: "They want a man who is sensitive to them but at the same time exhibits traditional masculine traits." Even those fashionably dutiful men, such as Stein, who took Sensitive Man as a role model were, in large measure, playing out a charade.

To "win the favor of women," many men felt they had to renounce the traditional role, recalls Warren Hoge, an editor for the *New York Times.* "How successful men were at making that change, I don't know. But my impression is . . . it became important for men to advertise the fact that they were sharing responsibility at home, becoming nurturing fathers and husbands. I don't know at that point what became feigned performance and what became real performance."

Rault Kehlor, a television production worker in his early twenties, agrees that many men assumed the sensitive pose "to get babes," but he thinks the result was generally good. "If you make that sort of decision to be that way, whether it's to get babes or if you really want to be able to share feelings and you're sick of the macho image, it doesn't really matter. It's all positive," he said.

Without question, many men were fed up with macho posturing. And some sincerely resolved to explore, like Dustin Hoffman's Tootsie, what they fancied to be the feminine side of themselves. Even assuming that most men wanted to acquire it, however, sensitivity is not exactly the easiest thing to master. It's not like, say, driving a standard-shift car, when a few days behind the wheel basically prepares you for the winding highways ahead.

Moreover, even at the height of Sensitive Man chic, popular culture continued to extol the classically macho archetype. James Bond and his countless successors and imitators—cool killers, often alone, generally aloof, who smiled as they kicked butt—remained heroic figures to adolescents and adults alike.

"In high schools that we've gone into, the heroes that . . . males cite are people like Arnold Schwarzenegger, Sylvester Stallone, Jean Claude Van Damme, Wesley Snipes," observed Neil Tiff, director of the Fathers' Resources Center in Minneapolis, Minnesota. Such figures, Tiff pointed out, "don't have very healthy conflict resolution skills." Yet, many men identify more with them than with the androgynous types who write "About Men" columns in the *New York Times.*

Danixia Cuevas, a legal services attorney in New Jersey, sees scarce evidence in the real world that the macho man was ever replaced by the sensitive gent. "I represent poor women who are often the victims of domestic violence and each and every one that comes to my office, they have their stereotypical machista pig: 'You can't go out.' 'You can't go out with your relatives.' 'You can't work.' 'You better cook, clean.' 'You better wash my clothes.' 'You better iron.'"

"Among the poorer culture there is still a machista male role that is very much alive," Cuevas noted. Even among middle-class professionals, she said, male chauvinism is flourishing—though perhaps it is more subtle than in years past. "I had a case in court," Cuevas recalled, "and it was the first time I had met my adversary, who was a white man. . . . I had a dress on. I had low heels . . . I looked professional . . . like I [do when I] go to work. . . . He said to me, 'Oh Ms. Cuevas,' and he touched my hand, 'it was such a pleasure dealing with you.' And he's flirting with me. I was like, '[I'm] . . . a lawyer. Deal with me at that level. I am a professional.'

"And it happens over and over again. Not only to me, but to all my friends. The same things happen. They'll just look at you and just the way they treat you, like 'You're this young Latina woman. Let me take care of you. Let me show you the ropes around our little old boys' network.' I really don't think that it's unique to the legal profession because I've had other friends who do other things, and they all tell me the same thing in different forms. So I don't think things have gotten that much better, unfortunately."

One reason that things haven't gotten "much better" is that it's so easy to slip into familiar roles—even for men and women who have had it pounded into them that gender stereotypes are bad. Kevin Bruyneel, a twenty-nine-year-old graduate student in political science, notes that members of his peer group—"academics, people who are generally conscious of the women's movement, conscious of gender roles and gender stereotyping"—find it awfully hard to live their professed beliefs. "And so people who you would think would make an effort or who do try to make an effort to fracture some of those roles in their own relationships fall back into stereotypes quite easily." Bruyneel confesses that he has been with women who complain that whenever they talk about emotional needs, he tends to keep his feelings to himself, forcing the women to do most of the work. "Now that may be more me than the masculine stereotype," he said, "but that is generally the masculine stereotype. So I see a definite fracture in the way in which the political and the sort of intellectual discussions of the change in gender stereotypes manifest themselves. . . . There's a gap, or there's just a problem, in translating from the idea to actually engaging."

With many men, a gap exists as well between their willingness to bend gender rules for female colleagues and to bend them for their wives. Rosanna Rosado, a vice president of New York's Health and Hospitals Corporation, finds it fascinating that some men respect her career, but want their wives to stay home. She finds it even more interesting that they insist on treating their wives and daughters by such different standards. "They have their daughters in college, and want their daughters to be successful, but they don't want their wives to work. They don't want their wives to have any real [professional] role. . . . I think there is a contradiction there."

Yet, hypocrisy may not be the only explanation for the contradictory attitudes observed. People who are moving in the dark toward the unknown are unlikely to chart a straight course. They are apt to zig and zag and, at times, totally reverse direction and to wonder whether they even know where they should be headed.

Many Americans never expected to have to take this journey into the gender wilderness. Men especially were caught unaware. When the women's movement exploded, many men had no idea what to make of it. They "didn't have a clue at that time about what was going on in their lives, but they started reacting," theorizes Stephen Johnson, the clinical psychologist who founded the Men's Center Los Angeles in Woodland Hills, California. Washington psychologist and MenCenter founder Alvin Baraff believes that many men viewed the tumult among women much as they would view a parade—as an event with lots of fanfare that eventually would go away. "Well, guess what, it didn't end," he says. As men began to realize that the women's movement wouldn't go away, they had no choice but to try to adapt.

The creation of the Sensitive Man was one such accommodation. And though he was not quite as ubiquitous as Harry Stein and company seem to believe, he was, in certain circles, a rather smug, if not altogether authentic, presence—and nowhere more so than in the "About Men" column of the *New York Times Magazine.* "Within months of the column's June 1983 launch," scoffed Stein, "it was being emulated in publications everywhere, its counterfeit voice aped by whole legions of actual men trying to show themselves to advantage before actual women."

Even the *Times* editors are not convinced that the voice was genuine. Warren Hoge, formerly editor of the *New York Times Magazine,* contrasts "About Men" with the "Hers" column—in which women would frankly open up and offer access to their souls. "Imagine the counterpart column from a man. I never saw it," says Hoge. Men "don't bleed well publicly," agreed Abbott "Kit" Combes, the column's first editor. "There's an inbuilt fear of really revealing yourself, which it seems that women don't feel so fiercely. Men are comfortable writing about their fathers, their sons, sometimes their ex-wives, and sports. It's a rare one that gets really inside and opens up."

Not that the *Times* had set out to delve into man's inner soul. The original objective was more modest and somewhat less resolved. With feminist concerns surging during the 1970s and 1980s, the *Times* editors realized that, sooner or later, the reverberations would come blasting through the male world. They sought an innovative way to cover the impact.

Edward Klein, who was the magazine's editor during much of the 1980s, recalls kicking the issue around with the paper's executive editor. "Abe Rosenthal and I felt that while the women's movement and the impact and effects of the women's movement were being widely explored in a variety of forums, no one had bothered to explore the impact of the women's movement on men." The effect, they realized, had to be profound. "You can't alter one side of the sexual equation without altering the other as well," Klein notes. So they came up with "About Men," seeing it as something of a counterpart to "Hers," which was then running in the daily paper.

"The goal of the column is to muse about the male life, and to try to make sense of it; to be introspective and informative without being stodgy and strident," wrote column editor Combes, in a March 1983 planning memo. "Are men reexamining their masculinity in light of the movement for female identity? Have men ever, in fact, defined their 'role'? Do men have a clear-cut notion of what it means to be a man?" Combes saw his writers tackling such questions. He also envisioned numerous articles, however, that would be distinct from the "inward-directed" essays on the male experience.

There would be stylishly written pieces of reportage on

such male-oriented subjects as "what it is like to attend the races at Ascot, or how an Egyptian copes with more than one wife, of a Frenchman's mania for bicycle racing, or taking your son to watch a baseball team's spring training." In addition, he anticipated articles offering advice on male toys and gadgets.

Once the column was launched, the magazine was inundated with submissions, and the editors soon discovered that they were publishing a number of similar compositions. "We found ourselves awash in oversensitive guys," says Klein. As the editors acknowledge in a 1987 collection of the columns, the magazine caught hell for favoring "wimps over red-blooded American males." It's easy to see the critics' point. In the aforementioned collection, Paul Theroux confesses, "I have always disliked being a man. The whole idea of manhood in America is pitiful, a little like having to wear an ill-fitting coat for one's entire life." Michael E. McGill observes that "men make poor best friends." Noel Perrin acknowledges his membership in "a large class of men and women . . . who are essentially androgynous." Thomas Flanagan discovers that he is a "wimp." The abundance of such self-consciously penned light-as-taffeta trifles helped foster the impression that sensitive guys were sprouting all over the landscape.

What was actually sprouting, as we have seen, was something a good deal more ambiguous and more diverse. Though some guys were trying their best, for any number of reasons, to fit the sensitive-guy stereotype, others were having nothing to do with it. And many men, probably the majority, found themselves somewhere in between—trying to puzzle out not only how real men should act, but how modern women should behave. At the same time, they were struggling with their reactions to a society that had decided that men were fair game for ridicule and abuse.

Journalist Michel Marriott takes the male mistreatment somewhat personally. "There are times when I look at commercials and I become incensed, because I feel like I've come [to] a certain place, and I think men have come [to] a certain place; and there are certain things that we don't do, or that we don't do as much of. And we understand when we do them that they're wrong and we shouldn't do them. Yet now it's almost like under the idea of fair play, the thing is reversed. I mean like that Hyundai commercial about a man's sports car being proportional to the length of his genitalia is sexist in the most abhorrent way. If they did that kind of thing [with] a woman," said Marriott, and implied that a women's choice of automobiles "has to do with what she's hiding in her blouse, and put that out as a commercial, it would be just blatantly sexist and should be condemned. But yet there's sort of a wink, a nod and a giggle when it's done against men."

By the same token, Marriott noted, he was disturbed by the Diet Coke commercial that features a hunky construction worker removing his shirt: "I see that, and I see like that's okay." Yet, in Marriott's view, it is anything but okay. Settling accounts by making men endure the kind of sexism once reserved for women strikes him as counterproductive.

"For a time I did a lot of work at home and I got to see a lot of day-time television," he says. "That is no man's land. . . . You could not have shows like that every day, where you have men who come on and complain about women, and how they abuse you. . . . But somehow, the impression is—maybe because of all the oppression that went on in the past—that [men are] fair game. And I think it has an effect on men. I'm starting to see more and more men's groups popping up, as if they're an oppressed group. You know, men organized to watch the media for anti-male stuff; because I think men are beginning to feel put upon by this stuff. You know, as women are assuming more responsibility and power in society, they're committing a lot of the same sins that we're being condemned for. And hopefully our behavior is beginning to change."

Without question, the behavior of many men is changing in ways that virtually everyone would concede are for the better. Sociologist Michael Kimmel, writing in the *Washington Post* in 1993, observed, "Few 1990s men fit the traditional picture of distant father, patriarchal husband and work-obsessed bread-winner; fewer still have dropped out of the working world completely into full-time daddydom and househusbandhood. Rather than a suburban conformist or high-flying single yuppie, today's organization man carries a briefcase while pushing a baby carriage. He's in his late thirties or forties, balding, perhaps a bit paunchy since there's no time these days for the health club. He no longer wears power ties, and his shirts are rumpled. While he considers his career important, he doesn't want to sacrifice time with his family. His wife may have a demanding job, which he supports; but he may wonder if she thinks he's less of a man than her father, and he may resent her for the time she spends away from the home."

In some respects Kimmel's portrait of the 1990s man is as fanciful as that of the Sensitive Man. It clearly applies only to members of the professional class, and only to a small portion of them. For even within the same socioeconomic group, men are simply too variable to sum up neatly with one grand phenotype. But at least Kimmel admits the possibility that men are ambivalent and being tugged in conflicting directions. One problem with the so-called Sensitive Man was that he was too pure, too noble, too unconflicted to be of this world. Another problem was that he was responding not so much to a real social or economic need as to a cultural fashion. It was as if certain men said to themselves, "Oh, women now seem to want a sensitive man; let me become one for a while." In real life, people are not so mutable. If they are going to go through all the trouble of reinventing themselves, they usually have a damn good reason to do so.

Those males who actually are in the forefront of the role-reversal revolution do not necessarily bear any resemblance to the creatures conjured up by supposedly hip magazine writers. They may not be particularly androgynous or eager to share their feelings at the drop of a hat. They may, instead, be more like Jaime Quiñones, a strapping construction worker and ex-marine, who leaves no doubts about his masculinity but who freely admits that, in a metaphorical sense, his wife wears the pants.

Quiñones, who is in his early thirties, is a product of East Harlem, the Bronx, and the U.S. Marine Corps—which he joined at the age of eighteen. In summer 1994, he was well into his fourth year of marriage to a woman—Rosanna Rosado, vice president of the Health and Hospitals Corporation—whom he happily acknowledged is more professionally accomplished than he. The afternoon we spent together at his home in the Bronx, he was busily at work preparing for a barbecue. He was also weary, having spent his entire week's vacation painting, fixing things up, and getting the back patio in shape. "I did this all for her," he said, referring to his wife, as he surveyed the results of his labor. But his major job, Quiñones made clear, was to care for his two-year-old son.

Not that he is a stay-at-home husband. He wields a jack-hammer for eight hours a day. At the end of his shift, he is sure to be home for his child. "Rosie, you know, she has her career," said Quiñones. "I don't have a career. I've done many jobs. I've done security jobs. I went into construction. I did a plumbing job. And now I'm back in construction again. I decided to take the hard route. Instead of going to college, I went to the service." She, he explained, "is in demand all the time. See, I'm not. She's always busy. You know, weekends, people on the phone." Since he knows she cannot be a traditional mother, he has followed the same schedule ever since his son and name-sake was born.

Every morning at 4:30, he awakens. "I make his milk. I

make my coffee. . . . I give him his milk. I change his Pampers if he's really wet. I go take my shower. I go back down, have my other cup of coffee. And then I get in my car." At the end of the workday, he rushes home and takes a quick shower and allows himself a few moments of private time before picking up his son at 5 P.M. from the baby-sitter down the street. The rest of the evening is devoted to taking care of his child. "If Rosie comes home early, I'm lucky. But she comes home at nine or ten o'clock sometimes. I have to put the baby to bed."

When he was growing up, Quiñones could not have envisioned such a role for a man. His father, he recalled, "had that old attitude. . . . The man is the breadwinner, and the woman stays home and has the babies. And that's the way it is. And when he comes home, she has to take care of him all the time. Everything—the socks, the clothes. You know, ironing, the food." Men with such expectations "won't cook. They won't throw away the garbage. They won't even clean up their plate."

When his parents were divorced, Quiñones and his sister found, however, that a male was not necessarily a monarch. He was raised primarily by his mother (though his father was sometimes present), and she made him do what his father no doubt would have considered women's work. "I took care of myself, buying my own clothes," said Quiñones. "I always cleaned up my own room."

The Marine Corps reinforced that training and "had a lot to do with where I am now," noted Quiñones, who recalls his time in the service fondly. "I was on top when I was a marine. I had a good score, plus my attitude. And everything else that was going on." The Marine Corps taught him independence. "I had to depend on myself. I had to clean up. I had to have my uniform spick and span and ironed every day [and be] clean-shaven every day. . . . And they instilled that in you. They taught me discipline, courage, honor and the whole shebang."

Getting together with Rosado, he said, strengthened those traits. At that point, he was ready to accept responsibilities he had not been willing to accept earlier, though he had been married once before. He married his first wife, he explained, "out of chivalry." She became pregnant. "I married her because of the baby. I thought that was going to be the best thing, but it wasn't. She wasn't what I wanted." At the time, he was a heavy drinker. "So my head wasn't straight at all. The liquor had me bad." The drinking, combined with his military obligations, made it impossible for him to be a good parent to his daughter. "I wasn't around there for her when she was growing up. I was in the service, we got married, I left back to the service. I was away almost a year before I saw her again." The marriage ended in divorce, and he connected with Rosado, whom he had known in high school but had never seriously dated.

Soon things became serious. "We got married, and she straightened me out," he said with a laugh. "After four months, she said, 'That's it.' And that was it." He gave up alcohol, and he became more purposeful. Previously, said Quiñones, he had not been particularly focused on working, but Rosanna helped him prepare for interviews and insisted that he do his homework and show up. Afterward, whenever he went for a job interview, "I had it all planned out. 'Cause she taught me all that. After I straightened up, any job I went after, I got." "*Any* job," he repeated, with evident pride.

He also began to contemplate the possibility of being a real father. "I really never thought about it until Rosie and I got together. And I thought about having a boy." "If I could have a boy," he had said to himself, "that would be great." He recalls having read somewhere that people "were put on this earth to take care of our children, to raise them up. And once we're done, we've done our job, and we can go on." To Quiñones, that seemed to sum up his role perfectly: "I got my job. I do my thing. I come home and take care of my son."

His wife, he added, "wants me to take care of her. But most of my time is to take care of Jaime. She can take care of herself. I don't have to be doing all these errands for her, running around for her. . . . The way I feel, when you have children, you have to spend most of your time with them. You have to nurture them." He boasts that his son, who is not even three, can jump and land on both feet. The child care magazines, he points out, say that doesn't happen until the age of four. "And he's doing it now. He's more advanced."

Asked about his aspirations for his son, Quiñones said, "He's going to be just like his mother. He has his mother's brains and his daddy's brawn. Rosie's the smart one in the family. I'm still the macho guy who hangs out in the street with his leather jacket up and stuff like that. I'm still like that, when I get with my friends. But around my wife, you can't be all macho. Cause she slaps that down."

Does the role reversal bother him? "What you gonna do?" he sighed. "You gonna put the woman down and stop her from what she wants to do, and then make her feel miserable?" If so, "she's not going to give you the love you want. You have to make them happy first. That's the way I feel. You have to make her happy first, and the rest will come along. She gave me my son. I'm happy now. And I have another one on the way. And if I have another son, I'll really be happy. I told her she blessed me when she gave me my son. "

He "can't speak for the other guys" in his situation, Quiñones stated, but certainly he has heard the comments—people who say in astonishment, "What, your woman makes more than you? And you're working. Come on!" "I don't have no time for that," he scoffed; "I mean I can't think about that. You know, she's making more money. Great. Let's get more things. Let's save more." If someone says, "'Oh, your wife makes so much money. If your wife is making this kind of money, what are you doing?' I don't know what to say."

He has no regrets about the situation. At times he finds himself thinking, "I can't believe where I'm at right now. Got a house, got my car. And my wife has a great job. 'What does you wife do?' 'Well, she's a vice president.'" His job, he notes, is of a different universe. "The job I'm doing, I'll be lucky if I hit sixty. 'Cause it's a lot of shit down there. Asbestos, dirt, and dust and heat, and the steam. I go down there and it's like three hundred Fahrenheit down there. That's the way it feels. It's killing me."

Yet he insisted he loves his work. "It's like the Marine Corps, you know. The thing I like about my job is the camaraderie with the guys, you know. I don't have many friends. I didn't lose a lot of my friends; I just stopped hanging out with them because they're all into the same thing: drinking quarts of beer, doing a lot of nothing. You know, I'm thirty-three years old. . . . Plus I don't drink anymore anyway. But they're still doing the same thing. Coke and the smoking. And they're into the same old things. You got to stop. That's the only way you're going to grow."

The unfortunate consequence of growing up for men, however, Quiñones conceded, is that it becomes harder to hold on to friends. "You need your buddies. . . . You don't need them all the time, but you need them sometimes."

He returned to the point later in the conversation. "I think we need somebody to talk to. The camaraderie. That's what it is. That's what it's all about. You know, I was in the service for four years. Man, I had the best guys. Until this day I still dream about the service. I dream about the guys and everything. We had the companionship, man. You need that. Every man needs that. "

Women, he says, seem to have more time for friendship. "You know, I don't have time for that. I tell the guys, come by my house. You see my car. I'm always here. They don't come by, you know. . . . That's why I have my job, you might say. You know, my job is my friends. And I see them eight hours. I don't tell them everything I do, but I know I need them. You can't tell your wife everything. Your wife is not going to understand you like a guy does."

When asked about the women's movement and women's liberation, he responded, "I think they fucked up the man when they did that. They fucked up the man, 'Oh, you don't cry. You never cry. You never show me your feelings.' Then you start showing them your feelings [and] they say you're a punk."

He laughed. "My wife, she tried that shit on me. But I don't go for it." Yet, as his wife attests, Quiñones has not exaggerated his caretaker responsibilities or his willingness to support her in a traditionally male role. Nor, she argues, is he, in that respect, unique. She has seen other men of her generation (and within her own family) gracefully take on duties that men once eschewed.

"My father is a great dad and all," she said, "but my father didn't know how to work a washing machine. He was not helpful in the house. My mother was a traditional mother. She worked, came home, cooked. My dad watched the Flintstones while she helped us with homework. My relationship is very different. My brother's relationship with his wife is very different. Our men—my husband and my brother in his relationship and my brother-in-law in his relationship—they are partners. We're partners, and I think there is a generational difference. . . . It's not like, 'The washing is not my job.'"

She acknowledges that her husband sometimes seems thrown when she requires nurturing. "I think sometimes my husband is surprised when I react too emotionally to something. Yes, I do expect him to take care of me—not in a financial sense and not in all of the traditional senses, but I think that, like any woman or like any man, I need a hug. I need attention. I need to be told I look good. I need to be told that I'm appreciated. Yes, I expect him to take care of me."

*   *   *

One moral of Quiñones's story is that real people—even real macho men—have a way of undermining stereotypes. No one-size-fits-all paradigm could possibly capture how all males are or should be responding to today's world or today's women. Yet some men clearly are changing, and, for the most part, they are driven less by a desire to emulate images of a "new" trendy man than by the demands of daily life—which for men, regardless of their social class, increasingly means considering how to accommodate a woman's professional aspirations.

Chapter 5

DO WE REALLY WANT
MR. MOM?

Barbara Caplan of Yankelovich Partners Inc. sees compelling evidence in her survey statistics that many men are grossly insensitive to the needs of working women. "They want it all," she says, meaning that men want women to work but also to take care of the children and the home.

She clearly has a point. Numerous women these days work two "shifts"—one at work and another at home. Yet to try to understand what is happening between the sexes today as a simple case of one gender or the other "wanting it all" is to misunderstand how much stock each sex has in clinging to tradition and how vigorously both sexes conspire to escape the practice of true equality.

Though the working woman has become the norm, society still continues to define men largely by their ability to pay the bills. "Even in the vast majority of families in which there are two wage-earners, the father is still seen as a primary bread-winner, if only because of continuing disparities between the salaries of male and female workers," commented Michael Lamb in *The Father's Role,* his 1987 book.

"Whatever his other roles in a family, a father is first and foremost expected to provide economic support. When he fails to do so, society considers him irresponsible, and the government evokes legal procedures to collect payment. If a father fails in other fathering roles, it is assumed that the mother will be there to fill those roles, to look after a child's other needs. But failure as a breadwinner is a mark of not measuring up," proclaimed a 1994 National Research Council report.

In 1978, *Time* polled a randomly selected group of registered voters and asked what qualities were important for "a real man." Sixty-seven percent said "being a good provider" was very important, and 29 percent rated it as somewhat important; only 3 percent said it was not important. Yankelovich Partners (which, in a previous incarnation, conducted the *Time* survey) does not now ask that question on its annual "monitor poll," an in-depth in-person survey of 2,500 Americans. It does, however, ask respondents to choose among several attributes that may define masculinity and many continue to link masculinity to breadwinning. In 1993, 43 percent of the respondents said "being masculine" means being a good provider for a man's wife and family, up from 35 percent ten years earlier. (The men's and women's responses were identical.)

I asked Caplan for her interpretation of the figures. She said that she took them to mean that women, particularly those in their "family formation years," were, in effect, saying that if the man makes enough money to support the household, then the woman could spend more time taking care of the kids. Although there are millions of exceptions, evidence indicates that men and women, on average, do indeed view work differently. Men tend to work longer hours, to be more concerned about job security, and to place more emphasis on (and be more optimistic about) their chances for advancement, according to a survey by the Families and Work Institute.

Lisa Jacobs, a twenty-seven-year-old publicist and writer, observed, "I think that the guys of my generation are confused, and so are the women. . . . Women's careers are really important, but many of us came from very traditional backgrounds, and there is this subconscious desire to emulate the parent. But there is also this recognition that things are changing. So, deep down,

I think there are a lot of women out there who see their primary role as that of supporter of the husbands and caretakers of the children, and the career comes secondary. But many women are not conscious of this. It's not perceived. *It's not the way women are supposed to be today.* And I think a lot of men . . . say that they don't want to have that burden of supporting a family. They want a women who's strong and who has her own career and her own ideas. But I think with them there is this underlying desire to have this he-man role, the king of the household role."

Thinking men and women have always known that, barring an extraordinary set of circumstances, people don't transform themselves overnight. So it is not exactly startling news that the feminist revolution is far from complete. Nor, given the dynamics of sexual politics and the general paucity of intergender empathy, is it surprising that men and women alike are concluding that they are getting a raw deal.

Women who are toiling in thankless jobs and raising children also find themselves not only struggling against discrimination at work, but facing unrealistic expectations at home. And men, faced with demands that they give up masculine privilege, wonder whether they are being offered a devil's bargain: Give up the benefits of being a man but retain all the disadvantages. So they question the brand of sexual equality that doesn't relieve them of the need to be the primary breadwinner or entitle them to a presumption of equal competence as a custodial parent.

In an age when many women are every bit as career oriented as the hardest-charging men, the idea of man as breadwinner seems more than a little quaint. Yet, as we have seen, the image refuses to die—although the increase in dual-career households has forced modifications in the archetype. These days, man is not necessarily *the* breadwinner, but *a* breadwinner, and not always the principal one at that. The result is not unqualified relief at shedding an outmoded and burdensome role, but often disorientation.

Some men, young and old alike, find the new flexibility troubling. An aspiring pop musician in his late twenties said he was worried that women with careers were abandoning their natural role. "I don't know how this may sound, how women may like it or not, but that is not what they were made to do," he said. "Society right now is like, 'Okay, we want women to work. We want women in high positions, to make them feel important.' So, they give them positions. At the same time as they give them these positions, you still have the man who is so used to being at work [that] he has to work a little harder. Therefore that makes the woman work harder. It's pushed into the minds of women now that they feel that they have to be equal to us, when they don't have to be that." A woman's "duty," he said, is to be domestic "because she has certain instincts beyond men, as far a childbearing, as far as child caring goes."

Other men, who are nowhere near as conservative as the would-be pop star, nonetheless, fret over how working women will affect them. A thirty-three-year-old unemployed engineer declared: "I've met women in the workplace who are very good at what they do, and there have also been some who are idiots. I've never really tied it to their gender. The only thing I have a problem with is basically reverse discrimination. They want to fulfill quotas and things like that at different companies, and you know, because I'm a Caucasian male, I'm the least desirable in that respect. And that's the only thing that really bothers me."

Not all men, of course, are rattled by the progress of women into and within the workplace. But most would agree with psychologist Stephen Johnson's assessment that "it's a whole new ball game for men" and that things are not made any easier by conflicting expectations that burden men with traditional roles and then condemn them for being traditional.

As journalist Michel Marriott observed, if the family starves, people tend to blame the man. Yet, because women are ubiquitous in the workplace and share the breadwinner burden, the provider role is no longer a reliable anchor for male identity. Society, however, does not seem disposed to sanction a new masculine concentration. Men are not seriously being urged to focus less on work and more on their families.

As Lisa Jacobs remarked, "There are a lot of men out there who would love to be househusbands, who would love to put family in front of career. But they can't. . . . There's a stigma against it." Certainly, society still looks askance at men who want to take much time off for, say, paternity leave or, for that matter, to do anything else that is not particularly career oriented—despite the fact that large numbers of men are unable to find work.

Many modern young professionals, despite their professed belief in sexual equality, cling reflexively to conventional roles. A professional woman in her early thirties recalled a point when her self-employed husband's business was not going well. She was not only worried, she confessed, but angry. *How dare he not carry his share of the load!* In retrospect, she said, she was ashamed of her reaction, for she knew that had her earnings dropped, he would not have complained about supporting her. The difference, of course, was that he was *The Man;* paying the bills was his job.

Ieva Massengill, a Chicago accountant, has noticed that some of her confidantes, both young and old, assume that a man is somehow deficient if he is not carrying most of the household's financial burden. She tells of one friend whose husband had been laid off, who was so angry at him for not contributing to the couple's finances that she was considering leaving him. Another, she said, had turned down a relatively good-paying job to stay temporarily unemployed while she awaited an opportunity at a more agreeable position. The preferred job paid considerably less, but it was more in keeping with her aims for personal fulfillment. "Women get angry if they're not allowed to follow their dreams," concluded Massengill. "They get pissed off if the husband can't support their unemployment."

Sean Casey, a law student in his midtwenties, reflecting on his relationship with his fiancée, said: "She goes to law school, too. But . . . I do one hundred percent of the finances. I'm in charge of buying the house. I have to buy the car. . . . I do every single financial thing. I tell her constantly, 'Don't worry about what school you go to. Your job should be nothing more than fun.' . . . But I feel more of a duty to make money."

A big-city prosecutor confided that he was thinking about changing jobs. Although he enjoyed his work immensely, it didn't pay very well, and since he was considering marriage, he needed to make more money. His prospective wife, an actress, he pointed out, did not have his earning potential.

He observed that upon taking on familial obligations, the men in his office typically left. "The women don't. I don't think that it's necessarily male chivalry that makes men leave lower-paying positions, public service positions . . . and then go into a higher-paying job. I think it's necessity. And I don't think women would be any less inclined to do it." The "biological reality" of childbearing and the fact that men, by and large, could get higher-paying jobs virtually obligated men to focus more on money than did women, he said. "It's what men are conditioned to do."

Such conditioning explains much about why so many men still don't take women's professional aspirations seriously. James Challenger, president and founder of Challenger, Gray & Christmas, Inc., a Chicago-based outplacement firm, said that he has often encountered a sense of resentment toward women among men who had lost their jobs. "There's still a feeling, especially among the older men," Challenger noted, "that women don't have to work and don't really want to work, that they're just doing it because it's something to do."

When such men lose their jobs, he said, the experience can be cataclysmic—"like a loss of the genital." "It's been their duty to bring home the money. Whether or not he has a spouse who is bringing in equal or more . . . when he loses a job, he's not doing what he's supposed to be doing in the world."

For Kip Trum, group vice president of Drake Beam Morin, a New York-based outplacement firm, shame was the word that came to mind. "It's genuine shame that people suffer about being out of work. And that can become crippling," said Trum: "the shame, the anger, the fear which adds up to terror. . . . They can still function, you know: 'Oh, how's it going?' 'Oh, it's going fine; best thing that ever happened to me. This is terrific.' Then they have to sit down and start making some telephone calls." And that is "not easy to do."

Nonetheless, observed Challenger, laid-off men suffered less now than they did in the past: "There were people twenty years ago who couldn't tell their neighbors that they lost their jobs. In some cases they couldn't even tell their spouse. . . . Now we no longer see that type of thing occurring as often."

Even in today's topsy-turvy job market, a man who does not work for any substantial period of time risks not only social censure but his career. Women, meanwhile, have been granted more leeway, if only because of the widespread, albeit unstated, assumption that they generally are not serious about their careers at any rate. It's all right, goes the reasoning, for a women to be distracted by a family, but a man should always keep his eyes on the prize. The result is a workplace that discriminates in different ways against men and women alike and that fosters the very stereotypes that enlightened corporations say they wish to erase.

In a 1990 study, Joy Schneer and Frieda Reitman examined the impact of a brief period of unemployment on careers of MBA graduates of Pace and Rutgers universities, where they then taught. Though work interruptions hurt both men and women, the researchers discovered, they hurt men more. Men who had been out of work for a few months earned, on average, 25 percent less than did other men, whereas women who had taken a break from work earned 15 percent less than did other women. Controlling for experience, responsibilities, and hours worked reduced the work-break penalty somewhat, but nowhere near totally.

Part of the reason women were hurt less is that women generally were paid less—regardless of whether they had taken time off or not. Even those with seamless work histories made 15 percent less than did never-unemployed men—though they made more than briefly unemployed men. In contrast, men and women with a gap on their résumés made roughly the same amount.

At the time of the survey, 98 percent of the male respondents had full-time jobs, compared to 77 percent of the women. To make the cohorts more comparable, Schneer and Reitman eliminated from their analysis those who were not currently working full time; they also removed anyone with more than one work break—reasoning that chronically out-of-work respondents might skew the study. Even after the culling, sharp gender differences remained. Twice as many women as men reported a career interruption. For women, child-rearing responsibilities was the most common reason for leaving a job; for men, corporate restructuring was generally the cause. Not a single man had put his career on hold to raise a child. Though men with a résumé gap reported lower levels of career satisfaction than did those without one, women showed no such divergence.

"The findings suggest [that] men with nontraditional career paths may be facing discrimination in the workplace," concluded Schneer and Reitman. The researchers also surmised that the women had not expected to work continuously; on the contrary, they had anticipated taking time to raise a family and accepted the career penalty for doing so. Men had no acceptable reason for being out of work and were not pre-pared to bear the professional consequences. "I think there was this feeling that there's something wrong with a man who loses his job," Reitman noted.

In 1994, Schneer and Reitman reported on a follow-up sur-vey. By then, the respondents were in midcareer. Their average age was forty-four, compared to thirty-eight during the original survey. Those whose careers had been interrupted early on still made substantially less than did those whose had not. Midca-reer interruptions also depressed earnings, though not quite as much as early-career gaps. As in the earlier survey, Schneer and Reitman found no men reporting a career interruption to care for children. They did find one important difference from their previous study, however: In an era in which firings had become epidemic in corporate America, the men who been laid off seemed more accepting of their fate.

The MBAs Schneer and Reitman surveyed were not every-day American wage earners. Their incomes—typically around $100,000 a year—were much higher, and their aspirations were presumably higher as well. Still, to the extent that their experi-ences are generalizable, they say volumes about how far Amer-ica remains from achieving equality in the workplace. Women, whatever their work history, seemed, for the most part, des-tined for a lower track than did comparable men. And men, whatever their disposition, appeared to be barred from claim-ing family time that women took as a matter of course. For men, any work interruption, including a layoff, constituted an unforgivable transgression—which one paid for literally for the remainder of a career.

The same reasoning that prohibits men from taking time off apparently also prevents them from adjusting their schedules for child care. A 1991 survey by the U.S. Bureau of the Census found that only 2 percent of employed fathers of preschoolers allowed child-rearing considerations to influence their work schedules. Mothers were ten times as likely to say they had adjusted their work schedules for their children. Even among fathers who cared for their children while their wives worked, only 6 percent said they had arranged work to accommodate those responsibilities.

A national survey of 3,400 workers by the Families and Work Institute also found that men were less inclined to make such accommodations than were women. Among male and female employees with children under age thirteen, women were roughly twice as likely as men to say they would sacrifice earnings and advancement for more flexible work arrangements.

When men have been offered time off or flexible work hours, they have been timid about taking them. In 1993, the *Washington Post* reported on several major companies that had implemented policies that, theoretically, at least, freed up men for family duties. The companies uniformly found that the men didn't respond. Campbell Soup Co., which offered employees a three-month unpaid leave for family-related business, found that 95 percent of the women who were eligible took advantage of the perquisite, but not a single man did. At Levi Strauss, the male response was not much better.

Few experts believe things have materially changed since the Family and Medical Leave Act took effect in late 1993. That legislation guarantees up to twelve weeks of unpaid leave to most full-time workers at large companies to attend to certain family business (including a child's birth or adoption or a family member's illness). Many business organizations fought the measure, and it was vetoed twice—by Ronald Reagan and George Bush—before Bill Clinton signed it. The law no doubt has been an immense comfort to many families, but it has not yet resulted in a swarm of men staying home with their children.

That may not be entirely men's fault. Our society is sending men mixed messages. It tells them that their children are the most important thing in their lives, yet marginalizes them if they put their families first. Given such conflicting signals, it's hardly surprising that men aren't eager to take on more parenting duties.

One government lawyer whose superiors actively encourage their subordinates to take paternity leave was struck by the fact that most eligible men took it; but such offices clearly are not the norm—and certainly not in the private sector.

A 1990 *Los Angeles Times* poll found that 39 percent of fathers in Los Angeles and Orange counties claimed they would prefer to stay home and raise their children rather than work full time outside the home. When asked, "How much do you think the job you are doing as a parent has suffered because of the demands of your work career?" 51 percent of the men said "a lot" or "some"; 57 percent said they felt guilty for not spending more time with their children.

Obviously, most of the men who say they would quit work and stay home with their children are voicing nothing more than a fantasy. They have heard too many times, and from too many different people, that real men belong at work—not in a nursery.

James Levine, director of the Fatherhood Project at the Families and Work Institute, coined the term—"daddy stress"—to describe the inner turmoil men experience when they feel trapped between family and work. Though working men and women experience work-family conflict in roughly equivalent numbers, says Levine, "men don't talk about it." Employers often compound the problem by informally restricting family-friendly policies to women.

"Employers expect that women are going to be the ones who are going to ask for those accommodations," said Levine, "and if accommodations are going to be given, they'll be given to women." Some men, he acknowledges, do take the unconventional path, "but by and large we're seeing guys sort of trapped."

In a November 1994 article, "Family-Friendly Firms Often Leave Fathers Out of the Picture," the *Wall Street Journal* portrayed a corporate world that is hostile to fathers who want to care for their children. Some companies, in apparent violation of the law, reportedly told men that the family leave legislation applied only to mothers. Others simply made it clear that long hours at work—regardless of the impact at home—were absolutely necessary for a man to get ahead. Conditions were so bad, reported the *Journal,* that *Child* magazine gave up trying to award firms that supported good fathering because not enough such companies existed to ensure a decent competition. That finding comes as no surprise to Edward Pitt, the Fatherhood Project's deputy director, who argues that until men start seeing good fathering rewarded instead of penalized, they will be reluctant to be the fathers that they should.

In this age of high-powered professionals, many women are pursuing careers that are more demanding and often more lucrative than those of the vast majority of men, and most are no more inclined to surrender their careers to domesticity than would be comparably ambitious men. Nonetheless, my prosecutor friend is right when he says that men, in general, are more "conditioned" than women to do the "economic thing." Although there are plenty of workaholic women in modern society, there are many more workaholic men.

The Families and Work Institute survey of workers, for instance, found that men spent an average of forty-five hours per week on the job, whereas women averaged thirty-nine. Men also typically commuted longer distances. Even after lower-level workers and part-timers were eliminated from the mix, men still worked longer hours than did women. Among full-time professionals and managers, men averaged just over fifty hours to just under forty-six for women.

Women, as expected, typically put in much more time at home—though husbands and wives often had conflicting perceptions of the respective burdens they shouldered. Of the men with working spouses or partners, 69 percent said that their mates took major responsibility for cooking, whereas 87 percent of the working wives said they did. Similarly, 78 percent of the working women said they were responsible for cleaning, as opposed to 63 percent of the men who said their wives did the cleaning. Such discrepancies notwithstanding, men and women agreed on two key points: that husbands of working wives helped out more at home than did husbands of nonworking wives and that wives, irrespective of employment status, did much more around the house than did men. Even in those homes where the wives were the principal breadwinners, the wives tended to do the lion's share of the household work.

A 1992 survey of more than 400 senior female executives with an annual average compensation of $187,000 found that those who were married and had children were still largely responsible for child care. The husband was the primary caretaker in less than 8 percent of the cases. Still, 49 percent said that they and their spouses equally shared child care duties.

When the same organizations (Korn/Ferry International, the executive recruiting firm, and the University of California at Los Angeles graduate school of management) conducted a similar survey in 1982, things were somewhat less egalitarian. At that time, fewer than 3 percent of the female executives with children said that their spouses were the main caregivers, and 42 percent said that child care was an equally shared obligation.

The 1992 study found other indications that custom was loosening its grip. In the decade between the two studies, the number of women who were titled executive vice president had more than doubled—from 4 percent to 9 percent of the total, and the number of women senior vice presidents had increased from 13 percent to 23 percent. (The aforementioned figures refer to the proportion of executive and senior vice presidents among high-ranking women, not among the total population of senior executives, whose ranks remain more than 95 precent male.) The fifty-six hours worked by the women in an average week equaled those put in by men in a 1989 survey of senior executives at America's largest corporations.

A comparison of the various surveys also yielded some striking male-female contrasts. The women, on average, earned only two-thirds the pay of the men (whose annual compensation was $289,000), but they were also younger (44 compared to 52) and held somewhat less exalted jobs. The most conspicuous differences, however, had to do with family.

Ninety-one percent of the men were married, compared to 60 percent of the women, and 95 percent of the men had children, compared to 63 percent of the women. Of those women who were divorced—13 percent versus 3 percent of the men—nearly half said that their careers had been a factor in the breakup of their marriages. One-third of all the women said they had postponed childbearing for their careers, and over a third had taken a leave of absence—generally for maternity or other family reasons. Only 6 percent of the men had taken time off, and only 9 percent of those took it for family-related reasons. Most took it either for education or government service.

Unlike the women in the Schneer-Reitman studies, most of those surveyed by Korn/Ferry reported no negative consequences for taking time off; 70 percent said it had no effect, and 18 percent said the effect was positive. Obviously, however, since Korn/Ferry included only management's stars, the poll effectively eliminated those whose careers had been sidetracked for family-related or any other reasons.

Notably, for all their accomplishments, the women seemed less than enthralled with corporate life. Even though they were younger than the male executives, they were more eager to leave. Over three-fourths, compared to fewer than a third of the men, said they wanted to retire before age sixty-five. Only 14 percent aspired to be chief executive officers, compared to

46 percent of the men—a disparity conceivably related to the belief among 93 percent of the women polled that a "glass ceiling" existed for women.

The picture that emerges, in short, is one of a corporate world in flux, in which women are being increasingly accepted and promoted, yet their aspirations and mobility remain restricted. Not only are women less likely than men to move on to the CEO's chair, they are, quite literally, less likely to move. Women senior executives were asked to relocate less than one-fourth as often as male senior executives. They also traveled far less frequently for business. Whether the lighter travel schedules reflected residual corporate sexism or deference to the women's domestic commitments is impossible to say, but clearly, many of the women were routinely juggling eleven- and twelve-hour workdays and considerable domestic duties. For whatever reasons—perhaps exhaustion with the juggling act, suspicions of a glass ceiling, weariness with corporate politics, or a more familial set of priorities—most were looking forward to getting free.

Nonetheless, the majority of the women and men were happy with their professional accomplishments. Many seemed to be delicately balancing both traditional and nontraditional roles. To a degree unseen in less affluent circles, they had worked out co-parenting arrangements with their husbands. The accommodation may have been made easier by the fact that most of the women had already assumed a substantial part of the "male" role. Nearly three-fourths of the women were the main breadwinners in their families. Even so, the men were not stay-at-home spouses. Virtually all were employed—the vast majority as professionals and managers.

Outplacement executive Warren Radtke said he was struck by the way many such "high level professional women" were, in effect, changing the rules and by how easily their men (the "secure" ones, at least) adjusted to their lesser status. "I know one man who is building their house on Martha's Vineyard all during the week, and he's just delighted to be doing that in addition to doing his other 'lower level' job," Radtke said. His own son, Radtke added, "has a very good job, but [his wife] is going to be a partner in one of the major New York law firms. He's going to be the child care person. He's going to be the household manager."

Few men have wives who pull down salaries of several hundred thousand dollars a year. Most men who are becoming "household managers" are not embracing a lifestyle choice; they are doing so out of necessity. Peter Baylies, a full-time homemaker in North Andover, Massachusetts, was laid off in 1992 from a large computer company. At the time he had a nine-month-old son and a schoolteacher wife, who suddenly was the family's sole support. Given the cost of professional child care, the decision to stay home was easy; adjusting was not.

Initially, says, Baylies, he found it "intimidating" to be outnumbered by women when he took his son out to play. He also felt isolated, so he reached out to other full-time fathers by launching a newsletter—*At-Home Dad*. The quarterly, which Baylies claims has a circulation of 500 and is rapidly growing, offers commentary, recipes, child care tips, and news that Baylies deems relevant to men like him. The Winter 1995 issue reported on a survey comparing forty-nine "at-home dad families" with forty-four families with stay-at-home moms. The small study provided the following upbeat news:

"A strong bond is developing between at-home fathers and their children. When compared to fathers that work outside the home, children of at-home dads turn to their fathers twice as often for nurturing and comfort. This is creating a special bond between at-home dads and their children, one that fathers have not known before." The newsletter also noted that "children still turn to their mothers more often for comfort no matter who the primary caregiver is. . . . Results show that in at-home mom families, children will wake their mothers for comfort at night 83% of the time. In at-home dad families, children still go to their mothers 55% of the time."

Baylies said he has discovered that the primary reason men stay home is that they were laid off; others were disabled, and some simply concluded that working and paying for child care make no economic sense. But once they are forced into becoming homemakers, many of them find it fulfilling. In his own case, Baylies noted, he realized that he was weary of the "dual-income lifestyle." What was the point of having a son, he asked himself, if he could not be around to help him grow up?

At this point, said Baylies, who is in his late thirties, he enjoys his life and has few thoughts of returning to the office. "I hope I can stay home forever." But he recognizes that companies that claim to encourage men to take time for their children are generally liars. "When you go back to work, you pay for it." And he acknowledges that some of the men in his network are worried about having to pay the price. Still, he claims, most feel no envy for the men who are married to their work.

For the time being, only a limited number of men will feel free to follow Baylies's example. The man-as-provider role is too deeply etched in the collective psyche. Even the most open-minded sorts seem to have problems with any other model. In 1989, *Psychology Today*, in search of the "ideal man," conducted an unscientific poll of its ostensibly avant-garde readership. Househusbands got an unambiguous thumbs down. "Your ideal man is still supposed to win the bread, although he doesn't have to strive to provide his family with a high standard of living," the magazine concluded.

Yet, even if most men are not prepared to be homemakers, many are deciding that what they are is not very fulfilling. When NPD Group, Inc., a research firm headquartered in Port Washington, New York, polled 2,500 workers, it found that the general level of satisfaction was not high. The poll also discovered that women were more content with their lot than were men. Forty percent of the women said they were "very satisfied" with their work compared to 31 percent of the men.

It's not clear why that should be so. One possible explanation is that whereas most men with lousy jobs felt they could not focus their energies elsewhere, women could. Nearly a fourth of the women, for instance, were part-timers—compared to 6 percent of the men. That is not to say that all (or even most) women are in a position to reduce their time at or leave disagreeable jobs, but at least society does not hold it against them if they do. Even if they can't leave their jobs, they don't necessarily have to make the jobs their lives.

A study of women physicians by a University of California researcher showed that those who were most satisfied and less conflicted had set their priorities in such a way that either family or work came first. Apparently, which came first mattered much less than that they decided to give one precedence over the other. Most men, of course, feel they have little choice in the matter. Work must come first—for the obvious reason that being a good family man is contingent on being a good provider.

Obviously, discrimination against women is real. I am not suggesting that women have it better than men, just that they have more role flexibility—thanks, in large part, to the successes of the feminist movement. Men, however, are still stuck with role expectations that predate the feminist age.

Liz Golden, a marketing specialist for a diversity consulting firm in the Philadelphia area, blames men and women alike for the current state of affairs. "I think this will not change unless men get behind each other and say, 'This nonsense is killing us. It's got to stop. It's not worth it.' I don't see any way [of changing things] besides someone standing up and saying, 'I will not buy a house that is bigger than I can afford so that I have all of this pressure for the next thirty years to work seventy-five hours a week in order to maintain this house.'"

She also recognizes, she said, that little is going to happen unless both men and women wish it to: "Unless we're in it with each other." Alvin Baraff, the Washington, D.C., psychologist, thinks one important shift is already in progress. "As women move more into the areas that have been mostly [for] men, they are going to be experiencing some of the same feelings. They're going to have less friends. They're going to be less in touch with their feelings. They're going to have the same kinds of illnesses that men have."

Philosophy graduate student Tim Benjamin made a kindred observation: "Perhaps [women are] giving up more than they're going to get," he said. "In order to gain a certain amount of equality on a business level, they give up a certain amount of perhaps fundamentally feminine characteristics—a certain level of seductiveness, for example, or certain privileges of femininity." Benjamin believes it to be reflective of "a general trend that is occurring in the world toward homogenization, toward a truly equal society." And the end product, he believes, adds up to a form of "mediocrity."

If Baraff and Benjamin are right, the result—at least in theory—could well be the revolution that Golden envisions. For if men and women find ourselves foundering in the same sea of discontent, we should be better able to understand each other and better able to address our mutual plight.

There is scant evidence, however, that such a happy end is in sight. Instead of developing intergender empathy, many men and women seem to be cultivating higher levels of antipathy. As Aaron Kipnis and Elizabeth Heron put it in *Gender War, Gender Peace*, "Many women and men today express their issues by firing bigger and more articulate missiles across the gender gap, at each other." That tendency, although evident around some workplace concerns, is nowhere more obvious than in the sphere of romance.

Chapter 6

COURTING, COMMUNICATING, AND COPING WITH CONFUSION

L ove has always been fraught with both promise and peril, but, of late, relationships, particularly on college campuses, have come to be defined less by their hopeful possibilities than by everyone's worst fears.

During the past few years, one college after another has weathered controversies that pitted women against men. In May 1994 a graduating senior disrupted Pomona College's commencement by unfurling a banner on stage that read, "A Rapist Is Among Us." The student was frustrated at the institution's failure to expel a man who was accused of sexual assault. After a night of drinking, he had slept with a woman who he believed consented, but who, more than two years later, lodged a complaint with college authorities.

At the University of Maryland in 1993 a group of female art students plucked several men's names from a phone book. They carefully copied the names onto posters that they plastered throughout the area reading, "Notice: These Men Are Potential Rapists." One woman on campus, told that the innocent men were upset at being connected with rape, offered this bizarre rationalization: "I think if a man was secure he wasn't a rapist, he wouldn't be threatened by this list."

At Brown University and Carleton College, names of men who were said to be rapists went up on women's bathroom walls. Unlike at the University of Maryland, the men were not selected at random, but were fingered by women who claimed to have been victimized.

The particulars in these cases are all different. The poster makers at Maryland, who were enrolled in a class called "Contemporary Issues in Feminist Art," apparently thought that libeling men was a form of artistry. The Carleton women, on the other hand, had specific complaints; four eventually filed suit against the college for not protecting them against sexual assaults.

To some activists, however, the particular facts were almost beside the point, for it was not so much individual men who were wicked but men as a class, they maintained. And by now the response is as well rehearsed as the charge. Outraged men, protesting their innocence, angrily denounce their supposed tormentors. Men at Pomona College, for instance, shouted obscenities as women painted feminist slogans on a wall.

The expanding anger—not to mention the fear, hurt feelings, and raw sensitivities—has made courtship complicated. "There's a kind of walking on eggshells kind of feeling," said one women, describing the ambience among the young, enlightened set. In such an atmosphere, rules that promise peace and order can be comforting. And in the past few years, universities have tried, more or less, to supply some. They have been driven, in part, by requirements that all colleges receiving federal assistance have sexual assault policies in place, but they have been prodded as well by students demanding that schools do a better job of protecting female coeds. Such was the case at Antioch College, whose nine-page sexual offense policy set off a national uproar when it fell into the hands of reporters in 1993.

The document, in essence, was an etiquette guide for foreplay. Adopted at the behest of a group calling itself Womyn of Antioch, the regulations required specific authorization for every phase of sexual activity. "Obtaining consent is an ongoing process in any sexual interaction," the text advised. "Verbal consent should be obtained with each new level of physical and/or sexual contact/conduct in any given interaction, regardless of who initiates it. Asking 'Do you want to have sex with me?' is not enough. The request for consent must be specific to each act."

Comedians found the policy irresistibly humorous. Columnists thought it unromantic and hopelessly naive. Even students thought it more than a bit intrusive. "It's got its good and bad points. But it sure does slow down an orgy," one coed told a writer for the *Washington Post*. Historian Elizabeth Fox-Genovese believes that such codes signal a flight from individual accountability. "Instead of learning to behave themselves according to minimal standards of decency, students are being taught to obey a series of rigid rules, which effectively relieve them of personal responsibility," she observed.

Boston Globe columnist Ellen Goodman was one of the few pundits to defend the guidelines vigorously. She saw them as a means of creating a safe environment essential to sexual pleasure and as "part of an ongoing struggle to create a new single standard. A standard of sexual equality. A meeting ground, where no means no and only yes means yes, where we come to intimacy as equals and find sexual freedom in an atmosphere of safety."

There is no evidence that the Antioch guidelines succeeded in creating such an atmosphere. Most students appeared to take the policy less than seriously. As one undergraduate quipped, "I ask a girl if she wants to have sex, and if she says yes, I get busy." Whatever effect the guidelines may have on normal people, it's hard to imagine a determined rapist being deterred by a nine-page-long list of edicts. But the rules certainly did no harm. And if they facilitated some useful conversations and empowered some normally bashful people to say no, so much the better. Their real purpose, however, seemed to be largely symbolic. They promised clarity at a time of raging confusion regarding sex and proper dating behavior, and they reaffirmed the college's role as a guardian to its students.

Just one generation after the sexual revolution essentially threw college administrations out of students' bedrooms, why should so many students be interested in reestablishing the university's guardianship role? One obvious reason is that students may have realized that society is not nearly so benign as it once seemed. All kinds of dangers are now visible that the free-love generation was perhaps too naive to see. Awareness of rape, for instance, has grown exponentially—particularly rape by dates or acquaintances. No well-informed modern woman can dismiss the possibility that a normal-seeming man could secretly be a sex-obsessed fiend.

Certainly, the statistics don't evoke serenity. Between 1960 and 1992, the number of forcible and attempted rapes reported in the United States has steadily increased, from 17,190 to 109,060. (Rape, as defined by the FBI, can be committed only against females.) During those years, according to FBI statistics, the rate per 100,000 inhabitants went from 9.6 to 42.8—more than a fourfold increase. Reports of other violent crimes increased as well. The murder rate nearly doubled, the property crimes rate virtually tripled, the robbery rate quadrupled, and the rate of aggravated assaults more than quintupled. Overall, during the past three decades, the rate of violent crime increased by a factor of five.

Such increases cannot all be attributed to better reporting of statistics—not even for a historically and grossly underreported crime such as rape. The fact is, the United States is more dangerous than it used to be, and women are more at risk of getting raped.

The threat of rape has become the catalyst for a crusade that has swept many college campuses. Yet, as some observers of the campus movement have pointed out, the risk of rape is significantly lower on most campuses than it is in virtually any big-city neighborhood. So why, given that the danger is growing most off campus, have campuses become the center of the antirape campaign? One reason has to do with colleges' tradition of mobilizing against threats in the larger society. Another is that many people have been convinced that campuses are a good deal more dangerous than they are.

Statistics have been widely disseminated indicating that more than one in four women in college have been sexually assaulted. A number of critics recently have pointed out that the statistic is misleading at best. The high number of assaults is derived by lumping together rapes; attempted rapes; assaults before entering college; and "rapes" of women who, in many cases, don't believe they have been raped.

Nonetheless, the exaggerated statistics accomplish an objective that some people consider important. They create the illusion that untold numbers of college men are wantonly raping women and thereby make the point that beneath the deceptive veneer of even the most gentle and upwardly mobile man lies the heart of a raging beast. Like the poster "art" that aspires to label all men potential victimizers, they grant women incontestable moral superiority. And in an age in which gender roles are confused and expectations are murky, moral certitude apparently counts for something—even if that certitude is rooted in fallacy.

In fact, however, little about romance or dating behavior is as clear and unambiguous as the politicized rhetoric would make it. Once we agree, for instance, that yes means yes and no means no, what is the status of "maybe"? Some people give mixed or unclear messages at least some portion of the time. To make matters even murkier, judgment is often impaired by drugs or alcohol.

Survey research by the Campus Violence Prevention Center suggests that the majority of the times when serious assaults occur on campus, both parties have been drinking. Student athletes seemed to be responsible for roughly one-fourth of campus sexual attacks, and a disproportionate number of assaults occurred at fraternity parties. If the center's figures are accurate, getting students to cut back on booze and to be wary of athletes and frat boys may be the best strategy currently available to prevent rapes on campus. Aside from those who are drunk, sociopathic, or caught up in some form of mob behavior, most men are not disposed to rape. Once they understand that they are not desired, normal, sober men tend to back down. Whether they understand that when they should is a question I will take up later.

One bachelor in his thirties opined: "The vast majority of times you know if you're not welcome . . . and it's not necessarily a linguistic communication. . . . It's body gestures. It's, I don't know; I think all of us have been in situations where you start some sort of intimate activity, be it kissing or whatever, and it moves on to an escalation. And there may not even be any words, but a hand is put there or your hand is moved or 'no' or 'not now' or 'Please, I don't think so.' It's just always been my experience, 'That's fine.' Stop. I don't need to pressure people. I don't like trying to pressure people."

Given the uproar over date rape, it's not surprising that men's advocates would come up with their own contrarian approach to reducing the risk in romance. The National Center for Men's "consensual sex contract" is designed to deal with what Mel Feit, the center's director, calls a "significant problem in our society." If a women falsely accused a man of any sex crime, "whether it was harassment, sexually abusing children . . . , or rape, the response of law enforcement was to essentially believe the accusation," he said. "There was no due process." Feit is also concerned about men being forced to pay child support for children they did not intend to have.

The contract, which can be terminated "at any time by either of us except during the sexual activity contemplated by this agreement," provides several options for prospective lovers. They can agree to sex "but without intercourse" or without the prospect of marriage or to express an "emotional commitment that may eventually lead to marriage." They can choose to be monogamous or to be free to play the field or "to have sex in order to conceive a child." Alternately, they can decide that "neither one of us will try to force the other into parenthood." In addition, signatories can state whether the sexual encounter should be "discreet" or whether they "want the whole world to know about our love for each other." Lovers are also allowed to write in their own conditions. And they are invited to sign a pledge certifying that "the anticipated sexual experience will be of mutual consent" and promising not to claim rape, harassment, or assault as a result of the contemplated intercourse.

Obviously, not many people who are eager to make love with each other are going to wade through such a prolix and paranoia-inducing document, no more so than they are going to follow the Antioch rules precisely. Still, the fact that intelligent people are drawing up such documents says something depressing about how horribly afraid some of us are of the persons we are choosing to pursue. It perhaps says even more about the widespread state of confusion—not just about risks, but about the rules of relationships.

In an age when most enlightened people agree that sexual equality is a desirable goal, there is little consensus on how to define the concept in the context of a courting relationship. Does it mean that women should continue to wait for men to ask them out? Or does it mean that women should take charge and be as aggressive as men? If a woman issues an invitation, is she obliged to pay for the date? And if she won't pay, should a guy denounce her as cheap? What about seduction? Is a man obliged to accommodate an assertively amorous female? And if a woman initiates a sexual encounter, is it incumbent upon her not to be the one to say no?

Karissa Wang, a professional in her twenties who lives in the Boston area, considers herself liberated. When she goes out, she insists on paying her share. "I'm trying to be my own person," she says. Yet she could not contemplate approaching a man for a date. "I don't go and ask a guy. I kind of wait for them because I know that they will take it the wrong way, like I will be considered controlling, even these days. My friends also always wait for the guy to ask them out." She suspects that many men of her generation are conflicted, that they aren't quite as comfortable with equality as they like to believe. She has a male friend, for instance, who admires the independence and toughness he thinks Hillary Clinton embodies. "But he also would never date someone like Hillary. In real life . . . he would be threatened by her," Wang said.

Lisa Jacobs also doubts that men want the sort of women they claim to like: "It makes relationships very confusing, I think, because men will tell women, 'I want an independent woman.' A woman will tell a man, 'I am an independent woman.' But in small ways, these roles will get played out. I mean, 'Where will we go for dinner?' Very often, the man makes the choice. The woman is more likely to be agreeable, to be more flexible."

Just as women like Wang and Jacobs wonder how much self-reliance and toughness they should show, many men feel as if they must bite their tongues for fear of giving offense. "It's not something I lose a lot of sleep over," said one graduate student, "but I just have to look at a situation and look at where this woman is coming from with regard to certain feminist issues, where she stands or whatever, and also if she has a sense of humor and what sort of sense of humor, and that kind of thing. You just sort of read it out; like any situation, you read how you're going to talk with someone."

Another male graduate student says that in the initial stages of a relationship, "I find myself being somewhat restrained, even if I'm being playful, because it's going to be taken the wrong way. . . . Especially when I'm at school and meeting new people, new women students, I feel a need to be more formal and a little less relaxed. And certainly less playful." Such awkwardness may not be such a bad thing, he believes, if it prevents him from saying things that may be "misinterpreted."

Fear of being misconstrued is rampant in dating circles. Lara Behnert, an undergraduate at the Rhode Island School of Design, believes even the act of paying for a meal can become hugely significant: "In dating college-age guys it's funny because when the bill comes, they get very, very nervous," said Behnert. "The men don't know if it's an offensive thing to ask whether they should pay for it or whether it's offensive to not pay for it."

Since women are not of one mind about that issue (or many others), they cannot easily resolve the bafflement among men. Angela Fung, a student at Parsons School of Design, has noticed "a certain amount of confusion because certain women will think 'I'm a feminist or a womanist and so I want to go Dutch all the time.' Others will alternate [in determining] who pays; and . . . I know a lot of women who say, 'Well, I know what I'm worth. He ought to pay for it all the time.'"

Jacobs recalls a conversation with a "feminist friend" during which she found herself becoming angry at the woman's insistence that the man was supposed to pay on the first date. "You can't have it both ways," she said, and asked her friend whether she recognized "how ridiculous" her attitude was. "Yeah. But that's just the way it is," the friend replied.

Who pays and who gets paid for are questions that are not limited to first dates. I was surprised to hear a graduate of an Ivy League university say that she was no longer certain she wanted to marry her fiancé. It seems she had landed a nice job and was making a good deal of money—perhaps more than he would be making when he completed work on his MBA. "I'm not so sure I want to share all of this," she said without a trace of irony.

That she would have had no doubts about sharing his good fortune if the situation were reversed went without saying. Clearly, she had assumed that he would be earning the most money, and apparently the relationship was somehow less desirable, from her perspective at least, if he was not.

Such feelings obviously conflict with the notion of a world in which the sexes are equal partners. The presumption that a man should make more than (and generally pay for) *his* woman is a relic of the prefeminist epoch. Yet that presumption is shared by many men and women of all ages today. And not only does it undermine women's quest for economic equality, but it also makes cynics out of men.

A twenty-year-old high school dropout was explaining his disillusionment with women. "I still treat them with love and respect," he said, "but I used to put all my energy and time in my girl and making sure she was all right. But now I've just learned that basically you better worry about yourself, get yourself together, because as soon as they see you crumble, then, they start looking you down and move on somewhere else." By "crumble," it quickly became clear, he meant "lose a job." He had "a lot of experience" being unemployed, he said. "I had no job. I was trying, doing my best. And [with] girls, if you ain't got the money, you're nothing. They stay with you for a little while, but after a while they can't take that. 'See you later.' It's a lot of girls did that, and now I got a good job, I just bought an apartment, and all of them are trying to come back. And I was thinking like, I should dog them out now, but I don't, 'cause it's not in my heart to do that. I just stay my distance. I'm basically trying to keep myself on time; just concentrate on me."

In all likelihood, the young man's tale of woe contained a large dollop of self-justification. Who knows what behavior on his part might have provoked the behavior he described? Still, a lot of women clearly judge a man primarily on his ability to spend money (particularly on them)—a form of "objectification" every bit as crass as the ways in which men dehumanize women.

Even when money isn't the primary concern, it often plays a much larger role in the way women look at men than in the way men look at women. One woman was describing to me her conception of the perfect man. He was "smart, sexy, fun and emotionally aware, emotionally competent." I noted that she had included nothing about financial success and asked whether that was important to her. She paused momentarily and added, "I guess that has to be there, too. I think a lot of women today want that goal-oriented man even if they themselves are not goal oriented." As for the struggling, starving, smart, sexy, fun artist sort: "I just don't find that attractive. I think a lot of women don't find that attractive. Maybe if I had money—maybe if I were independently wealthy and didn't have concerns about that, but I need somebody who can be my partner in that [financial] way."

Surely not all women feel the need to hitch up with a man who has wealth or even a decent job; stories abound of women who have taken in destitute unambitious men. And as more women earn substantial incomes of their own, men's finances may become relatively less important. As lawyer Debra Allen put it, "When I look at a man, I don't really look to him to provide for me. I just hope that he has common sense around the whole money thing and he himself is financially stable and able to finance his own. I don't expect him to have to carry my weight at all. So I don't necessarily look at his net worth. It's more important to me that he be gainfully employed and able to handle his own finances."

Allen's attitude is becoming common these days. Yet even among such modern women who don't need or want a man's money, it's difficult to find many who are eager to support a man. They generally want him to have a job or at least to be employable. For huge numbers of men, however, a woman's desirability has very little to do with her state or level of employment.

Jacobs attributes much of the difference in attitude to continuing economic inequality in the society. "In today's world, men usually have higher-paying jobs than the women that they're with, and so, I think that also breeds an inequity in the relationship. . . . I was having a conversation with a woman friend of mine. And we were talking about how we're both independent, career women, but she was thinking, 'Wouldn't it be really neat to land a really rich guy and take a break.' And we're talking about our friends, of if we hear about a woman who got a rich guy, it's like, 'Cool. She made it.' And if you switch the roles, there is still this societal [disapproval]; society looks down their noses at a man who marries money. That's still not really accepted."

Money issues, of course, are not the only topic around which male and female perspectives tend to differ. Virtually nothing about sex, intimacy, and romance seems to be seen in quite the same way by women and men.

A twenty-five-year-old actor was elaborating on his notion of sexual equality. "In an ideal world there should be an even playing field in terms of things like casual sex, one-night stands and things like that," he asserted. Putting aside the question of whether anyone should be embracing casual sex and one-night stands in the age of AIDS, I was struck by how distinctly masculine that view of equality sounded. Obviously, a great many women enjoy casual sex. But, by and large, women don't define the license to have one-night stands as their idea of sexual equality.

Rault Kehlor, a gay man in his early twenties, remarked, "I think that attitudes about sex between men and women are coming from completely different worlds. None of my women friends can comprehend the idea [of random sex]. They can't even contemplate an act of random sex and not being affected by it. . . . Every guy that I have ever talked to—gay, straight, or whatever—can embrace this idea and understand that it is great for what it is." His attempts to explain the appeal to his woman friends, he said, had generally not been successful. They were often, he said, either baffled, hurt, or angry.

Distinctive male and female views of sex are probably inevitable, given the disparate messages that boys and girls receive. Tom Henry, director of the Philadelphia Children's Network's Responsive Fathers Program, noted "When our sons are not sexually active at a certain age, or a certain point, then the men start wondering, 'Is my son okay? Is he all right? What's going on here? Is he gay?' You know, it's that double standard."

The Rev. Jesse Jackson tells of being in a church with a highly respected minister who embraced a child during baptism and proclaimed, "This is a handsome little boy, ha. He's going to be a ladykiller." Why, Jackson wondered, would he say such a thing; why would he "fuel this foolishness" that ultimately results in boys seeing girls as "notches on their belts"? Such foolishness, unfortunately, has a deep toehold in our culture. And even though sexism is officially recognized as evil, it still sprouts in the strangest places.

Critics pilloried author Katie Roiphe for suggesting in *The Morning After* that there was something stereotypically female about some feminists' view of womanhood—that the image of women as fragile creatures in need of protection from predatory men long predated the dawn of modern feminism. Whatever one may think of Roiphe's larger critique of feminism, she must be granted her point. Avant-garde social ideologies—

from wherever they arise—have a way of melding the old and the new. No humans are capable of re-creating themselves (or their worldviews) totally from scratch. So even among men and women who consider themselves enlightened, we often see the residue of outmoded views—be it the feminist who wants men to pay her way because she's "worth it" or the young lawyer who believes his wife's job will be "fun" while his will be serious work.

Laurance N'Kaoua, who was raised in France but came to the United States to attend a midwestern college, has concluded that a lot of American women are "starving for traditionalism." "I know it sounds paradoxical and probably is," she said, "but my greatest cultural shock was when my best friend in college admitted to me that she went to college to find a husband." The pull of traditional roles, coupled with the gender polarization of an "extreme country," has created situations in which, as N'Kaoua sees it, "men and women hate each other . . . yet stay together out of social pressure." The whole situation, she said, was infuriating and perplexing. "There's a war out there, and at the same time they need each other. I think it's a little crazy."

While paging through a copy of *Essence* magazine, I was struck by a passage from a female writer describing a "blind date" arranged by her employer with a rap star. "I walked toward him—my bell bottoms swishing rhythmically and midriff perfectly arranged so my belly button would twinkle up at him. I *hoped* I was breathtaking. I imagined a smile spreading on those robust cheeks as I moved his way—the hips slightly swaying, my dreamy eyes focused. . . . I put my feminist need to not be objectified in check—just this once—and kept on stepping."

That passage nicely sums up why some men are baffled. What if she had not been of a mind to be "objectified" and her date had responded to her as a sex object? Or what if he had misread her sexy come-on for something more than it was? When journalist Michel Marriott complains of the dilemma of dealing with a woman who "one moment, wants this part of the man and one moment wants the other part . . . without sending the right signals," he is describing much of what is happening between men and women today.

In her bestselling book, *You Just Don't Understand*, Deborah Tannen commented, "Boys and girls grow up in what are essentially different cultures, so talk between women and men is cross-cultural communication." It is not only the talking that's difficult but understanding what the words, once said (or left unsaid), mean. Angry accusatory language does nothing to make that communication easier. It merely focuses blame. As Liz Golden, the diversity marketing specialist, observed, an approach that merely says, "You're the problem" doesn't leave much room for discussion or mutual understanding.

Even when men and women feel affectionate toward one another, they don't necessarily communicate well. "Conversation has a really different meaning often to men and women. For women, sharing ideas and information is often establishing intimacy," said Golden. It's "getting to know you so I can figure out if I can trust you or not. I think for men, that isn't always what conversation is for. . . . There isn't the same sense of, 'We are developing a sense of connectedness by sharing this common experience.'"

Instead, she says, men are more likely to wonder, "'Why are you asking me all of these questions? Why do you need to know all of these things?'. . . Talk for talk's sake is not always as easy for men. And I don't know if it's that we're wanting different things or not." Yet, "based on my norms, you know, talk is for being intimate. So if you don't want to talk, then it must mean you don't want to be intimate. But I don't think that's what it means necessarily. I'm judging from my framework, and it's very hard to step outside of that."

Tannen refers to the process of talking to establish connections as "rapport-talk." And, if Tannen is correct, women do indeed engage in it more often than do men.

In his immensely popular *Men Are from Mars, Women Are from Venus* John Gray observes: "To feel better, women talk about past problems, future problems, potential problems, even problems that have no solutions. This is the way women operate. To expect otherwise is to deny a woman her sense of self. . . . Gradually, if she feels she is being heard, her stress disappears. After talking about one topic she will pause and then move on to the next. In this way she continues to expand talking about problems, worries, disappointments, and frustrations." Men, on the other hand, "talk about problems for only two reasons: they are blaming someone or they are seeking advice." Otherwise, claims Gray, men pretty much keep their thoughts to themselves.

Jacobs confided in mock frustration, "I think that sometimes women are introspective to a fault. We need to find a happy medium. Sometimes I get together with my women friends and we talk and talk and talk about this and this and we never reach any conclusions. At some point it seems like it's destructive to be delving so deep."

This current generation of men may never acquire the capacity to delve as deeply into relationships as do women. Nor may most ever "get it" quite to the degree that many women want them to. Certainly, men are capable of understanding a good deal more than they have been given credit for, but they are not likely to be helped very much by activists who are more interested in placing blame than in inspiring cooperation. Nor are they likely to find that the answer to ambiguity and ambivalence in romance is the drafting of all-encompassing contracts or adherence to rigid rules about relationships.

The realistic view is that relationships between thinking beings will always be difficult. No two intelligent people ever agree on everything, nor can two separate beings always fully anticipate each other's needs—whatever their respective genders. It's not as if same-sex relationships, after all, are always models of concordance either.

One self-declared bisexual woman, asked whether her relationships with women were easier than those with men, reflected for several moments and replied: "The same rules aren't there. In my experience there are no rules. You have to make them up as you go." And that, she said, was as terrifying as it was liberating "because just like we all want someone to take care of us, we all want someone to tell us what to do sometimes. And when neither person knows what to do, you're both sort of navigating uncharted waters.

"I don't know if we have an easier time. I think the expectations are different, though. Maybe there's less rigidity. Maybe in that sense, it's easier. Still, a lot of the issues are exactly the same—just two people having to work things out; but there aren't rigid roles you have to fight your way out of. So maybe it is easier."

Fighting one's way out of rigid sex roles can be wearying, discomfiting work. Many men and women are far from convinced that the result is worth the effort. Even among those people, apparently a majority, who are persuaded that *something* must change, the details (How do you go about changing? How much change is enough?) are not especially clear. Given that, it is only natural that some people would turn to rigid rules and righteous rhetoric to impose certainty where it does not exist, or that others would focus on symbolic gestures ("Do you want me to open the door or don't you?") as opposed to more important yet more difficult questions about how men and women should relate.

The symbolic and the substantive are obviously linked; relationships need something of both. Sylvia Wagonheim, a lawyer, academician, and diversity expert, acknowledged that she, like many women, wanted a lot from a man: "I want to be a colleague on one hand. On the other hand, I want to be loved and protected and held, and doors opened for, and flowers sent to. You know, I want it both ways. Where a man wants to be macho, he also wants to be nurtured. He also wants to have a sexual partner. He wants to be approached and interacted with on a lot of different levels. So does a woman. If you and I are talking as professionals, I want you to respect me as a professional. If you and I are talking as dates, I don't want you to see me as a professional. I want you to see me as a woman, a desirable woman. And I want you to send me flowers. And I want you to do all of this kind of stuff.

"It might be my [baby-boomer] generation," continued Wagonheim, "but I really like it when a man opens a door for me. I like to walk out of an elevator first. I don't like it when men jump ahead of me. I don't care one way or the other in subways, but there *are* certain things. And I want to be taken in all my different faces. And I think men want all this, too."

Wagonheim is right. Men, no less than women, want to be seen for the complex beings that they are. Yet coping with the many "different faces" of modern men and women is a daunting task. Once upon a time, assigned gender roles scripted how things should go. These days, as people struggle to escape the confining strictures of the past, they toss various parts of the script away. And in the resulting uncertainty and instability, many relationships collapse. The U.S. Bureau of the Census now recognizes divorced as the fastest-growing marital-status category. Between 1970 and 1993, the number of divorced adults in the United States nearly quadrupled, from 4.3 million to 16.7 million. For men and women who are ostensibly committed to one another, staying together has never been tougher. Rhetoric that further polarizes people obviously won't make it any easier. At best, it will provide the comfort of a simple-minded answer as to why things have fallen apart.

Chapter 7

MEN WHO JUST DON'T GET IT

Perhaps nothing in recent times has contributed more to the war of words between the sexes than the suddenly ubiquitous debate over sexual harassment. In the aftermath of the Clarence Thomas–Anita Hill hearings, women everywhere took up the mantra, "You [meaning men] just don't get it." And men became defensive and confused. Some responded with waspish indignation—echoing the thoughts of Lance Morrow, who wrote in *Time:* "Women elaborately manipulate and exploit men's natural sexual attraction to the female body, and then deny the manipulation and prosecute men for the attraction—if the attraction draws in the wrong man. Women cannot for long combine fiery indignation and continuing passivity (attempting to have the best of both those worlds)."

In fact, men, in large measure, don't "get it," if by "get it" one means that they always perceive sexually charged incidents in the same way as do women. The perceptual gap, however, may not be as large as many women believe it to be. Though some studies indicate that what many women perceive of as harassment strikes many men as relatively harmless behavior, others reveal a much more complicated reality. Researchers at Augusta College, for instance, found that women predicted that men would be a great deal less empathic and more "negatively biased" than they actually turned out to be. Another study at Suffolk University found few gender differences in how sexual harassment was perceived—except that male protagonists were viewed less favorably by women than by men. Investigators at Illinois State University found that if a female target was friendly with a man, men were less inclined than women to view unacceptable behavior as harassment. The research, in short, seems to show that although men, in many circumstances, view sexually harassing behavior differently from women, most men are not particularly supportive of or sympathetic to it.

One problem with complaints of sexual harassment is that no one has a clear definition of what sexual harassment is. Under Title VII of the Civil Rights Act of 1964, sexual harassment consists of conduct that has "the purpose or effect of unreasonably interfering with an individual's work performance or creating an intimidating, hostile, or offensive working environment." What is intimidating or hostile to one person is not necessarily looked on that way by another.

So Morrow has a point. Sexual harassment is harassment only if the harassee feels harassed; in other words, if the attention is undesired. The perpetrator does not necessarily know how an act will be perceived until it's committed. In a culture that makes men the sexual aggressors and trains women to be passive, some men, even with the best intentions, will cross the line separating pursuer from harasser. For the line—barring, for the moment, clearly egregious behavior—is infinitely elastic. It lies wherever the person pursued or hassled deems it to be. And if she (or he) finds the other party attractive, the line will probably be in a different place than if she (or he) does not.

To compound matters, society has long judged male and female sexual aggression by radically different standards. There is a "double standard in the language," observes Dr. Jean Bonhomme of the National Black Men's Health Network. Statutory rape of a boy by a woman, for instance, is not considered quite as serious as statutory rape of a girl by a man. "If it's an adult male with an underage female, it's statutory rape," Bonhomme notes. "If it's an adult female with an underage male, it's 'giving the boy his first sexual experience' or 'making him a man.' They actually act as if that were beneficial."

In April 1993, a popular female swimming teacher in the Washington, D.C., area was convicted of statutory rape for a three-year relationship with a former student that had begun when the boy was eleven years old. Her sentence was thirty days (which could be cut in half by good behavior). The judge indicated that he was not inclined to make her serve any time at all, but was only doing so because of the "aggravating circumstance" created by her "relationship of trust" with her young lover. It's difficult to imagine a man who is convicted in a high-profile trial of raping an eleven-year-old female student receiving similarly lenient treatment or attracting (as this woman did) a courtroom of citizens offering their support.

Bonhomme is convinced that society's essential denial of young males' sexual vulnerability and the tendency to minimize the impact of exploitative experiences on boys can create men who are sexually insensitive. "A lot of the guys who are treated that way, what I've noticed is that they have impulse control problems around sex. They get the expectation that all women want it . . . and that type of thing. So they end up catching flack for sexual harassment or whatever," Bonhomme said. I have no idea whether Bonhomme's diagnosis is correct, but obviously men and women are taught different and, to some extent, incongruous lessons about sexual behavior. And the inevitable result is confusion.

The vague definition of harassment and the double standards that permeate every aspect of sex in America don't alter the fact that sexual harassment is a serious problem. They just make it awfully difficult to sort out.

In November 1993, the U.S. Supreme Court handed down a closely watched sexual harassment decision, unanimously affirming a person's right to sue for sexual harassment even if she (or he) has not been psychologically harmed. The case

(*Teresa Harris* v. *Forklift Systems*) was brought by a female employee of a Nashville company who was rattled by her boss's obnoxious behavior. He had called her a "dumb-ass woman," suggested that she used sex to attract customers, and made a practice of asking women employees to fish in his pockets for quarters. Teresa Harris finally quit, but a judge rejected her claim of sexual harassment because she had not been harmed psychologically.

By the time the case reached the Supreme Court, both sides agreed that sustaining psychological harm was not a necessary condition for sexual harassment. Many court watchers expected the justices to use the case to clarify the meaning of sexual harassment. Some groups had been urging that the perspective of a theoretical "reasonable *woman*" (as opposed to a "reasonable *person*") be made the standard for determining harassment claims. The argument, in essence, was that women see sexually obnoxious behavior in a different light than do men and that the judicial system is tainted by a male perspective and controlled by a "gender hierarchy." Thus, determining whether a work environment is hostile by relying on a gender-neutral ideal cannot possibly be fair to women.

The Ninth Circuit Court of Appeals in San Francisco bought that reasoning, but a good many legal scholars did not. To accept it, they argued, would be to imply that women are not reasonable persons or, at the least, that they are not reasonable in the same way as men. In effect, it would give stereotypes the force of law. Walter Arbery, writing in the *Georgia Law Review*, observed, "The reasonable woman standard conveys the message that certain conduct is actionable just because women are more sensitive." What is worse, said critics, is that the standard would make harassment claims virtually impossible to judge on anything approaching an objective basis, since such judgments would be dependent on defining how an imaginary and presumably somewhat sensitive woman would react.

The Supreme Court opinion, authored by Sandra Day O'Connor, sidestepped the "reasonable woman" issue and simply agreed that the judge had erred by requiring Harris to show psychological injury. "This standard, which we reaffirm today, takes a middle path between making actionable any conduct that is merely offensive and requiring the conduct to cause a tangible psychological injury," O'Connor wrote. Title VII was violated, she concluded, when the workplace was permeated with "discriminatory intimidation, ridicule and insult," that was "sufficiently severe or pervasive to alter the conditions of the victim's employment and create an abusive working environment."

In a concurring opinion, Justice Antonin Scalia acknowledged that the murkiness of the definition remained a problem: "As a practical matter, today's holding lets virtually unguided juries decide whether sex-related conduct engaged in (or permitted) by an employer is egregious enough to warrant an award of damages." But the ruling at least didn't burden juries with having to distinguish between "reasonable" persons and "reasonable" women. Nor did it endorse some of the more radical proposals that proponents advanced to expand the reach of the law.

Some scholars had urged, for instance, that virtually any sexual relationship in the workplace between supervisors and subordinates should be seen as a form of sexual harassment. Joan Van Tol, of West Virginia University College of Law, said that such relationships send the message "that the only way to advance in the workplace is to 'use' or 'surrender' one's sexuality." "This is the same message that victims of direct sexual harassment receive," she wrote in the *Industrial Relations Law Journal.* Consequently, she said, "preferential treatment of sexually compliant employees" often amounts to harassment, not of the "compliant" worker but of other employees who are disadvantaged by the lovers' relationship. How an employee would determine whether he or she was disadvantaged by someone else's relationship or by some other fact unrelated to sex (or a sexual liaison) is not evident, but Van Tol apparently believes that the threat of judges and juries is needed to restrict such liaisons.

Inevitably, the heightened sensitivity to sexual harassment has left some men feeling persecuted, and it has convinced others that the handling of sexual harassment claims can be every bit as abusive as sexual harassment itself.

One middle manager told me that his experience in handling a complaint had left him shaken. It started when a female employee told him she had been kissed, against her will, by a male co-worker she disliked. The manager took the charge to his superiors, who proceeded to investigate. Almost immediately, things snowballed. Several women took it upon themselves to canvass others in the office, seeking tales of other unsavory behavior on the man's part. By and by, the man was accused, though not formally, of harassing several others.

The manager was uncertain how to evaluate all the stories, but he was convinced that at least some were specious. One accuser, he said, had previously put two grapefruits into the top of her dress and pressed her body against the manager's office window to get the attention of the man she now accused of harassing her. At the time, the manager had written the scene off as "juvenile" but characteristic behavior from that particular woman. Others who were now complaining, he said, had engaged in similar stunts. Instead of the man's behavior being seen in the context of a banter-filled office populated with offbeat characters, suddenly he seemed headed for a lynching.

The case was never officially resolved. The man resigned rather than confront the charges against him. Though the manager thought everyone might be better off with the man gone, he was unsettled by the way the episode had played out. "It ripped the place apart. And it was really difficult to keep it going. The men became very defensive and very frightened. It's like the guys were wondering, 'What did I do three years ago that could now come back to haunt me?'"

Senior management, he was convinced, had handled the matter poorly. The bosses had been right, he thought, to take the original complaint seriously, but as soon as the grievances picked up steam, management apparently panicked. The attitude was "like, let's just get this guy out of here." To him, that reeked of something like McCarthyism, not of enlightened management practices.

An Illinois air traffic controller had an even more unsettling exposure to the politics of sexual harassment. In September 1994, the Aurora man, Douglas Hartman, sued the U.S. Department of Transportation in connection with a "cultural diversity workshop" that apparently sought to shock men into social awareness. According to the complaint of sexual harassment and employment discrimination filed in U.S. District Court in Chicago, during the three-day seminar in fall 1992, Hartman was subjected to "a barrage of anti-male propaganda." The Bible, he said, was "condemned as sexist and religion was characterized as a device of the power structure designed to keep people, particularly women, in their place."

In the course of the seminar, women were assembled in a conference room in a hotel and instructed to form a gauntlet modeled after the one made notorious by the 1991 Tailhook scandal. Men entered the room, one by one, and were "subjected to touching, groping, and other demeaning and unwelcome sexual harassment by the females in the room." Hartman said he was touched on his "legs, buttock and genitalia, with the females involved making sexually demeaning comments." Eventually, the men and women were brought together in a room where male sex organs, in "various sizes and states of arousal," were exhibited on charts, and the men were rated on a scale of one to ten. According to Hartman, he was called a "wimp, limp-dick" for protesting the treatment. After filing an EEOC complaint, he said, he was harassed even more and denied promotional opportunities. As a result, Hartman claimed, he suffered stomach problems, insomnia, headaches, and other stress-related ailments.

Few men are subjected to such misguided and abusive attempts at consciousness-raising. But many have found themselves under assault for little more than being men. As Menswork Center founder James Sniechowski noted, "Men are feeling betrayed all over the place, even though they don't feel overtly like they've done anything." In the workplace, he said, gender dynamics sometimes take on a life of their own: "The women come in and they often assume a victim's position, meaning, 'We are the oppressed, and as a consequence, what you do is going to oppress us no matter what you do.' So a lot of times these guys are opening up and saying, 'Tell us what you need,' and [women are] saying 'We don't believe you.' So they don't know how to get across the gap."

Such dynamics ultimately lead only to frustration. Liz Golden, the marketing expert, says she has became so "tired of fighting" that she often forces herself to find a less confrontational way of making points she deems important. "Every time the opportunity comes up to be self-righteous, I have to make a conscious effort to stop myself from saying, 'See, you don't really understand what it's like to be a woman, because if you did understand you wouldn't have said such a stupid thing.'" Emotionally satisfying as such rhetoric may be, she says, it leads nowhere. "It's like running in a circle."

Health and Hospitals Corporation executive Rosanna Rosado reached essentially the same conclusion: "One of my predecessors who was this very strong feminist, on every major women's group in the city and all of that, really castrated these men. She had this women's agenda . . . and she hit them over the head with it and constantly talked about sexual harassment, but like only to the men. I feel sensitive to that. I think that being a feminist is not being anti-men. . . . Not all men are the same. Not all women are the same. And I like to think that you [can] teach people."

What Rosado and Golden have realized is that relations are enhanced when language is demilitarized. Not that goodwill will eliminate all the gender gremlins that bedevil modern life and, increasingly, the modern workplace, but at least it will foster an atmosphere that makes it easier to determine whether miscommunication or malice is to blame for any particular untoward act. Miscommunication, after all, can be corrected; malicious behavior can be punished. But it does little good to cultivate an environment in which it is impossible to tell the difference.

Following a recent "Take Your Daughter to Work Day," I spoke with two women, both of whom had young sons and both of whom were reflecting on the meaning of the day. One woman, a journalist, was stymied by her daughter's insistence that her younger brother accompany them to work. Not wanting to fill the girl's head with notions of a women-destroying "patriarchy," she fibbed and told her that boys had a day, too.

The second woman, a computer professional from California, was convinced that her son, who was too young to talk, had somehow intuited that something important was going on. He had clung to her much more tightly than normal when she had left him with the baby-sitter. It was as if he were begging to be taken to work, she said. Though it was inconceivable to me that the toddler could have had any notion of what the day was about, I was struck by the mother's sense of guilt. I was struck also by the fact that mothers with children too young to understand gender limitations were wrestling with how to shield their children from gender politics. Whatever the parents do, of course, the innocence at some point will pass, and the children will learn, as their parents have, that gender is not a neutral trait. What they will also learn, if we are lucky, is that gender differences are not necessarily reasons for a fight.

Chapter 8

WHO'S GOING TO BE THE DADDY?

When lawyer Ron Henry asks, "How have we gone in one generation from 'Father knows best' to 'All men are rapists'?" he is posing the question rhetorically. He is also, perhaps unintentionally, making a linkage between the apparent upsurge in female-male hostility and the state of fatherhood in America today.

In at least one noticeable sense, the connection is undeniably real. The increase in divorce—and the power struggles, custody fights, fatherlessness, and feelings of abandonment that often accompany it—has let loose an avalanche of anger and resentment upon society. But the damage done by the breakdown of certain family values and of fatherhood goes much deeper, say some pundits, than we generally care to see.

The current buildup of male-female antagonisms, they contend, cannot be viewed in isolation, but should be seen as a product of a revolution that is undermining American mores— that is pitting not only men against women but children against fathers and, in large measure, society against itself. That revolution has resulted in the collapse of the connection "between masculinity and responsible paternity," in the words of David Blankenhorn, author of *Fatherless America* and founder and president of the Institute for American Values; and that collapse, in his view, has aggravated practically every social problem imaginable.

Blankenhorn's analysis is, to put it mildly, controversial—

and one well marinated in various tenets of conservative ideology. It strikes some critics as little more than a call for a return to the mythical good old days. Yet, even those who reject his thesis acknowledge that in focusing on children, he has latched onto an important issue. For though men and women are firing the weapons, children, more and more, seem to be emerging as silent casualties of the sexual revolution.

In the past four decades, the nation has seen an explosion in the number of youngsters being raised without fathers. No serious thinker considers that a healthy trend. Many see it as a major crisis, and one that affects us all.

Michael Lamb, of the National Institute of Child Health and Human Development and a respected expert on fatherhood, observes: "In the sixties, it was poor blacks. And while a lot of the concern today is still about inner-city black boys and the lack of male role models . . . everybody now knows somebody growing up without a father, or who is a father without his kids." Blankenhorn blames fatherlessness for a frightening array of pathologies—antifemale and antichild violence, low test scores, juvenile delinquency, mental health problems, reading disorders, and dependence on welfare. It may be the "principal cause of declining child well-being in our society," says Blankenhorn, who claims that father absence is a better predictor of violent criminal behavior than is either race or income.

The National Fatherhood Initiative, founded in 1994, which Blankenhorn chairs, has compiled mountains of statistics adding up to an indictment of father absence. Sixty percent of rapists, 72 percent of adolescent murderers, and 70 percent of youngsters in state reform institutions are products of single-parent homes, NFI claims. Poverty, educational failure, and health problems are also pervasive in homes where fathers are not around. In Blankenhorn's hands, the statistics are weapons with a purpose: to provoke America into action. And he has plenty of company helping to sound the alarm.

At a summer 1994 "Family Re-Union" conference in Nashville, one speaker after another decried the epidemic of fatherlessness. Kyle Pruett, of the Yale Child Study Center, alluded to "a hunger and a longing in the lives of America's individual children for a paternal presence that I don't think has ever been greater." Richard Louv, author of *Fatherlove,* spoke of children "walking around with a hole in their heart the size of a parent."

Vice President Al Gore called for a cultural awakening: "We must instill in the next generation of fathers the belief that fatherhood is a sacred trust, that it is their non-negotiable responsibility to support their children financially and emotionally, that children need and deserve a father's love." The Rev. Jesse Jackson, who keynoted the conference luncheon, delivered a paean to fathers and the ties that bind them to their children. At one point, he turned to the vice president and roared, "How could Al Gore dare to think he could change the world? *BECAUSE HE SAW HIS DADDY DO IT,*" he answered himself.

Much the same tone prevailed at a "national summit on fatherhood" sponsored by NFI in Dallas several months later. Wade Horn, director of NFI, pronounced fatherlessness "not just one of many national crises. It is *the* national crisis." Eloise Anderson, director of California's Department of Social Services, emphatically agreed.

"I don't think women really pay attention to the safety of their children in the same way fathers pay attention to the safety of their children," said Anderson, who apparently had a particularly irresponsible type of mother in mind. "Single moms in most homes are usually dating as well," she said. "They bring men into the home whom they really don't know. *Their children are not safe.*" She ended with a ringing defense of men and marriage: "If we don't reconsider marriage, and if we don't get rid of this whole notion that men are redundant, then I think there are two things that we can do: We can stop having boy babies. Or we should stop having children." If Blankenhorn and company have their way, all the hullabaloo will result in a national mobilization to reverse the trend of single-parent households.

Unwed mothers, of course, have always existed; but their number has previously been relatively small. And divorce, though always a possibility, was once rarer than eternal love. Between 1921 and 1923, approximately 160,000 Americans divorced each year. That amounts to a divorce rate roughly one-fourth of what it is today. The rate skyrocketed following World War II, but soon drifted downward—that is, until the 1960s. Since then (with the help of "no-fault" divorce laws), the frequency of divorce has more than doubled. At the same time, the percentage of children born out of wedlock has quintupled.

This is not to imply that previous generations had no children without fathers. As author Mary Ann Mason documented in *From Father's Property to Children's Rights*, colonists in prerevolutionary America often imported minors, who had no fathers or were willing to leave them, to work as indentured servants. And out-of-wedlock births, as economist Robert Lerman observed, reached a rate of roughly 30 percent in certain areas during the nineteenth century. Still, ours is the first generation to deal with a huge number of single mothers raising children without men.

In eighteenth-century America, for instance, fathers generally retained custody in those rare occasions when divorce occurred. Indeed, whatever their status or circumstance, mothers had virtually no claim to their children. As Mason notes, "An orphan in colonial America was defined as a child whose father had died, even if the child had a surviving mother." Well into the nineteenth century, American courts, citing property rights under common law, as well as the man's obligation to support his children, normally favored fathers when custody was in dispute. Fathers who were slaves, of course, were a different matter, with the owners of the mothers generally retaining ownership of the children. By the end of the nineteenth century, the tide had turned. Courts were under the sway of what Mason calls "the cult of motherhood." Women, judges and society assumed, were designed by nature to nurture, which implied that children, at least during the "tender years," belonged with their mothers. In recent years, American courts and state legislatures have adapted gender-neutral policies, but mothers, for a variety of reasons, still generally end up as the custodial parents. In 1993, 84 percent of single divorced parents with custody were mothers, whereas only 16 percent were fathers. Among those who were never married, fathers made up only 13 percent of the custodial parents.

Up to this point at least, never-married men have shown little inclination to organize and fight for parenting "rights." Divorced men have mobilized with a vengeance. Many are furious, both at their ex-wives and at a legal system they believe has robbed them of their children. They are loudly insisting that their children need them and that they have a right to their children.

H. W. "Sonny" Burmeister, president of the Children's Rights Council of Georgia, approaches advocacy with all the subtlety of a raging bull. "Look what our legal system does," he grumbles. "It aborts one parent, almost always the father; and it maximizes conflict. It says, 'If you can afford it, come in and play our game of destruction. We've got these gladiators called attorneys with the child as the trophy. . . . The power, the control, the money swing wherever the child goes.'"

Burmeister, a head hunter for computer companies, was divorced in the early 1980s. At the time, he had a four-year-old daughter and a two-year-old son. Although he initially agreed to his wife having custody, he later became convinced that her home was unsafe and tried to wrestle them away. As Burmeister tells the story, a Georgia judge dismissed his arguments by commenting, "'Mr. Burmeister, I ain't never seen the calves follow the bull. . . . Therefore I always give custody to the mamas. I think a bad mama is better than a good daddy.'"

"I spent thousands upon thousands of dollars to protect my children and then had a judge say that. So what I realized was that our court system was gender-biased. It was corrupt. Lawyers and judges and psychologists, people who were supposed to look after our children, have what I call a child-suffering industry," says Burmeister, who now spends most of his energies trying to reform what he considers a sexist system.

Much of his time is devoted to collecting information he believes will help persuade the public that fathers are not necessarily at fault when marriages crumble. In cases he has researched in Atlanta, says Burmeister, the wife was the one who sought the divorce more than three-fourths of the times after a marriage which, on average, lasted between four and five years. While such statistics say nothing about what drove so many wives to divorce, Burmeister believes that they at least demonstrate that most divorced men have not callously traded in old wives for younger models. "You hear [that] June Cleaver bore his children, put him through school, was devotedly married to him for twenty-five years, and then he leaves her and the kids for some twenty-two-year-old." That perception, Burmeister believes, is "bunk."

He is obsessed with statistics relating to custody. After sifting through two hundred cases one judge had handled, Burmeister concluded that she had never awarded custody to a father in a contested case. In those few instances in which the wives had voluntarily surrendered custody, the men were granted child support only 25 percent of the time. In those cases in which the wife got custody, child support was

awarded 93 percent of the time. The numbers he collected persuaded him that many common beliefs about failed marriages
are fallacies.

"I found that the system perpetuates myths about who's
seeking the divorce, about what type of marriage it is, about
how many kids are involved, about the economic condition of
those afterwards." His job, he concluded, was to set the facts
straight, to "raise consciousness" and force people to act. "The
way you do that," he claims, is to stir up and make people
"smell their own manure." The "manure" he refers to are laws
and policies, which, in his view, are "gender biased" and
antifamily.

The price of Burmeister's obsession has been the virtual
collapse of his business, but he doesn't seem to mind. "It was a
sacrifice that I was called to," he says. His former wife,
Burmeister confides, has moved out of state and essentially
beyond his reach. "What I do now is not going to affect my
children, but hopefully it will affect my children's children, and
the children of the world." He believes God is using him to try
to set things right: "I think that out of my tragedy, which was
done by the court system and society devaluing and disenfran-
chising the role of a father . . . came this ministry."

Stuart Miller, legislative director of the American Fathers
Coalition, shares many of Burmeister's views. A former real
estate developer, Miller blames his divorce settlement for the
collapse of his business. "As a result of the divorce I went
through, I saw one hundred-and-twenty men lose their jobs,"
he said. He is now a full-time volunteer advocate for men.

Miller's resentment was fueled not only by an ugly custody
battle with his former wife (which he lost), but with a second
battle with a girlfriend who, Miller claimed, "saw how much
child support I was paying after my divorce and figured she
could live on that kind of money as well." He won the second
legal skirmish, but the woman disappeared with their child,

and the federal government has refused to help him find them.

Those experiences led Miller to conclude that something was wrong with federal policies, as well as with a judicial system that saw him principally as a source of currency. He has no difficulty understanding why, faced with such attitudes, some fathers withdraw. They "feel pushed away and they can't take the pain on a daily basis," he said. That pain, said Miller, is "the reason I quit doing real estate development and I'm a full-time volunteer—to try to make an impact on the system so my children will not have to grow up and go through the pain I went through, and am still going through to this day."

Miller and Burmeister want a system that allows men to continue to be fathers (in virtually every sense of the word) even after a divorce. What that means to them is a system that encourages joint physical custody. For Miller, the rationale is simple: "They need to take the battle, the adversarial battleground of the children, out of that scenario completely. [Children] are not a winner/loser item. Both parents need to be involved in children's lives. And, very frankly, they need to be forced to be involved."

Burmeister is even more adamant. "We should assume that parents who want to divorce each other can, but they can't divorce each other from the children," he said. To prevent parents from trying to do so by moving out of state, he would make relocation grounds for losing all custodial rights.

Under such a system of joint custody, the financial incentive for fighting over children will vanish, Burmeister believes, since no one would pay child support: "Why would you need a transfer of money if you each have the child fifteen days?" He also sees less tangible benefits. Reconnecting children with their fathers, he says, could restore a sense of purpose to men's lives. "Look at ego status and self-esteem, particularly [among] low- and middle-income blacks and white males. Ninety-five percent of their whole identity is in providing for their family, being able to bring the bacon home, to have mom, the kids, a little white picket fence, a house; and the neighbors can say, 'Well, you know, John's a good guy.' We take that away from fifty percent of our fathers today," said Burmeister. "And we wonder why they won't pay their child support. We wonder why they aren't responsible."

The case for joint custody, as I will show later, is not nearly as incontestable as Burmeister makes it seem. Putting aside, for the moment, the matter of custodial arrangements, some critics see a fatal flaw in Burmeister's premise. The idea that men can leave their families and still be good parents is wishful thinking, argues Blankenhorn.

"I don't think there is a viable post-divorce fatherhood," he declared. "You need to live with your children and you need to have a good working relationship with the mother; and all the evidence that we have suggests that if you don't have those two foundations, you really can't be a very good father. And it doesn't matter how good a guy you are, or how hard you try. Unless you're some kind of superman who's really willing to become almost heroic about it, it's very hard. And once you remarry, or once your ex-spouse remarries, you can multiply by ten how hard it is. . . . If we're concerned about fatherhood in our society and the loss of fatherhood, what we need to be concerned about is not reforming our procedures for divorce— even though maybe we should have a few divorce reforms— but the main issue is to have more married parents raising their children."

An end to divorce does not seem to be in the cards any time soon. For though it is not quite as rampant as it was during its high point in the late 1970s and early 1980s, when half the first marriages were projected to fail, at least 40 percent of first marriages are still expected to collapse. The casualty rate for second marriages is reckoned to be even higher. In addition, births to never-married parents have risen dramatically—among virtually all ethnic and socioeconomic groups. In 1960, for instance, a single-parent household was over five times more likely to mean a household with a divorced parent than one with a never-married parent. By 1993, the proportions were roughly equal.

To Blankenhorn, such statistics underscore a colossal crisis—and one whose ramifications go far beyond protecting the rights of once-married men. On one point, however, he and the advocates for divorced men agree: Getting men more involved with their children is essential.

Bernadine Watson, a vice president of Public/Private Ventures, had the same insight in the early 1990s. The Philadelphia-based nonprofit organization strives to develop innovative solutions to public policy problems, but the issue of teenage pregnancy had P/PV's best thinkers stymied. People were telling her, "We've reached the end of our rope. We don't know what else to do," Watson recalled. Then it suddenly came to Watson and her colleagues that fathers were the missing link, that while numerous programs had been developed for unwed mothers, unwed fathers had been ignored.

It was clear, said Watson, that "the young men have a lot of influence on the young women—in terms of their aspirations, in terms of what they can do with resources. They have a lot of influence on the children. But nobody's paying attention to their economic viability, their social development, their ability to be productive parents, their ability to contribute productively to the relationship."

Meanwhile, Ralph Smith, president of the Philadelphia Children's Network, was investigating how to reduce the odds of failure in Philadelphia's public schools. He soon realized that the vast majority of schoolchildren with serious problems were from single-parent households. Shortly thereafter, he signed up PCN to become one of six sites across the country that would house a thirty-month P/PV-sponsored demonstration project targeting young unwed fathers. Each site was required to enroll at least fifty unwed fathers aged sixteen to twenty-five.

Tom Henry, a University of Pennsylvania official who agreed to become director of the program, himself had been a teenage father; he welcomed the chance to help others avoid the mistakes that he had made. Henry organized classes dealing with the basics of parenting, as well as seminars with successful men and women from various walks of life. He also instituted weekly rap sessions, during which no subject was taboo. Each young man became a personal mission, and Henry made a point of being accessible at all times—even if that meant taking calls at home at 4 A.M. Henry also shared his own history, including his success at maintaining a happy marriage for nearly thirty years.

Henry, in effect, became a nurturing older brother, helping his charges with everything from legal problems to acquiring high school equivalency diplomas. The effort seems to have paid off. When I visited the program in 1994, over half the men had gotten jobs. Some had enrolled in drug rehabilitation programs or extracted themselves from legal problems. Several credited Henry and his co-workers with giving them the confidence and financial wherewithal to get married. Others praised the program for providing them with an extended family. "Without this [program], some of us guys ain't nothing," one man bluntly remarked.

Brian Thompson, a twenty-year-old with an infant daughter, said the program had enabled him to envision a better future for himself and to be a better father to his child. But, for him, as was noted in Chapter 2, it had also served an even more basic purpose: It had allowed him to "surround myself with men" and to "be around men and see how men think."

Similar programs have sprouted across the country, and some report a great deal of success. In Cleveland, Ohio, the

Charles Ballard's National Institute for Responsible Father-hood and Family Development works with young men who are very much like those in the Philadelphia program. The men enter, for the most part, as unemployed high school dropouts; many are gang members, and few are in any position to support a child. After working with Ballard, the vast majority return to school, find jobs, and accept financial responsibility for their children.

The success of people such as Ballard seems to stem from their intense faith in (and ability to relate to) the young men with whom they are working. Some of the best programs are run by men who were unmarried fathers themselves, but nonetheless managed to turn their lives around. They expect no less from their protégés, whom they infuse with high expectations. They also create an environment in which the men feel free to reveal their deepest insecurities and to ask for help. "For a lot of us," observed Ralph Smith of PCN, college served as "a sheltered environment for a long time . . . a stable site where you could make mistakes, and where you could grow up, and where you could establish supportive relationships." Henry, he noted, had created something similar with the Responsive Fathers Program.

Despite Henry's apparent success, Smith knows that the impact of such efforts is limited. He also knows that even with someone like Henry trying to look out for them, young, unmarried inner-city fathers face daunting challenges. "One of the things I think we learned is how fragile these relationships between the young men and young women are, and how little support there is for these relationships," Smith said.

First, he noted, the couple is not married, so the child is considered illegitimate. The parents are almost certain to be financially unstable, and the man is likely to have a criminal record and an uncertain work history. Even though they may struggle to stay together, they come with "all of that sort of

baggage." To make matters worse, the child support enforcement system then "drives these young people into court
around paternity and around child support." Is it so surprising,
he asks, that many of the men disappear?

It is certainly no surprise to Blankenhorn or to his colleague
at the Institute for American Values, Barbara Whitehead. In a
widely discussed 1993 article in *Atlantic Monthly* provocatively
titled, "Dan Quayle Was Right," Whitehead spelled out her
analysis of the problem.

Fewer than half of today's children will grow up with both
natural parents, she observed, and many who were devastated
by a divorce will never bounce back. Children raised without
fathers are "more likely to drop out of high school, to get pregnant as teenagers, to abuse drugs, and to be in trouble with the
law." They are at a higher risk of physical or sexual abuse and
are more likely to have emotional problems. As adults, they
will experience more difficulty than normal in establishing satisfying relationships, forming stable marriages, or holding onto
a job.

Even those who are taken in by a stepparent are not as well
off as are those who stay in intact homes, said Whitehead. Children "living with stepparents appear to be even more disadvantaged than children living in a stable single-parent family,"
she wrote. "Stepfamilies disrupt established loyalties, create
new uncertainties, provoke deep anxieties, and sometimes
threaten a child's physical safety as well as emotional security."
Moreover, stepchildren are at a high risk of another harrowing
ride on the marital-rupture roller coaster. Nearly half the children who acquire a stepparent will go through yet another
divorce. All that instability, Whitehead argued, damages, often
irreparably, the bond between father and child and leaves children exposed to untold suffering.

Nonetheless, divorce has become a defining characteristic
of modern life. Between 1960 and 1993, the percentage of chil-

dren living with a divorced parent nearly quintupled—rising from just over 2 percent to slightly over 10 percent. In the same period, the percentage of children living in single-parent homes tripled—from 9 percent in 1960 to over 27 percent in 1993. More than one-fifth of white women, more than one-third of Hispanic women, and more than two-thirds of black women who bear their first child are husbandless, and many seem destined never to marry.

Richard Weinberg, director of the Institute of Child Development at the University of Minnesota, recalls watching two young girls acting out a domestic scene. One turned to the other and asked, "Who's going to be the daddy?" "Oh well," her friend replied, "we don't need a daddy. Do we?" Weinberg found the exchange a sobering commentary on today's society.

He may, of course, be reading too much into the offhand comment of a child. But with more and more children being raised in households that have no fathers, the girl's question easily takes on an almost cosmic dimension. How necessary are fathers in a world where women can do virtually anything a man can do? For Blankenhorn, the answer is obvious. And he sees the upsurge in violent crime as the prod that may force America to try to solve the problem.

"When you have a society that is just increasingly fearful about crime . . . it's just not that complicated for the average person to put two and two together," he said. The two things he sees people putting together are violence and fatherlessness—which he views as being inextricably related. "No one study . . . proves it to everyone's satisfaction," he concedes, "but many studies show this again and again."

Although Blankenhorn is trying to mobilize public opinion around fatherhood, he resists describing any such mobilization as a movement. "Populism was a movement. The civil rights movement was a movement because you had people in beauty parlors, and church halls, and just in the local community taking action, going out and doing things. We have not gotten to that point. And we may not get to that point because, in a way, this is about how you live your life. It's not about getting a law changed necessarily; it's certainly not primarily about that. And it's not about defining yourself as a victim [who is demanding to be] treated more fairly. In that sense, it's different from the women's movement.

"We're not saying we've been mistreated or anything like that. We're just saying that this generation of children is spending less time with their fathers than any generation in American history and that this is a national tragedy, for children, for men, and for the society—and that we all, starting with men themselves, must change course on this problem of fatherlessness. A lot of it's personal and has to do with your basic philosophy of life, so it's hard. I don't know if it's going to become a movement. But what it really is now is some people who want to make the argument in the public square that says fatherlessness is the most urgent social problem of our generation. We must reverse this trend. That's really our argument. And we will see whether or not there are people who agree."

An evangelical Christian group called Promise Keepers is making a similar argument in the public square—or, to be more precise, in several of them. In 1994, more than two hundred thousand men flocked to Promise Keepers' rallies, and more than six hundred thousand were expected in 1995. The huge crowds represent a spectacular growth for the men's ministry founded by Bill McCartney, the former head football coach at the University of Colorado, whose first conference in Boulder in 1991 drew about four thousand men. A million believers are expected to turn out for a 1996 rally in Washington, D.C., at which men will recommit themselves to their families. McCartney set the tone by resigning his $350,000-a-year coaching job at the end of 1994, saying he intended to spend more time with his wife.

Promise Keepers took its name from the fact that "guys talk a lot, but they do not keep their promises, especially when it comes to children," said Don Cardenas, a spokesman for the organization. The ministry aspired to change that situation by prompting people to open their hearts to the Lord. "We found that all kinds of external types of commitments—getting back to fatherhood, to the family—were just temporary types of things," said Cardenas. Lasting change, he explained, had to be spiritually based and accepted "within."

That spiritual foundation, Cardenas suggested, was what made Promise Keepers different from secular pro-fatherhood organizations, but there are other dissimilarities as well. In fact, among the many groups promoting fatherhood, differences abound. Promise Keepers, for instance, believes that a man's place is at the head of the household. The patriarchy, from its perspective, is part of God's natural order. A *Los Angeles Times* writer described the attitude as something of a "throwback to the days of 'Father Knows Best.' Dad is still in charge, but he's kinder, gentler and a lot more spiritual." In contrast, Wade Horn, NFI's director, insists that he has no interest in "reestablishing patriarchy." He is interested in connecting fathers to their children but primarily in the context of a marriage, except in the most aberrant cases—giving him quite a different agenda from the groups that focus primarily on divorced men or unwed fathers.

The groups' disparate objectives underscore the fact that fatherhood or fatherlessness, for that matter, is very much a mixed bag. Fathers who live with their children, for instance, obviously father differently from those who don't, just as divorced fathers typically have a different relationship with their children than fathers who were never married. Despite the dreary statistics around fatherlessness, all the news is not bad. It would be wrong, in other words, to assume that an entire generation of fathers have failed. An increasing number of divorced men are gaining custody of their children—though, as I will show, the odds continue to favor women. And a growing number of married men are taking care of their children while their wives are at work.

A 1993 census report stated that one of every five preschoolers whose mothers worked outside the home was cared for by a father—a substantial increase from the previous decade when the ratio was roughly one out of seven. Among married couples in which the wives work, the proportion of young children cared for by fathers rose by over a third, from 17 percent to 23 percent between 1977 and 1991. More than 50 percent of fathers among the long-term unemployed served as the primary caretakers of their preschool-age children. Among every significant category of fathers—including those not married to the mothers of their children and those who worked full time—the numbers involved in child care have increased.

Fathers' involvement in child rearing will no doubt continue to grow. Many of America's fastest-growing jobs are in service industries currently dominated by women. Women will most likely continue to take a large proportion of those jobs, and many will continue to work after the birth of their children. Large numbers of fathers will have no other economically viable alternative to shouldering more child care responsibilities. Others, out of a sheer desire to experience the pleasures of fatherhood, will find ways to be an important presence in their children's lives.

Obviously, not many fathers are trading in business suits for aprons. As I discussed in Chapter 5, some men simply are not inclined to put in much effort at home, and many employers tell men, in effect, that a prerequisite for success is the willingness to forgo domesticity. If men are not exactly telling their employers to go to hell, they are not necessarily happy with the bargain. Fatherhood Project director James Levine, who coined the term "daddy stress," said that many men in corporate

America feel "trapped." They are uncertain how to approach their bosses to ask for time off to attend a PTA meeting or to go to a child's soccer game. "If they can hear an example of some other guy that's been able to do that, that can be very empowering," he said.

Ellen Galinsky, co-president of the Families and Work Institute, sees evidence of the same phenomenon. Men, she says, "want more time with their kids. They're not wanting to be the stick figures that their parents were to them." At the same time, however, surveys show that "the behavior hasn't caught up with the attitudes."

The very fact that so many men now have such enlightened attitudes about fatherhood is a sign of an important shift in the culture. If these men are not yet living up to their own ideals, one reason is that much of society has still not accepted the possibility that a dad can be as nurturing as a mom—or even ought to aspire to the "mommy's role."

In some sense, as society shifts, we are seeing a war for men's souls. One set of forces is bringing men closer to their children than they have been in generations. And another set is driving them away. The result is that there are several categories of fathers: some who are married and nurturing, some who are altogether missing, and a huge number who are somewhere in between. Included in the last category are the divorced men who fervently wish to be good fathers.

As was noted earlier, Blankenhorn believes that their yearning amounts to little more than pipe dreams, and, for many fathers, he is probably right. Psychologist Judith Wallerstein's pioneering ten-year study of divorce provided ample reasons for concern. Among the well-to-do divorcing northern California families who opened up their lives to her scrutiny, she found a high level of psychological distress—even years after the divorces had taken place. Many children, upon learning of the breakup, became fearful of being abandoned. Animosity between parents made things worse. At some point in the divorce process, over half the children saw violent parental conflicts; most had never previously seen such violent behavior.

Nonetheless, many of them adjusted relatively successfully. Within five years after the divorces, one-third of the children were functioning well and had good relations with both parents. Some were better off than they had been when the parents were married. But more than one-third were in a sorry state. Many were clinically depressed and failing at school and in their personal relationships. A large number of their problems, Wallerstein concluded, originated with the parents. Despite the divorces (or perhaps because of them) nearly one-third of the parents were bitterly battling each other, and they made little effort to shield the children from their fights. Caught in the throes of their rage ("a rage that feels good," was Wallerstein's description), many parents were apparently oblivious to its destructive effects on their children.

Adolescence and young adulthood were particularly difficult times for the children. By that time, many were coping not only with a second divorce (half the children in the study saw either their mothers or their fathers divorce again), but with the need to make a life for themselves, and they tended to be wary of relationships. Nearly half the children "entered adulthood as worried, underachieving, self-deprecating, and sometimes angry young men and women," wrote Wallerstein in *Second Chances*, her book-length analysis of her study. Boys initially seemed worse off than girls. "Ten years after divorce," wrote Wallerstein, "close to one half of the boys, who are now between the ages of nineteen and twenty-nine, are unhappy and lonely and have had few, if any, lasting relationships with young women." But many of the women experienced what Wallerstein termed a "sleeper effect." As they approached adulthood, they discovered that they feared marrying someone like their fathers or questioned their own ability to be good mothers and wives.

The father's role in divorced households was particularly difficult since the father was rarely the custodial parent. Instead, he typically became a visitor and gradually grew more and more distant from his children. Fathers, Wallerstein found, were painfully divided: They were "eager to stay close and embrace their children and eager to let go of them." Fathers, who felt pushed away (the women in two-thirds of the cases had initiated the divorces) tended to retreat. Ten years into the study, most of the children had poor relationships with their fathers. During adolescence, when children hungered intensely for their fathers, the fathers tended not to be easily available. Stepfathers, in many cases, could not fill the void. Children who were nine or older at the time of the divorce generally resented the unaccustomed father figure. Ninety percent told Wallerstein that life had not improved by having the new man around. (In contrast, 90 percent of the younger children appreciated their stepfathers' presence.) Whereas girls were often accepting of their stepfathers, boys, for the most part, were not.

The postdivorce picture, as Wallerstein made clear, was not necessarily bleak. But the children's well-being was heavily linked to the birth parents cooperating with each other. For men who wanted to stay in their children's lives, the challenges could be disheartening. Noncustodial fathers who were unwilling to make heroic efforts to stay involved were, by and large, destined to become shadowy phantoms looming somewhere in the distance.

Dr. James Egan, former chair of the Department of Psychiatry at Children's Hospital National Medical Center in Washington, D.C., believes it is almost impossible for a father to undo the damage done by divorce. "What is more important than whether the father is there or not . . . is why he's not there. Outrageous as it may sound, a dead father, who's been killed in war or in an airplane crash or in an accident, is a more effective father than a relatively devoted divorced father." At least when a father died, explains Egan, a child does not feel he has been rejected.

Egan agrees with Wallerstein's assessment that a stepfather generally cannot fill the void. "The least favorable family structure is the one that in our culture we have glorified: the Brady Bunch—mine, yours and ours." Ranking family types in order of desirability for children, Egan judged that "by and large, the best is an intact family. Second best is a dead parent. Third best is both [parents] divorced neither remarried, with considerable involvement with both parents. Next in [order] of preference is remarried with no other children. Least desirable is remarried with children." Given that reality, suggested Egan, mothers whose primary motive for remarrying is to give their children a father should probably be discouraged.

Dr. Jean Bonhomme, himself a child of divorce, gives poignant testimony to its effects. The reason he is "not married and I don't have children myself," said Bonhomme, has much to do with the suffering that his parents' divorce caused him. Bonhomme was about ten at the time his parents separated and was living in Brownsville, the rough Brooklyn neighborhood that spawned boxers Mike Tyson and Riddick Bowe. "As a ten-year-old, having to face that environment without the protection of a father, I felt kind of like a clam without a shell." Not only did he feel vulnerable, but he felt bewildered. "Growing up was much more difficult because I had to make all my mistakes myself."

To compound matters, Bonhomme recalls, he was told that his father was worthless: "Very soon after my father left, my mother would be screaming at me if I even said anything nice about him. Now, that really was a gut wrencher, because here was a man I had been told to obey without question, to love: 'This is your father.' And all of a sudden I can't even speak nicely of him. I'm denied permission to love him. I actually ended up participating in my mother's abuse after a couple of years. I started to tell him that when he drove home, I hoped he crashed the car. My mother used to love to hear that kind of talk."

It seemed that his father could do nothing right. "When my father used to try to help me with my school work and would take me places to study with other students so I could keep up with my courses, my mother would accuse him of sabotage," says Bonhomme.

As a child Bonhomme "dreaded the prospect of growing up like my father." Yet today he credits his father with a substantial part of his success. "I think the ten years that I had with my father made the difference," he says. Bonhomme has come to appreciate, among other things, the value of his father's influence not only as a man but as a Haitian. "He grew up in a society where a black man could be anything. A black man was the president, a black man was the policeman. A black man was the judge. . . . He grew up in a society where 'A black man can't' was just unheard of." Only as an adult could Bonhomme truly appreciate the challenges his father had faced going "from a society where a black man could be anything to a society where a black man couldn't be anything." Despite his father's problems adjusting to such a society and his eventual banishment from his life, his father managed to instill in him some values that allowed him to achieve.

When we spoke in summer 1994, Bonhomme said he had become a supporter of "shared custody," essentially of the type advocated by Burmeister, by which the parents, in effect, are told: "You're both going to have access to this child, and if you fail to cooperate . . . you are the one who will lose custody." Such an approach, Bonhomme argued, would penalize parents for not cooperating as opposed to rewarding them—as the present system does—for fighting it out in court.

A legal presumption of joint custody, however, is far from a solution. For one thing, it requires a great deal of cooperation between parents; yet if it is legally mandated, it will be imposed on many parents who are at war.

Researchers Eleanor Maccoby and Robert Mnookin studied 1,100 divorcing northern California couples for a period of several years during the late 1980s. They discovered high rates of conflict among over a third of the parents who adopted or were forced to accept joint physical custody arrangements. The study stemmed, in part, from curiosity about the impact of relatively new California policies that encourage both parents to maintain close contact with their children after their marriages are dissolved. One result was that numerous parents were induced to accept joint custody when they would have preferred to raise the children alone. "An award of joint physical custody in and of itself does not create cooperative co-parenting," concluded the authors of *Dividing the Child.*

Dale Mrkich, after analyzing similar Montana policies favoring joint custody, concluded that forcing parents to share child-rearing responsibilities could often work against the best interest of the child. "Joint custody has not enabled divorced parents to maintain a nuclear family by legislative fiat," wrote Mrkich in the *Montana Law Review.* And unless joint custody is mandated, many parents will have nothing to do with it. The vast majority of mothers don't want it, and most of the fathers who say they want to care for their children don't seem inclined to pursue custody in court.

More than one-third of the fathers told Maccoby and Mnookin that they wanted joint custody, and nearly one-third said they wanted to be the sole custodial parent. Eighty-two percent of the mothers wanted sole custody, and less than 2 percent wanted the father to have sole custody. Fewer than 40 percent of the fathers who said they desired sole custody actually filed for it, however, compared to 80 percent of the mothers who followed through. Similarly, more than half the men who claimed to want joint custody either made no custody request or requested sole custody for the mother. The result, of course, was that even with a legal presumption that seemed to favor joint custody, mothers ended up with sole physical custody in roughly two-thirds of the cases. Joint custody was awarded 20 percent of the time, and the father received sole custody in nearly 9 percent of the situations.

Any number of factors could account for the large gap between the husbands' expressed desires and their actions. Some of the men may have been lying to the researchers. Others, upon reflection, may have concluded that they were not up to the challenges of child rearing. Many may have sensed, or had been told by a lawyer, that it was fruitless to go against a woman's wishes because, in a custody dispute, she generally gets what she wants.

"What happens routinely is that when a man walks into a lawyer's office and says he wants to fight for custody of his kids, most lawyers will advise fathers, 'Don't even try, because there is a maternal preference; and unless you have a very compelling case, you will wind up spending twenty or thirty thousand dollars and you'll walk away with nothing,'" said Mel Feit, of the National Center for Men. "A lot of men have come to us and said, 'I wanted custody. I was just talked out of it,' including one man in our organization who was the primary caretaker."

Indeed, Maccoby and Mnookin found that despite the gender-neutral wording of the law, the mother was more than twice as likely to prevail in those cases where the parents were in conflict. Continuing cultural bias favoring mothers as parents may be one reason, as Feit suggests, for the lopsided custody outcomes. Perhaps a more important reason is that during the period of separation, wives generally serve as the custodial parent, and judges are reluctant to interfere once child care patterns are established. Knowing that fact, some divorce lawyers routinely advise husbands who are seeking custody not to leave the marital residence unless they are forced to do so.

The never-married father, of course, is in a wholly different situation. Whereas the divorcing father is ending a life with the mother of his children, the unmarried father has typically never constructed one. He may not even be acknowledged as a parent. And if he is, it is often in the narrow context of his responsibilities for child support. Any legal custody claims he may have are likely to remain academic.

Occasionally, of course, exceptions surface—such as the widely covered 1994 case of Stephen Smith: a twenty-year-old unmarried father in Michigan who won custody of his three-year-old daughter because the mother put the child in day care while she attended college. The teenage mother, who previously had raised the child with little help from Smith, was allowed to keep her daughter while the judge's decision was appealed.

In many respects, as the press pointed out ad nauseam, Smith's case was something of an aberration. Unwed fathers typically are even less inclined than are divorcing fathers to fight for any measure of custody—and are less likely to prevail if they do.

The efforts of such organizations as the National Institute for Responsible Fatherhood and the PCN notwithstanding, never-married fathers generally don't get much encouragement to stay a part of the lives they have helped to create. PCN's Tom Henry argues that society is pushing such men away. He cites, for instance, the effects of the 1975 amendments (Part D of Title IV) of the Social Security Act of 1935, which spawned the Child Support Enforcement program, which attempts to establish paternity, locate fathers, and collect child support. All women who accept or apply for Aid to Families with Dependent Children assign their support rights to the state, which gives them up to fifty dollars a month of anything collected from the fathers of their children. It "doesn't take a Wharton grad," says Henry, to figure out that a woman gets significantly more money if the father provides it directly (albeit covertly) to the mother than to the state.

Henry calls the CSE program's approach, a "bait-and-switch tactic." "At the height of an emotional high" when a child is born, says Henry, the government tries to get men to sign a paternity acknowledgment "and the minute they finish signing, before the ink is dry, we say, 'I got you. Now, okay, you're just like all those other fathers who come here and are not going to take care of your children. We've got you now.'" His colleague Ralph Smith agrees that the system has its priorities scrambled. If society endeavored to get them "attached to their kids" as opposed to trying to confiscate their money, many of the young fathers would "do the same things that the rest of us do," says Smith. "They begin to find ways to provide the support their children need. And not all of the support their children need is financial support. Sometimes what the children need is someone to take them to the doctor and sit in that health center for two hours while mom goes to work."

The confiscatory nature of the child support system, Smith says, has led to the phenomenon of "underground fathers"— men who are in some sense present but fearful of being discovered—for to surface would harm them and their children. There must be a better way, he argues.

"We could use the child support system to provide mediation to young couples, rather than beating them up, providing six or eight hours of mediation counseling. And if you can't work out something, then we'll impose it. We could do that; but we don't. We could take paternity establishment and unhook it from the child support system. Right now the only time when society pretends to care about paternity establishment is when it involves child support. . . . Why don't we celebrate paternity, encourage people to establish it, and then come back and say, 'Let's think about child support down the road'?"

Smith's argument can be summed up with one point: If you can get young fathers attached to their children, they will end up providing much more than the state could ever hope to collect. Certainly, he is correct in observing that current policies are not working very well. The Child Support Enforcement program, if nothing else, is a very expensive way to collect money, and it is notoriously ineffective when dealing with unmarried fathers. A study by the Congressional Research Service calculated that in 1991 states netted $384 million from the program, while the federal government lost $588 million. The program, in short, cost $204 million more to run than it managed to bring in.

Never-married fathers, who tend to be poor, are generally not assessed much—if anything. While three-fourths of divorced women are granted child support payments, only one-fourth of never-married mothers are awarded payments, and only three-fourths of those see any portion of the money. The average amount collected annually is in the neighborhood of $2,000.

By emphasizing the relationship with the mother and child instead of focusing primarily on the money, Smith believes that in the long run everyone (the child, the father, the mother, and the state) will end up winners. Some of the young men who have gone through his program make a strong case for his position. One twenty-one-year-old, for instance, took great pride in the fact that he had gotten a job and was contributing to his child's support. "It helps me inside to know that I'm trying," he said.

Older men who are divorcing are in a different position from Smith's protégés. Obviously, most are not interested in remarrying the mothers. And they, unlike many young unmarried fathers, have already established a relationship with their children. They know what it means to be a parent, and they are not seeking a program to help them shoulder their responsibilities.

Divorced men's groups point to the fact that involved fathers tend to pay their child support and uninvolved fathers don't as a proof of their position that unfair child custody decisions drive fathers away. They note that approximately 90 percent of the fathers with joint custody pay at least some of the child support they owe, compared to about 80 percent of those without custody but with visitation rights. Fewer than half the fathers with no formal contact with their children pay anything at all.

Although it is true that fathers who stay in touch with their children are more likely to pay child support, it does not necessarily follow from the statistics that joint custody is what brings them closer or encourages them to be financially accountable. It's also possible that they are just more caring and responsible fathers. In other words, it's conceivable that those who were close enough to their children to work out joint custody arrangements in the first place are also those who are the most concerned about their children's welfare—and therefore are more likely to cough up money for child support.

Blankenhorn, in short, is probably right in arguing that tinkering with custody arrangements will not make divorced men into good fathers, though he is probably wrong in arguing that proper fathering can occur only within marriage. What seems more important is that parents should cooperate fully and avoid conflicts that can result in trouble for their children.

Unfortunately, such cooperation is difficult to come by in the adversarial cauldron of divorce. Instead, the process typically begins in anger and gets hotter as it progresses. Even when the battle is over, the parties continue to seethe. If the divorce process accomplishes anything, it "provides parents with two or three years of training at fighting each other," Michael Lamb observed.

When custody is at issue, the fighting can be especially brutal, especially when lawyers enter the fray. And often the discussions have little to do with the welfare of the children. Instead, they have to do with anger, jealousy, and tactics designed to win legal points or inflict the maximum amount of suffering. Psychologist Richard Weinberg recalls once being asked to help mediate between two lawyers who were fighting over their children. It was, he said, one of the most frustrating experiences of his life. "Nowhere in that conversation . . . was there any discussion about what was good [for or] in the best interest of the child. It was strictly selfish one-upspersonship between the two attorneys who knew the law better than I certainly did. I threw a tantrum; threw them both out of my office and told them that they both needed to take a half hour to go into separate rooms and to think . . . about the child. They both came back into the room crying, tears going down their faces."

Sometimes, when custody is at issue, parents will use any weapon within reach—including charges of sexual abuse or perversion—to give their spouses a black eye. Even when the legal struggle is over, reasons for resentment remain. The person who is assessed child support, almost always the man, is often angry. Not only has he been separated from his children, but he must continue to pay money to his former wife. Often he is convinced that the money is not going to his children at all, but to support the extravagant habits of a woman he, in many cases, has come to abhor. The spouse who has retained custody, generally the wife, has reasons for anger as well. The amount of money she is receiving, typically in the neighborhood of $3,000 a year, is paltry compared to her needs. And the fact that she often has to badger the man to get it only adds to her aggravation. In addition, whatever problems induced the divorce in the first place have a way of resurfacing, if only in memories, causing the rancor that characterized the terminal stages of separation to endure.

Even the public dialogue—about deadbeat dads and worthless men—only fans the flames. Increasingly, spokespersons for fed-up men seem inclined to answer the rhetoric in kind. They point out, among other things, that women can be deadbeats, too, and they question the fairness of a system that boots them out of the house and then insists that they pay. In fact, in those relatively rare cases when noncustodial wives are assessed child support, men have no easier time collecting it than do women. One-third get none of the money due them, which underscores, if nothing else, the folly of reducing conflict between former spouses to the caricatures of a gender war.

In all the overheated rhetoric, and in the outpouring of raw emotions, parents sometimes have a hard time understanding that the conflict can hurt their children—especially when they tell themselves they are fighting on the children's behalf. At such times, it's virtually impossible for them to see that what the children need most are two parents who are working together to give their offspring a better life. Yet the evidence is persuasive that if the parents can manage to defuse the tension and continue sharing responsibility for their children, and can create a semblance of post-divorce stability, the inevitable trauma of divorce can be mitigated substantially.

Ross Parke, a psychologist at University of California, Riverside, observed, "Divorced families that have reduced the acrimony between the parents are often better off than those in intact families with a high degree of intra-family conflict. . . . "There is an enormous amount of literature emerging suggesting that family conflict is not good for kids," he added. "It's particularly true for boys because boys often tend to be exposed to the family conflict more than girls. That is, parents will fight in front of their boys more than they do their girls. . . . So if you can mediate it somehow and organize it such that the kids still have contact with their fathers . . . but acrimony can be reduced, that's the ideal situation. And nobody's come up with a perfect model of how to do that."

Assuming the tension can be defused, co-parenting after divorce is still not an easy process. Maccoby and Mnookin discovered that even before the divorce, mothers and fathers have different ideas of their respective contributions to child rearing. Eighty-four percent of the mothers reported they were the more involved parent, whereas 58 percent of the fathers said that either *they* were more involved or that both parents were equally involved. Barring something approaching perfect communication, the perceptual disparity can only increase if the parents are no longer together.

Despite the difficulties in keeping both parents involved with their children once the couple has separated, most experts these days believe the results more than justify the effort. A child needs more, they have come to recognize, than just a mother's love. And even other male role models don't really take the place of a father.

Fathers are uniquely positioned, maintains Dr. James Egan, to be a source of support for the mothers before childbirth. "When that function is not present, or that function is not taken care of adequately," noted Egan, mothers are more likely to be depressed, insecure, and incapable of effectively parenting their children. During a child's second year, says Egan, the father is not only an anchor for the mother, but helps the child to begin to decrease its dependence on the mother. Fathers also play a major role, he said, in the consolidation and internalization of standards and principles.

Much of a father's impact, the experts now know, is not immediate, but seems to express itself fully only when the child becomes an adult. Weinberg, for instance, sees much of a girl's relationship with her father as something of a "rehearsal for relating to males later on in her life." He cites the "sleeper effect," documented by Wallerstein, as evidence that girls who are raised without their fathers often have a hard time in relationships. Other things that fathers do have more immediate value. Fathers and mothers tend to have different styles of play, and children apparently benefit from both.

Dr. Jean Bonhomme observed that in many instances, "the

women will talk with the baby and coo at it and communicate. The men will play with the fingers and the toes and make sure everything's working all right like they're doing a top to bottom check." Parke has seen similar differences. Mothers, said Parke, are often more didactic or instructive, whereas fathers are generally more physical and less predictable. The physicality seems to help young children learn to regulate their behavior. "What we think is going on is that they are learning to regulate emotions in the context of play. They're learning how to read emotional signals that other kids are sending. And they're able to send clearer signals." Whatever the reason, young children who play regularly with their fathers seem to have more confidence and to get along better with children their own age. And, certainly, by many measures, young people who have fathers they can turn to are better off than those who don't.

"Men have been accused of encouraging aggression in their children," said Egan. In fact, he asserted, it is when fathers are not present that out-of-control aggression seems to surface. In particular, he believes, "it is the fathers who are largely responsible for the containment, control, and modulation of sexually aggressive impulses."

Even in later life, fathers continue to be important—to women as well as men. In the Korn/Ferry International survey of executive women cited previously, the prominence of the fathers' role in the daughters' success was striking. Asked whether anyone had influenced their decision to pursue a career, more women cited a masculine influence than a female role model, and the majority of those naming males named their fathers.

Despite the emerging research on the importance of fathers, American men are torn. Some, as was noted, are moving in the direction of increased involvement with their children, and others are simply moving on. According to one study published in the *Journal of Marriage and the Family*, 35

Chapter 9

IF WOMEN FEEL MORE PAIN, WHY ARE MEN SELF-DESTRUCTING?

Stuart Miller of the American Fathers Coalition was explaining how distraught men sometimes become when divorce separates them from their children. "A lot of the studies will show that fathers feel pushed away, and they can't take the pain on a daily basis," he said. Men in such a frantic state, he noted, had sometimes killed their children and themselves. "Now to you and I it's shocking how a father could do that," he added, "but the psychological impact of custody and divorce is devastating to so many people."

Psychologist Stephen Johnson was also talking about men in pain because of divorce and what he called "a breakdown of traditional family values, of a family structure that held a community together." For men, the situation had changed immensely since his father's era. "My father came out of World War II and, as did most men, it was about establishing family and creating career. And the great American dream at that point was the carrot, you know, on a string. These days, men, and especially what has become branded as Generation X, have a certain amount of hopelessness, helplessness, that's there. The outlook is somewhat bleak. So they're asking questions: 'Is it worth it?'"

New Yorker Darnell Whitten made a similar observation. When he was in graduate school, he said, "I heard a lot of students say that they didn't think they would do as well as their fathers, that something's really gone wrong." That realization, noted Whitten, seemed to hit men a lot harder than women "because, just speaking in general, men expect to be able . . . to reach their potential. They expect to do that, and they're expected to do that, where women have not always been expected to reach their potential."

In one conversation after another in interviews done for this book, when the talk turned to men, it often also turned to despair. A number of my informants observed that many men—though certainly not all—were struggling with what they perceived as an immense weight bearing down on their shoulders. As psychologist Alvin Baraff put it previously, "It looks good on the outside, but men are not walking around that happy on the inside. . . . We don't have a happy bunch of men."

The leap from unhappiness or even despair to suicide is a large one—and one that most men clearly don't make. Yet, anyone who investigates the dimensions of male distress must at some point grapple with the question of suicide. Why are American men more than four times as likely as American women to kill themselves? Why are they twice as likely to die in accidents? Are so many men so miserable that they simply no longer care to live?

Baraff clearly believes the answer is yes. Shortly after he started his Washington, D.C.-based MenCenter practice in the early 1980s, he saw just how disconsolate some men were. They would come to his office and pour out their tales of woe, and "the stories had a depth to them, and a sadness to them, and an alienation that I just wasn't hearing before I started MenCenter," Baraff recalls.

Such sadness and alienation, if unrelieved, can end in self-destruction. The suicide statistics are evidence of it. And those statistics, Baraff believes, understate the problem, since many suicides are not recorded as such. Perhaps half the nation's fatal accidents and car crashes, he guesses, are "unconscious suicides."

In reflecting on his own life, Baraff has concluded that, had things worked out somewhat differently, he might be dead—"probably not a suicide, but *something* would have happened." Following his divorce and the resultant loss of his children, he recalled, "I felt extremely guilty. I felt terrible, because I had always wanted to be a father. That was one of my goals in life, to be a father. And it was just a shocker to me to find that I was going to be an absentee father. And I believe that had I stayed in the town that I was living in, I would not be here today. I would have been dead. And I would have been dead in some kind of way that men die." By "some kind of way," he means a car accident or perhaps of drinking too much—ways of killing oneself that the average person would not equate with suicide.

The male penchant for self-destruction is particularly striking in light of research that has consistently found that women report sharply higher rates of serious depression than do men. It becomes even more intriguing in light of studies showing that women attempt suicide much more often than do men. So why are a larger number of men ending up dead? Why, to reiterate Feit's question, are so many more men putting guns to their heads and blowing their brains out?

The experts, unfortunately, are not sure—though, in their search for answers, they have sifted the research on depression and suicide to a fare-thee-well. What they have come up with is the proverbial riddle in an enigma.

For as long as scientists have been measuring "major" depression, they have found more of it in women than in men. The ratio in the United States was at one point thought to be three to one; it is now reckoned at roughly two to one. The numbers vary in other countries, as does the overall depression rate. For New Zealanders, for instance, the rate of depression is more than twice the rate for Americans. But the trend is always the same. Wherever the measurements are taken, women are doing worse. Myrna Weissman, a psychologist at Columbia University, is convinced that the statistics are valid and reliable. She notes that in every country she has studied, including Taiwan, Korea, Lebanon, and France, there are more cases of major depression in women than in men.

Nonetheless, some people believe the numbers don't reflect reality. Men are too ashamed, they say, to admit that they are depressed and therefore hide their despondency at virtually any cost. "Men's depression may be much higher than we thought," said clinical psychologist Ellen McGrath. After White House lawyer Vincent Foster killed himself, many of McGrath's male clients glimpsed something of themselves in Foster and hungered to talk about his situation. McGrath, who once chaired an American Psychological Association task force on depression in women, thinks that her male clients' reaction highlights a real problem.

Because men are not supposed to be depressed, they often refuse to recognize it or deny that they have it. "They think there's so much shame. They won't talk about it," said McGrath. As result of that denial, they eschew treatment and then plunge into despair. That despair, she believes, often leads to "attempts at medication" with alcohol and other mind-numbing drugs. The end result can be total disability. (She refers to the denial, despair, drugs, disability sequence as the "four Ds" of male depression.) Given such male propensities, said McGrath, the search for depression in men is often a search for "masks and equivalents," such as substance abuse, accidents, generally self-destructive behavior, and carelessness on the job.

If much of the male depression is, in fact, "masked" and therefore undetected, it would follow that the male-female disparity is not nearly as large as most mental health professionals believe it to be. And if a huge number of men are suffering in secret because they are not diagnosed, that might explain why more men end up dead—despite the statistics indicating that women are more depressed.

Peter Muehrer, an expert on suicide and depression with the National Institute of Mental Health, dismisses that theory. "Do men mask [depression] by using alcohol and other drugs? That's been a very popular belief for some time," he says, "but, from a research perspective, that hasn't been confirmed. Obviously many men do experience depression and exhibit the same kinds of symptoms we see in women."

Weissman insists that the male-female depression gap cannot be explained by male masks. "We documented that it's a very consistent pattern," says Weissman. "It can't just be [an] artifact. And it isn't just because men drink and women don't drink as much. We don't really know what the reason is, but we do know that it exists, and it has to do with the fact of women being perhaps more sensitive to the breakup of interpersonal attachments, and they're expressing it with depression."

A cross-national inquiry by Weissman and her colleagues confirmed that men and women have "different help-seeking patterns" and that more males than females abuse alcohol. It also acknowledged the possibility that "some unknown proportion of depressed men may have appeared in the alcohol rates and not been identified as depressed." But the Weissman study, published in the *Journal of Affective Disorders,* flatly rejected the possibility that the entire difference was due to such phenomena.

Weissman herself once thought male masking behavior might explain the discrepancy, but her research has convinced her otherwise. "There is no evidence that depression is an equivalent of alcohol [abuse]. And even when you control for alcohol, you still find the increased rate in women as compared to men. I don't think that that's a viable explanation. And if you look at some countries where alcoholism is very low, like Taiwan, you still find the sex differences."

Those differences, nonetheless, may be diminishing. Work done by Weissman and others has found that men born after World War II may be more susceptible to depression than were their elders. The reason, Weissman believes, may be related to social disintegration. "I think depression has to do with the breakup of attachments, and there are many more opportunities for the breakup of attachments now than there used to be. There are more people living alone. There are more divorces. There's more separation. And there's more what I call 'divorces without marriages.' There is more serial monogamy, and serial non-monogamy. And there's later age of marriage."

McGrath agrees. The post–World War II generation, she noted, is the "first generation of divorce," the first in which a huge number of people came from "blended families." In addition to having to deal with familial instability, they also have had a higher level of exposure to drugs and alcohol and have faced a confusing array of "sex-role challenges."

Such instability seems to have increased the disposition not only toward depression, but toward suicide. A recent study of patients at the Albert Einstein College of Medicine, for instance, found that early parental loss contributed to the risk of suicide. Given that depression sometimes leads to suicide, it's perhaps obvious that something that increases the likelihood of depression might also increase the likelihood of suicide, although depression does not necessarily result in suicide.

Only a small percentage of severely depressed people end up killing themselves. As Muehrer, the psychologist at the National Institute of Mental Health, pointed out, "Suicide is an extremely rare event." Fewer than thirty thousand Americans commit suicide a year. "So whether you're a male or a female, the likelihood [that] you're going to commit suicide is very low, which means that any single factor . . . is a very weak predictor of suicide by itself." Put another way, nearly 15 million Americans are thought to have suffered serious depression at some point in their lives, but only a very small proportion of them have decided to take the ultimate step to end it. Hence, it's not exactly clear what effect a narrowing of the depression gap might have on the suicide rate—not, that is, unless someone can figure out the difference between depressed people who will most likely commit suicide and those who almost certainly won't. No reputable psychiatrist claims to have a fail-safe method of determining just what combination of risk factors will tip a person over the edge.

Dr. Robert Plutchik, of the Albert Einstein College of Medicine, has "come to the conclusion that we have a situation with regard to suicide which is a little bit like what they talk about in chaos theory, that is, you have a whole large number of variables, or factors which influence suicide. . . . Some of them may seem to be more important than others if we make measurements of a large group of people, but for a given individual who may have a lot of factors operating, it is sometimes a small change in a relatively unimportant variable which determines whether the suicidal act actually occurs."

Even so, the gender difference demands an explanation. For though the disparity may tell us nothing about any particular individual's decision to die, it makes a possibly damning statement about the effect of modern society on men—or at least on men who are especially at risk. And it raises an unavoidable question: Even if only a minuscule proportion of the population is taking its own life, why should the vast majority of those suicides (in America and most other countries) be men?

One common answer is that men are more effective at destroying themselves because they tend to choose more lethal means. Men are more likely to use guns, for instance, whereas women are more inclined to take pills, and as Dr. Frederick

Goodwin, former director of the National Institute of Mental Health, observes, "it's a lot harder to kill yourself with pills than with a gun." Also, the effects of most pills can be reversed—meaning that pill poppers can change their minds even after the act. "In [certain countries in] South Asia and South America where the preferred [ingesta] is something like a herbicide . . . , for which there are no medical treatments," the suicide gender gap essentially vanishes, said Dr. David Shaffer, a Columbia University psychiatrist. People may still have second thoughts, noted Shaffer, but nothing can be done about it.

Why would American and European women be drawn to relatively benign methods? Alexander Rich, a psychologist at Indiana University, believes that women are often fearful of damaging their bodies, a peculiar instance in which vanity may literally be life preserving. Men, he believes, have fewer such fears. Since men are also more naturally aggressive, they use more deadly force. In addition, Shaffer suggested, alcohol and drugs play a much larger role with men than with women: "In our own research with young adults and teenagers, substance abuse and alcohol seem to be very powerful determinants [but only] . . . in males."

Males have an array of other traits (some behavioral and some biological) that seem to make them especially vulnerable to self-destructive urges. They are more impulsive and more prone to behavioral problems in general. "Young males just don't think before they act," said Muehrer. "The idea that their actions could end up killing [them] may not be readily apparent to them."

In elderly men, the higher suicide rate may be linked to retirement or diseases of old age. As Plutchik observed when an older man commits suicide, "it's usually either because he's very sick, in great pain, has an incurable disease and is terminal, or has felt that after retirement his life is meaningless." Women, he added, "don't deal with aging in the same way as men."

Men also seem less adept than women at dealing with depression and are less likely to have friends who can pull them through it. "Women are much more encultured to acknowledge feelings, including depressive feelings," observes Goodwin. They feel no disgrace in turning to their friends or to a therapist. The male "is much more likely to stiff-upper-lip it and deny depression."

Goodwin speculated that in tribal times, strong silent types had a real advantage. "Tribes where men were the most quiet, most silent," he surmised were also the most successful. When hunting game, chatter is "not very helpful." Unfortunately, men are still programmed to be strong, silent hunters, to feel more comfortable skulking about than opening up.

Male biology is also treacherous. Testosterone apparently makes men more likely to be violent, and that violence is turned not only outward, but inward. Also, a shortage of serotonin (a vasoconstrictor and neurotransmitter) may sometimes lead men astray. "Men have significantly lower levels [of serotonin] than women in their brains," Goodwin pointed out. "And if a man is going to get depressed, it is more likely to be a male with low serotonin."

Psychologist Rich surmised that shame may play a disproportionately strong role with men. Men are not only ashamed of being suicidal, they become intensely embarrassed if they try to kill themselves and fail. In his research with so-called parasuicides (suicidal people who had not yet succeeded in killing themselves), Rich found that men and women exhibited different preoccupations about suicide. Women were "afraid of mutilating their bodies and causing [themselves] physical harm"; they were not particularly concerned with social disapproval. In contrast, "men are very concerned with the social disapproval."

But all these factors do not fully explain why men are so much better than women at killing themselves. Sure, men are more violent and may be more impulsive and are apparently more likely to abuse alcohol and drugs. Such factors could account for the higher male fatality rate if men and women were equally given to hopelessness, despair, and depression. But they are not, according to the people who measure such things.

By the same token, the male affinity for more effective tools of self-destruction could explain the rate if, in fact, equal numbers of men and women were trying to commit suicide. Yet, researchers in the field insist that women make many more attempts; some experts put the figure at three times as many, whereas others put it even higher. The suicide statistics should somehow reflect that fact—unless, in reality, many of the "attempts" are not quite what they seem, that is, unless men, generally speaking, are more serious about suicide than are women.

Is it possible—as Rich's research suggests—that we have created a society in which men are so fearful of not measuring up that many would rather succeed at suicide than be perceived as failures? Have we made it so difficult for men in pain to cry out for help that many prefer to vanish into nothingness without a peep? Have we somehow sent out the signal that a cry for help is somehow disgraceful if it comes from a man? And have we therefore made it much more possible for women than for men to stop just short of the final step?

David Clark, director of the Center for Suicide Research and Prevention at Rush–Presbyterian St. Luke's Medical Center in Chicago, believes that may be the case. Women probably profit from the fact that there is "a little less social prohibition against weak, resigned behavior" in them than in men, said Clark. Not that people who are about to kill themselves spend a lot of time worrying about how it will look, "but these social influences are there, and they exert subtle influences."

Men simply are not supposed to feel pain, whether it's physical or psychological. They are not supposed to need help.

"Guys are prone to grit their teeth, bite the bullet, bear the pain, even if we're talking chest pain and physical health conditions," said Clark. That tendency is "going to be a little more pronounced around psychological disorders than health care, but it's the same issue." The need to seem tough and in control, suggested Clark, makes men especially disinclined to fail at suicide. From their perspective, there is no point in "making a suicide attempt and having that on your record unless you're really going to die."

Researchers have long known that the vast majority of people who "attempt" suicide don't succeed. Experts who have calculated the proportion of attempts to completed suicides put the ratio at everywhere from twenty to one to fifty to one. Yet mindful that previous suicide attempts put people at special risk, they have tended to take "parasuicides" at their word. Still, clearly, some suicide attempts are much more serious than are others. And the more serious attempts, it seems, are much more characteristic of men. Part of the problem of assessing such a possibility is that it is often impossible to determine just how serious a suicide attempt is. One group of researchers who did try to establish a rigorous definition discovered, noted Muehrer, that people's claims to have attempted suicide cannot be taken at face value. That finding, he said, "leads us to ask, 'Well what are we actually measuring on these surveys [of suicide attempts]?' Are we really measuring deliberate behavior that would attempt to cause death? And based on this study, which is the best of its kind, the answer is no."

That study, conducted by a team headed by Dr. Patrick Meehan, an adviser to the Centers for Disease Control, surveyed the freshman population at a major university and found that over half had, at one time or another, experienced suicidal thoughts, though not necessarily with an intent to act on them. Ten percent reported having attempted suicide at some point in their lives. Only one-fourth of them, however, reported having needed medical attention, and only one-tenth of those who had "attempted" suicide ended up hospitalized overnight. In other words, most had not managed to do enough damage to themselves to make it believable that they were really determined to die.

Conventional wisdom among suicide researchers holds that there is no monumental difference between those who commit suicide and those who merely attempt it. As one research paper put it: "Although there are some differences, there appear to be more similarities. For example, the distribution of diagnoses between those who attempt suicide and those who actually suicide is quite similar." Clark, however, believes that the lopsided numbers are telling us something. "It's clear to all of us that the attempters and completers are more different than alike," he said. "I think people who decide to kill themselves, do it. They find an efficient means. And I don't think there is an enormous sex difference there." He rejects the theory that men are more likely to die because they are more inclined to choose guns over pills, pointing out that both men and women who actually succeed at killing themselves are more partial to the use of guns than any other method.

Certainly, logic dictates that if men and women are equally knowledgeable about how to kill themselves and both groups say they are trying, *but men are dying much more frequently than women*, then both groups cannot be equally determined to succeed.

I am not attempting to minimize the agony that anyone goes through who is contemplating suicide. Nor am I questioning the wisdom of taking any suicide threat seriously. People who threaten suicide, after all, are a lot more likely to go through with it than are people who do not. Still, when you ask the question, "Why are so many more men dying if more women are trying to kill themselves?" one of the few answers that makes sense is that the men, generally speaking, are trying harder. The question then becomes: What have we as a society done to make men feel that they must succeed—even at suicide? And the logical follow-up question is, "As we continue to emphasize the importance of success for women, will women's suicide rate begin to approximate that of men's?"

The answer to the last question may well be yes. There is some evidence that women are beginning to change their approach to suicide. In the future even more women may turn to guns, and more may end up dead. That would be an extremely unfortunate result of equality. Society obviously would be better served by figuring out how to keep more members of both sexes alive.

Plutchik thinks that part of the solution may lie in research that sorts out the specific catalysts that drive individuals to suicide. In the same way that people accumulate risk factors, he theorizes, they can also amass "protective factors." Hence, the potentially deadly effect of the loss of a father before the age of ten may be mitigated by the development of a social support network or by learning to reach out for help.

Another part of the solution depends less on individual strategies than on the society at large, for it would entail altering society's very idea of success, or at least of success for men. At a minimum, it would mean getting men to recognize that an obsession with achievement can be deadly if it is not accompanied by a willingness to acknowledge and alleviate distress.

Chapter 10

BATTERED MEN, BITTER TRUTHS

Since the slayings of Nicole Brown Simpson and Ron Goldman in 1994, much of the world's attention has focused on the dangers of male obsession—not with success, but with a woman—and on aggression that is not turned inward, resulting in suicide, but toward a love object, resulting in murder. For countless families who have been spared the anguish of such violence themselves, the Simpson-Goldman case brought the danger home.

Domestic violence obviously did not begin with the Simpsons. In ancient Rome, historians report, husbands were legally entitled to kill their wives; the expression "rule of thumb," many believe, comes from the maximum thickness of a rod with which (under English common law) a man could beat his wife. Still, in America, until recent times, spousal abuse was hidden away in a shadowy nook of the nation's consciousness. The women's movement forced it into the open, and the Simpson case thrust it to center stage.

I had my first experience with domestic violence in the mid-1970s. As a young man on vacation in New York City, I had fallen in with what I took to be a hip crowd. Frank, an ex-con who had reinvented himself as a poet, and Patty, a chanteuse at a Greenwich Village nightspot, were among the more exotic of my newfound friends. One afternoon, as the three of us passed the time in Frank's apartment, the conversation turned to Patty and her abusive boyfriend. Why, I wanted to know, did she stay with someone who regularly beat her? "He wouldn't beat me," she shot back, "if he didn't love me."

I found the answer incomprehensible, but let the matter drop, unable to understand how someone so obviously intelligent would allow herself to be so mistreated. Years later, I received a plausible answer when reading *Behind Closed Doors,* a book by domestic violence experts Murray Straus, Richard Gelles, and Suzanne Steinmetz, based largely on work done at the Family Research Lab at the University of New Hampshire. Straus and his colleagues theorized that children who were beaten for disciplinary reasons or who saw their fathers knock their mothers around sometimes became adults who believed "those who love you the most are also those who hit you." I had no idea whether Patty had come from an abusive household, but I got a clear picture of her current hell.

A few evenings earlier, her lover had pulled a gun on guys he believed were cheating him at poker. So when I heard a loud pounding at the door, I immediately feared the worst.

Before anyone could respond, her boyfriend's voice rang out demanding that Patty join him. When no one answered, his tone grew testier, and he threatened to break down the door. At that moment, Frank grabbed a knife from the kitchen cabinet, and I tried to brace myself for mayhem, as I imagined the lunatic, guns blazing, bursting through the door.

Nonetheless, we told Patty to stay put; but she, it turned out, had other ideas. Frank and I eventually stepped aside. The police, whom Frank had managed to call in the confusion, came just as her boyfriend dragged her into the street and punched her full in the face.

I have no idea what ultimately became of that troubled couple, but for years, whenever I heard the term "domestic violence," I remembered Patty and her boyfriend: the menacing man and the submissive woman, bound together in pathology. The idea that a woman could be the aggressor and a man could be the victim never came to mind.

So I was intrigued to hear numerous men's advocates argue that women were as physically abusive as men. As one men's group member put it, "Domestic violence ... exists in both directions. It's as damn near as equal to a two-way street as you can find." When I pressed him on how that could be possible, given the average man's obvious physical advantage, he replied, "There are so many answers to that [question] that unfortunately lots of people don't want to hear—like knives and guns are great equalizers. If you look at murder, how many husbands and wives [kill each other], you very nearly have an equal split." We didn't hear more about these statistics, he insisted, because the press generally ignores them. Also, he added, "because of the societal stereotype that it's always the man who's the aggressor, when a man is victimized, he doesn't report it typically." Indeed, men under attack frequently find themselves in a double bind: "We've had situations where ... guys are being attacked by their wives. The guy calls the police to say, 'My wife is attacking me.' The police come out and arrest the guy, and that's done as a matter of policy."

Much the same argument was made by MensCenter founder James Sniechowski and his wife and colleague, psychologist Judith Sherven. In an op-ed piece they coauthored for the *Los Angeles Times*, they cited statistics purporting to show that "husbands and wives were abusing one another in roughly equal numbers." Spousal violence, they argued, was not something unilaterally perpetrated by an "evil, brutal male," but was a reflection of a couple "bound in their dance of mutual destructiveness."

When I talked with the twosome, Sniechowski mentioned a male acquaintance of his who, in the midst of a horrible divorce, was beaten by his wife. He knew another man, a former college football player, who was similarly abused. Neither retaliated, he said, because they had been raised not to hit women. He was aware of yet another couple who were "battling it out." The man would split the woman's lip, she would hit him with a toaster, and they would pummel each other. Yet, he said, "We do not address the entire dynamic. " Instead society was "characterizing the pathology as a unilateral problem of the man." In focusing merely on brutal men, he said, we were wrongly telling the women in such relationships, "There is nothing wrong with what you're doing. Only with what he's done."

Abused men are showing up in emergency rooms claiming to have tripped on the stairs, he insisted. And because battered men are so reluctant to come forward, "the media image, the public image is that men are doing all the harm." As a result, he contended, politicians are "creating legislation and policy not dealing with reality" and worse, setting up a "backlash" from men.

Sherven said that the mutually destructive behavior is not necessarily limited to physical abuse. Women, she said, are capable of great "emotional violence" and can be "evil and vicious with their mouths." Frequently, she said, such relationships were abusive verbally long before the physical violence started.

When I asked psychologist Stephen Johnson whether he believed an epidemic of male battering had broken out, he replied, "I don't know whether it's an epidemic. I feel that men are probably the silent victims. Men shy away from talking even more than women do because of the shame involved." Abused men had called him from out of state, Johnson said, because they were too ashamed to seek help in their own hometowns. Sometimes they lived not only in fear of violence, but of being denied access to their children if they spoke out. They would call, he said, and murmur, "What do I do? She's threatening to take the kids away."

Once some of the hype died down from the Simpson case, Johnson conjectured, people would be able to look more clearly at the real dynamics of family violence, and they would see not only what men have done to women, but "the kinds of things women have done to them." In fact, confided Johnson, he was working on a book tentatively titled *Dangerous Women and the Men Who Fall for Them*—intended to be an examination not necessarily of physical abuse but of the phenomenon of "dream women becoming your worst nightmare."

Johnson felt nothing but compassion for women in abusive relationships. It was "poppycock," he asserted, to blame women for getting beaten, but a tragic reality, he added, was that "a lot of times women will not let a man walk away."

Dr. David Gremillion, a physician who teaches at the University of North Carolina, has treated numerous victims of physical abuse, and many don't fit the aggressive man-passive woman mold. "In most of the cases that I see," he said, "both partners are violent." Certainly, he had seen relationships in which the woman was submissive and the man was dominant, but he had also seen the damage that violent women could do, such as wounding a man with a knife. "Many men are quite passive within the context of their intimate relationships with women," he asserted, and they generally are reluctant to discuss the assaults against them.

Men are particularly at risk when they are physically weak, he thinks. Elderly men, who are senile or simply debilitated, are often cared for by abusive women, frequently their wives. The "power dynamics within the relationship have been reversed," said Gremillion, and sometimes the caretaker becomes violent. Men who are enfeebled by AIDS, said Gremillion, who sees a large proportion of gay males in his practice, are also frequently at the mercy of female attendants, and their caretakers, sometimes their mothers, can end up tormenting them.

Like Johnson, Gremillion refuses to categorize what is happening to men as an epidemic of domestic violence and insists that "any violence within a personal relationship is a serious problem." He believes the problem of battered men has been very much ignored. America's politics of "gender polarization" and its refusal to acknowledge that men can be victims as well as abusers, he believes, make coming up with intelligent solutions to domestic abuse exceedingly difficult.

Patricia Overberg, director of the Valley Oasis Shelter in southern California, agrees. "I know there are battered men out there simply because I was doing some counseling of women who are batterers," said Overberg, who claims to run the only shelter in the United States that welcomes both men and women. She recalls one client, a hundred-pound woman who was beating up a two hundred-pound iron worker. "Size really has nothing to do with it," she noted. "A man is brought up not to touch a woman. She is taking advantage of him, usually with a weapon."

In her shelter, Overberg said, they treat battered husbands precisely as they treat battered wives, and she has discovered that the women residents don't mind. Although the women may be surprised to discover that a man is a neighbor, they "go out of their way to be as warm as they can."

Very few men, however, have sought Overberg's help. When we talked during summer 1994, she could recall a total of five men who had stayed there over the past several years. Not all those men had been battered by women. One had been beaten by his father because he was considering a sex-change operation.

That so few men are willing to ask for assistance, she said, reveals nothing about the dimensions of the problem. "Men don't come forward and tell," she asserted. "One of the things that men have to deal with that women don't deal with is the ridicule of their fellow men, getting laughed at." Moreover, women obviously are more at risk of injury than are men. So fighting domestic violence has traditionally been a "women's mission." "We're about the only one even pushing for the men," she said.

Her interest in getting the problem addressed is not merely based on pity for battered men; she also fears for the children who are trapped in such dysfunctional families. Women who abuse men, she had found, are likely to abuse children. Overberg advocates a "family systems" approach, a philosophy that focuses on the entire family's problems as opposed to just demonizing the presumed aggressor.

For some people, the very idea that a woman could terrorize a man is so inconceivable as to be laughable. I myself wondered what could really be going on with these men who claimed to be smacked around by their mates. Resolving to seek some out, I decided that the logical place to start was St. Paul, Minnesota, where a colorful character named George Gilliland had opened the only shelter in the country expressly designed for battered men.

Even before I met him, I was aware that Gilliland was widely considered to be something of a loose cannon. In a 1991 profile, the *St. Paul Pioneer Press* traced his emergence as a men's advocate to his 1988 arrest for attacking his then-wife. Gilliland insisted that *he* was the victim in that incident, that he had been hit over the head with a board. Soon after spending thirty days behind bars for fifth-degree assault in that case, he founded an organization that eventually came to be called the Domestic Rights Coalition. Gilliland, the *Pioneer Press* dryly observed, "brings to the coalition a wealth of firsthand experience with domestic abuse cases: Two former wives, a former girlfriend, a son and a daughter-in-law have obtained court protection against Gilliland because of alleged violence by him or the fear of violence. His youngest son, Christopher, says Gilliland beat him regularly as a boy."

The article carried a quote from Gilliland's son describing

his advocacy work as "his way of trying to get revenge on women." "The idea that there are abused men out there probably is true," Christopher Gilliland told the reporter, "and they may need help just like women who are abused, but he is not the person to be doing it." A local expert on domestic abuse denounced Gilliland's organization as "a rather dangerous group," adding, "They are trying to create a myth that men are just as frequently battered as women." Two years later, the *Pioneer Press* featured Gilliland again, this time on the occasion of his conviction for disorderly conduct for threatening two female domestic abuse workers.

Coverage of Gilliland in the *Twin Cities Reader* was even less flattering. Shortly after he opened his shelter in December 1993, the weekly publication commented, "Though Gilliland portrays himself as a champion of abuse victims, his record suggests that his credibility as an advocate is itself rather battered."

When I called on Gilliland in July 1994, he seemed eager to dispel the notion that he might be some kind of antifemale crackpot. A compact, wiry man with a blunt homespun manner, he readily acknowledged that battered women deserve every bit of assistance they are receiving. His willingness to care for battered men, he insisted, should not be seen as an attempt to deny the legitimate grievances of those women or to shelter the people who abuse them. "We counsel men here. We don't let them off the hook when they do retaliate against the women. We hold them responsible for their behaviors. We teach them alternative ways of handling explosive situations," he said.

Gilliland said he had wanted to organize the shelter for years, but had previously been unable to pull together the resources to do so. Minnesota's mandatory arrest law, enacted in 1989, brought home to Gilliland the need for a sanctuary for men. In most cases, the law requires that the police arrest someone if they believe domestic abuse has been committed. That someone, Gilliland insists, is generally the man—regardless of who was the aggressor.

Even if the man has a split lip and the wife is drunk and out of control, says Gilliland, the man is likely to take the ride to jail. "A lot of times they will tell the guy, 'Hey, why don't you just leave for the night? Leave the little lady alone, and come back tomorrow when things have cooled off,'" which to Gilliland is little more than an invitation to the woman to "turn around and do this to you all over again."

"Once in a great while," said Gilliland, "you'll get a cop or a deputy who will arrest the women—but seldom. I've had prosecutors tell me that they don't want to prosecute women because it's politically unpopular, and they want to keep their jobs. They also don't want to get into problems with judges as far as judges having to sentence these women."

He envisioned the shelter as a place where innocent men with nowhere else to go could come for refuge. "Opening this place gives the cops and the deputies a chance to lessen the stress of the situation that once they leave may escalate into a physical encounter," said Gilliland. "It's easier for them to let a guy know, 'Hey, there's a place you can go for a few hours, stay overnight, whatever, get some help. . . . Why don't you go do that? We don't want to arrest anybody. We don't want to take you to jail.'"

In the seven months since he opened the sanctuary, Gilliland said he had housed some thirty-five men. One was a man beaten by another man, but most of the men, he claimed, were assaulted by women.

"The dynamic involved has been real interesting," he said. "The guys get as screwy as the women do when they're being battered and slapped around and kicked in the nuts and . . . stabbed by women. They have come here for a couple or three days, and in the meantime the phone starts ringing. Women are calling and trying to get a hold of their husbands or boyfriends or whatever, and trying to track them down, and see what they're doing, and see what's going on with them." Consequently, he said, all calls were screened. Nonetheless, many of the men would return the women's calls and believe their promises of reform. "These guys are dumb enough to go back and it gets worse and never gets better. Sometimes chemicals [meaning drugs] are involved, sometimes not. Other times mental problems are involved, and sometimes not."

The three-story facility was clean and well cared for. Its ambience was reminiscent of a youth hostel or perhaps a barracks. Toiletries, including shampoo, conditioner, shaving cream, a tooth brush, deodorant, tooth paste, and a comb and towels were neatly laid out on each bed. "A lot of times a guy has to leave and he doesn't have these things available," Gilliland explained. The place could accommodate eight men, he said. One large room, with three beds plus a baby crib, was reserved for men with several children. Smaller rooms could accommodate men who came alone. Gilliland puffed up proudly as he talked of his plans for renovating the building: Perhaps he would carpet the steps or redo the third floor. He hoped to make room for even more men.

Yet, despite his expansionary aspirations—having optimistically named the enterprise "Men's *Shelters* of Minnesota"—Gilliland was uncertain he would succeed in keeping his doors open. Although he had established a sliding fee for residents, many of the men who came were unable to pay their way. He had garnered a substantial amount of community support in the form of food and other essentials, but financing was another matter. "We've got a real severe financial problem. Unless it gets cured fairly soon, the place is going to go into foreclosure," he said.

Some of his problems, he presumed, were the result of his being politically incorrect. "Politicians don't want to jump on the bandwagon and support the idea of male victims. The battered women's organizations label you immediately as antifemale and antifeminist and [anti] battered women, which I'm not, of course."

In addition, Gilliland had something of a personal image problem—to put it mildly—which he attributed to "yellow stinking journalism" and an ungrateful son whom softhearted, gullible dad continued to try to help. "And, invariably, every time I do it, he boots me right square in the fanny for it," fumed Gilliland. As for the arrest for assaulting his former wife, Gilliland let loose with a string of invective directed at her and her daughter.

It was abundantly clear that Gilliland believed himself to be a persecuted man. Viewed from his vantage point, he was savaged by the press, harassed by government officials, and frequently lied about in court. Those lies, he suggested, accounted for the unusual number of protective orders obtained against him: "The last I knew I had about thirteen of these things. If you want to get an order of protection against me, you could do it within the next hour. . . . What the media [don't] say, though, is that I turned around and also filed for orders of protection. And those were also put into effect against the same people that applied for them against me."

Gilliland freely admits to being a recovering alcoholic and intimated that his upbringing had something to do with it. "Well, hell, I grew up in a very abusive home. My mother was a drunk and my dad wound up divorcing her when I was eleven years old, and from the time I was eleven until the time I was eighteen, when I graduated from high school, that was a living hell to be living with that woman." He insists, however, that he should not be judged by the past and swears that he has been sober "for eighteen-and-a-half continuous, uninterrupted years."

Sometimes when he was drinking, he conceded, he did

some pretty stupid things. Yet "no matter how broke I was, or how sick and screwy I was, the system held me responsible for my behavior. They put me behind bars for writing out NSF [not sufficient funds] checks a couple of times, a few days here, a few days there. They put me behind bars for getting in fights in bars, disorderly conduct. I'd spend a few days in jail here, and a few there. They held me responsible no matter how sick I was. I did the time, whatever."

It seems to him that women are treated differently. And that, he insinuated, is one reason he is so devoted to his cause. The justice system is conspiring, he believes, to help lawbreaking women avoid responsibility for their behavior. Women "know that rarely if ever will they get arrested," he contends, "no matter what in the hell they do, short of killing a man. And even when they kill a man, they've got all these battered women's organizations and everybody else with ready-made excuses as to why it was justified." His shelter and his Domestic Rights Coalition, he implied, are lonely outposts against male victimization. It is not surprising that his clients tend to share that view.

At the time of my visit, Gilliland had several victims standing by. None was staying at the shelter. The current shelter residents, he explained, were uncomfortable talking for publication, but all had stories to tell of horrors suffered at the hands of women.

An athletic-looking college student of nineteen, who had been married for little more than a year, said that his wife had poured cold water over him as he slept. The eighteen-year-old wife was "a real religious, judgmental type person" who had decided that her husband was no longer "close to God." The cold shower apparently was meant to being him back to his senses.

His protests only made her behavior worse. She "bit, scratched, hit, kicked me numerous times," he said, "usually after we'd get into a verbal argument." At present, he was living with his mother, though "If I wasn't so young and didn't have my ma, I'd probably be right here [at the shelter]."

Another Gilliland disciple, a thirty-nine-year-old bus mechanic, had married a nurse a few years earlier. Shortly after the marriage, she stopped working, and he suddenly became the sole support of her and her twenty-year-old son. He also discovered that his "pretty, nice" wife had a "temperamental" side.

When he would come home a little later than planned, she would throw things at him—vases, cans, whatever she could grab. On one occasion when she spotted him talking to a strange woman, she went into a jealous rage and kicked him. "I went into the house and I caught it square in the nuts," he said.

When she went berserk, he would call the police. Generally, they would take note of his bleeding face, ascertain that she was unharmed, and ask him if he had somewhere else to go. One such call, however, had resulted in her spending the night in the county hospital's psychiatric unit—an experience that made her even more vengeful.

Over time, her actions grew increasingly irrational. One evening, she blew up in a bar because he refused to make the bartender turn up the jukebox. During the entire seven-mile ride home, he claims, she punched him in the head, pulled his hair, scratched him, and threatened to jump out. He treated the episode as a test of his driving ability. "I did a good job, too. I timed all the lights so I didn't have to stop, so she couldn't jump out. We got home, and she's still whaling on me."

One morning, he said, she attacked him with a knife; he protected himself by hitting her with his open hand. He insisted that the blow was not a form of retaliation but only self-defense. "You know, she's never been to the hospital," he said defensively. "My wife is one hundred and thirty pounds, five four. You know, I'm very capable of putting her in the hospital."

Many of her problems, he indicated, stemmed from her drinking: "She drinks every day. *Every day.* She claims she needs it to go to sleep. I don't know. She's a drunk." She was so out of control, he said, that on Father's Day, when his two children from a previous marriage had made a long trip to visit him, he decided to send them back home rather than subject them to her violent rages. "My kids don't need to deal with this," he said. "And, so they made a six-hour trip for nothing."

Shortly thereafter, he said, she whacked him with a large metal candleholder, and he resolved he had had enough for a while. He left for several days, and when he returned, she had obtained a restraining order against him. Some time thereafter, as part of the separation agreement, he was told to pay $800 a month in maintenance, which left him with $600 a month for himself. So he moved back into his parents' basement. "I'm just trying to get through this thing," he said, "get away from her, get my life back together."

A third Gilliland client worried about his emotionally unstable wife, whom he was in the process of divorcing, harming his two-and-a-half-year-old daughter. At one point, annoyed at their daughter's behavior, the woman had threatened to kill her, he said. "I called child protection. They told me that unless your wife is holding a knife or some threatening object to your daughter's throat or whatever, those words don't mean nothing." One day, he said, his wife became so angry that she threw a coin-filled bank at him and broke his toe. On another occasion, he claimed, his wife grabbed his daughter without provocation and "dragged her into the bedroom and spanked her butt a couple of hard times. My daughter was screaming, and I went in there and asked her what was going on. . . . She pushed me out of the way, and she told me, 'I don't tell you how to father; don't tell me how to mother!'"

He attributed her instability to her upbringing: "My wife came from a broken home. Her parents both were alcoholics.

She had never had a relationship with her dad. . . . It was a horrid situation for her." As a consequence, he suspected, she had not fully matured. "When she would have a problem, I'd have to handle it. When someone hurt her, I would have to deal with it. When it came time to make any decision, I had to make it."

When she found him wanting, he said, "she would torment me. She would cut me off sexually." And she had grown increasingly abusive. Men had nowhere to go when confronted with such situations, he said. "We have no options, except to go to jail or walk the streets. And without support, whether it be counseling or [being] able to sit down and vent, things escalate and get out of hand.

"I guess my reason for being here," he said, "is that I have no faith in the system. I feel that men are extremely prejudiced against." He had arrived at the shelter earlier, he noted, and had found the door locked. He contrasted that to what he imagined a woman's shelter must be like. A distressed wife, he conjectured, "would be all comforted and nurtured and taken care of and advised."

Over the next few weeks, I spoke with several other men who claimed to have been physically abused by women. One had stayed at Gilliland's shelter. The rest had no connection with Gilliland, but their stories were strikingly similar. Many of the relationships were afflicted with drug or alcohol abuse or haunted by demons from troubled childhoods. Invariably, the interviewees spoke of frustration with authorities who were unwilling to take them seriously and of their difficulty finding anyone who understood their distress.

After writing about battered men in *Newsweek,* I received a call from a banker in Ohio who said he needed someone he could talk to. His wife, he said, often belted him, and he had no idea how to handle it. "I've been lying to people, lying to my kids, telling them, 'Mommy's having a bad day.' All these years, I've been taking the crap because that's what we're supposed to do." The fat lip she had given him, he said, was not nearly as serious as what the blow had done to him emotionally. "We're supposed to pretend it doesn't happen." He had "called all around and there's no place to go," he said. "The world doesn't get it. . . . Of all the things I've experienced in my life, I was most emotionally unequipped for this. The courts won't help. Lawyers will laugh at you. Domestic abuse people don't want to talk to you."

I gave him the number of a men's center, and he thanked me and said, in a tone more suggestive of a question than a statement, "I can't be the only one who's going through this."

Another man, who claimed his wife had clawed and beat him until blood streamed from his face, said he could get no one to listen to his story. The police refused to take a report from him; the judge treated him with disdain; and his own attorney, who was helping him fight for custody of his children, told him, "You've got to buck up, be a man. Let's not bring up this domestic violence stuff. Otherwise, the judge will think you're a wimp."

An ex-marine who had stayed with Gilliland had a three-year-old daughter by his crack-abusing girlfriend. Whenever the couple argued, he said, she became violent. "It's been going on ever since my baby's been in the world, three years." And though he was a big man, well over six feet tall, he would take the blows. "I don't believe a man's supposed to be hitting a woman," he said. "I don't know anything about that. The only way I know to fight is to protect my life."

She would scratch, kick, and bite him and throw things at him, and when the police arrived, they would arrest him, despite the fact, as he put it, that "I'd be scratched up and looking like I'd been fighting a lion." Once, following his arrest, he had to go for abuse counseling. "That's like sending a rape victim to counseling for a rapist," he railed. "It was degrading and it was humiliating."

His mate had not always been involved with crack, he said, but she had always had a violent temper. The crack, he was convinced, had made matters infinitely worse. Once, for instance, when he refused to give her the car keys so she could go for drugs, she had socked him. "She hit me straight in the eye. I said, 'I ought to knock you out.'" Instead, he called the police. "They didn't even file a report," he said. When he called a women's abuse center, he said, "they went to laughing."

His first wife, he said, had also been a drug abuser. "I went through that with [her]. . . . I just didn't want to do that again." Finally, he fled to the shelter and stayed for several weeks. It gave him a chance, he said, "to ease my mind."

Like the other "battered" men, he was convinced that the deck was stacked against him. "The court system is just not designed to help men," he said. "How is it going to be equal when you're stereotyping one group, one gender? You're saying all men are guilty just because we're men. And that ain't right."

A New Yorker, who was also involved with a drug abuser, had an equally grisly story to tell. At various times, he said, his wife had cut him, hit him on the head with a telephone, threatened him with a hammer, and thrown scalding water on him. Once, he said, she had put a gun—which turned out to be a replica—to his head. After she threatened him with a knife, he called the police and they were both arrested.

The abuse and the subsequent battle for custody of their son filled him with such rage that he contemplated hiring a crack addict to take revenge on his wife. Instead, he sought out a therapist who helped him to control his anger. His experience taught him a bitter lesson about the volatility of the combination of drugs and fury. He was convinced that with the rise in alcoholism and drug abuse among women, battering of husbands would increase.

"I could have beat my wife. I could have killed her," he said; but his Catholicism had stopped him. Nonetheless, he confessed, he now understood how some men could get to the point where they ended up killing their women.

A onetime drug abuser whose former wife also used drugs recounted an even more harrowing story. When he told his wife he was going to leave, he said, she slapped their young daughter so hard that the toddler went flying into the air. "She said, 'That's what's going to happen if you go and leave me, you know.' I flipped out and I slapped her. And who gets thrown in jail? Me. Yeah, I slapped her for that," he ranted unrepentantly.

Without doubt, some battered men's tales are either lies, distortions, or exaggerations. In early 1995, for instance, police in Suffolk County, New York, took a 911 emergency call from a man claiming he had been slapped around by his estranged wife. A police officer arrived and was given an audiotape of the encounter. On the tape were the sounds of an argument and of the man screaming, "Don't hit me! Don't hit me!" Later, the man's wife produced a videotape of the same meeting. She said she had taped it because she feared violence from her husband. Her tape showed that the shouting occurred not in response to any attack from her but as she was leaving. The police concluded that the man was trying to perpetrate a fraud and charged him with filing a false report.

Such bizarre incidents notwithstanding, I am persuaded that the so-called battered man phenomenon is real. I am also convinced that in many cases the abuse is mutual and that few of the most victimized participants are engaged in anything remotely approaching a normal, healthy relationship. Drugs and liquor clearly contributed to the horrible situations in which many of the men I talked to found themselves, as had a scarcity of coping and relationship skills. Some men apparently considered violent behavior a perfectly appropriate response to frustration unless it reached a point where somebody was seriously harmed. Others had gotten tangled up with women who had obvious emotional or psychological problems—women whose conduct was so extreme that warning bells should have sounded long before the battering began.

How typical, I wondered, were those men's relationships? How many men are being battered? And how (if at all) do these men's problems mirror those of battered women? Several studies promised to shed some light on the issue, but those studies, I discovered, must be interpreted with care. The reality is that no one truly knows the answers. No one has faultless numbers; everyone has, at best, estimates or conjecture. And some of the more shocking statistics are about as solid as quicksand.

Three of the most widely quoted studies of marital violence were designed by researchers connected with the Family Research Laboratory at the University of New Hampshire and were conducted in 1975, 1985, and 1992. The 1975 survey is generally considered to be a seminal inquiry into violence in the nation's families. For that survey, researchers conducted 2,143 in-depth in-person interviews with persons over age eighteen who were living with a member of the opposite sex.

They interviewed either the woman (in 1,183 cases) or the man (in 960), but not both. Instead of asking a person whether she or he had been battered, interviewers asked about specific actions engaged in as a result of anger or disagreement. They then grouped the responses using a classification system called Conflict Tactics Scales. Such actions as pushing, grabbing, shoving, and slapping were deemed to be "minor" assaults. Behavior more likely to cause an injury—kicking, biting, threatening with weapons—was classified as "severe."

The scholars discovered that, by their definitions, roughly 9 percent of families admitted to having engaged in "minor" marital violence over the past year; over 4 percent had seen severe violence. What most surprised them was that husbands and wives seemed to be violent at more or less the same rate.

Of those households reporting assaults, 49 percent claimed that both partners had transgressed, 27 percent said that only the husbands had been violent, and 24 percent said that only the wife had acted. In addition, husbands more frequently accused wives of "severe" assaults than wives accused husbands of such actions. Despite the seeming equivalence of behaviors, husbands clearly did much more damage. Straus and company pointed out, for instance, that women were about seven times as likely as their husbands to end up injured.

The 1985 survey of 6,002 households was conducted by telephone. It produced the encouraging news that household violence seemed to be decreasing, especially violence perpetrated by husbands. Whereas the respondents said that nearly 4 percent of husbands committed severe assaults in 1975, they said that 3 percent engaged in such behavior in 1985. Severe assaults by wives showed a less dramatic drop. A close look at the statistics for husbands revealed that the entire decrease could be accounted for by men reporting fewer aggressive acts. In other words, although husbands claimed they were less abusive, wives disagreed with that assessment.

Critics dismissed the finding as insignificant, attributing it not to a change in male behavior but to a change in men's willingness to admit to wife beating. They also questioned whether a telephone survey was the best way to get to the truth.

The 1992 study addressed both objections. The survey of 1,970 subjects was conducted in person. Not only did it confirm that seriously violent incidents by husbands had decreased since 1975, but it came up with an even lower number than the 1985 survey. Fewer than 2 percent of households were alleging severe acts of aggression by husbands. The gender difference in reporting continued. This time, however, husbands admitted perpetrating slightly more violent acts, while wives said their husbands had committed significantly fewer. Severe assaults by wives took an even more curious turn.

Whereas husbands said they had decreased from 1985, wives claimed they had increased. Both husbands and wives said "minor" aggression by women had gone up. More than 4 percent of the women were reported to be engaging in serious violence, compared to roughly 2 percent of the men.

The investigators at the University of New Hampshire were uncertain what to make of the fact that violence by husbands seemed to be going down even as assaults by women against men seemed to be on the rise. Nonetheless, they saw a silver lining—at least in the drop in reported serious assaults against women. In a paper presented in July 1994 at the World Congress of Sociology, Murray Straus and Glenda Kaufman Kantor suggested that the decrease seemed to reflect, in part, the success of steps taken "to condemn and punish assaults by husbands and to provide alternatives for battered women such as restraining orders and shelters." They were disturbed, however, that minor assaults by husbands remained essentially unchanged.

Straus and Kantor were also dismayed at the findings that showed that the rate of assaults by women was not going down. "Part of the reason may be that there has been no effort to condemn assaults by wives parallel to the effort to condemn assaults by husbands," they wrote. They also wondered whether the increase in "minor" assaults by women was perhaps "an unintended consequence of the increasing equality of men and women. Unfortunately, equality means that women tend to acquire not only more male economic characteristics and power, but also less desirable male characteristics."

In another academic paper, presented at the American Sociological Association meeting in August 1994, Straus and Kantor, along with David Moore of the Gallup Organization, examined a number of surveys that looked at American attitudes toward marital violence. They discovered that though approval for husbands slapping wives had steadily gone down, approval for wives slapping husbands had not. Whereas only 10 percent of Americans in 1994 thought a husband might be justified in slapping his wife, nearly one-fourth of Americans thought a wife might be justified in hitting her man.

Straus and his colleagues interpreted the results of the poll to be a reflection of the general public's "tendency to assume that a wife slapping a husband is primarily a symbolic act which is physically harmless." And they deemed America's complacency toward women's violence to be hazardous—not just to men, but to women.

"When women engage in what they may think is a harmless and justified minor assault such as slapping, they are inadvertently helping to reinforce the implicit cultural norm which makes the marriage license a hitting license," they wrote. Their point, of course, was that if a woman slaps a man, sometimes the man will hit back, and things could quickly get out of hand.

Straus had made the same argument in "Physical Assaults by Wives: A Major Social Problem," an essay published in a 1993 book titled *Current Controversies on Family Violence.* "To end 'wife beating,'" he wrote, "it is essential for women also to end the seemingly 'harmless' pattern of slapping, kicking, or throwing things at male partners who persist in some outrageous behavior and 'won't listen to reason.'" He took pains to point out that he was not blaming the victim. "Recognizing that assaults by wives are one of the many causes of wife beating does not justify such assaults. It is the responsibility of husbands as well as wives to refrain from physical attacks (including retaliation), at home as elsewhere, no matter what the provocation."

In polite and scholarly language, Straus laid out the case for why he believed that assaults on husbands are a serious problem. Genteel as the language was, no one could miss the point that one of the world's leading researchers on domestic violence was explaining a critical change in his perspective.

Initially, Straus and virtually every other expert in the field had believed that battered husbands were not deserving of much empathy. They had assumed not only that husbands were generally not harmed, but that violence by women was primarily defensive in nature. In other words, they thought that women were either defending themselves against attack or the threat of one or they were retaliating against an assault that had taken place.

Now, Straus was saying he was no longer so sure. He had reviewed every significant study he could find—more than thirty in all—that looked at violence between husbands and wives. The only ones he had excluded were those of "self-selected" populations—groups that, because they were not scientifically chosen, could be expected to yield biased or skewed results. In every one of those studies, observed Straus, he had found that women assaulted men in about the same proportion as men assaulted women.

That fact was considered so controversial by some researchers, he noted, that data on assaults by women in several studies were "intentionally suppressed." One such study, conducted by the Kentucky Commission on Women, showed, Straus wrote, that "among the violent couples, 38% were attacks by women on men who, as reported by the women themselves, had not attacked them." The result, he revealed, had come to light only because independent researchers got the computer tapes and ran the numbers. Such intentional concealing of information "brings out a troublesome question of scientific ethics," Straus noted. In the courteous language of the academy, he had accused some of his fellow researchers of a cardinal sin. And he was far from through.

As Straus methodically worked his way through the data, he dropped another bombshell. "In previous work I have explained the high rates of attack on spouses by wives as largely a response to or defense against assaults by the partner. However, new evidence raises questions about that interpretation."

In the world of family abuse researchers, Straus's repositioning was tantamount to Ronald Reagan saying he no longer believed in supply-side economics. Straus had taken aim at an argument long used to explain away violence by women, and he was saying that at least some women's attacks on men seemed to be unwarranted.

Straus's "new evidence" was derived from several sources. One was homicide research examining cases in which women killed their husbands or lovers. In one inquiry that studied twenty-four incidents, the investigators discovered that several seemed not to fit their preconceptions. In only ten of the instances had the man initiated physical violence, and in only five was the killing a response to prior abuse or threats. Other studies, they noted, found that women who killed their husbands tended to be impulsive and violent. A majority, in one inquiry, had prior arrest records.

Straus also reviewed studies of women in battered women's shelters. Most such studies, he said, did not ask about assaults by women and, when they did, generally asked only about self-defense; but the few that tried to assess the magnitude of assaults by females, he noted, found the rate to be high. One survey, he reported, found that in the year before they came to the shelters, 50 percent of the women said they had assaulted their partners. "These assaults could all have been in self-defense," he wrote, "but Giles-Sims' case study data suggest that this is not likely."

"A large-scale Canadian study found that women struck the first blow as often as men," he wrote. "However, as in the case of the Kentucky survey mentioned earlier, the authors have not published the findings, perhaps because they are not 'politically correct.'"

Straus also reexamined his own 1985 data and recomputed instances of assault for the previous year looking just at women's responses. Since Straus included only the figures reported by women, he presumed the analysis would be free of any bias caused by underreporting by men. He found that according to the women in violent relationships, the husband was the sole perpetrator in just over one-fourth of the cases, the wife alone was violent in one-fourth, and both were physically abusive in nearly half the cases. Since the wife was the sole perpetrator in one-fourth of the cases, he argued, "a minimum estimate of violence by wives that is *not* self-defense . . . is 25%." When he looked just at "severe" assaults, the news was not much better. The wife alone was the guilty party 30 percent of the time, the husband acted alone in 35 percent of the incidents, and they assaulted each other in the remaining 35 percent. The news was even worse when he looked at who struck the first blow. Fifty-three percent of the times, he concluded, the wife struck first.

"It is painful to have to recognize the high rate of domestic assaults by women," wrote Straus, who dutifully noted that "the statistics are likely to be misused by misogynists and apologists for male violence." Nonetheless, he suggested, it is time to face the best available facts and to urge women to stop their violence just as society had appealed to men to stop beating their wives.

Despite his analysis demonstrating that women are more violent than he had previously thought, Straus provided scant support for those who believe that men and women are equally at risk from domestic violence. Instead, he strongly underscored the point that, in violent households, wives are more endangered than husbands. When he adjusted the figures to account for damage done, he concluded that women were more than six times as likely as men to be injured. He also concluded, however, that the injury statistics were much lower than the numbers generally disseminated to the public. In a given year, he calculated that a wife stood one chance in nearly 300 of being injured by her husband and that a husband's odds were one in nearly 1,700 of being seriously hurt by his wife. In hard numbers that meant that some 188,000 battered women were injured by their husbands, and roughly 30,000 men were injured by their wives.

In anticipation of the inevitable attacks from ideologues, Straus included a lengthy response to feminist faultfinding with the new information his research was turning up. He dismissed much of the criticism as uninformed, error-prone, and misguided, commenting that his critics were not providing "feminist critiques, but justifications of violence by women in the guise of feminism."

Straus noted with evident regret that some of his former champions now reviled him. His earlier work, he observed, was widely cited by feminist thinkers. But he had "published 'politically incorrect' data on violence by women and was therefore excommunicated from feminist ranks." Nonetheless, he proclaimed, "I remain one of the faithful, and have never accepted the excommunication."

Reducing the estimate of wife beating and increasing the estimate of husband battering is not an inconsequential act, and Straus was well aware of the possible political ramifications. He noted that without adjusting for injury, his survey had produced statistics showing that 6 million women were assaulted each year by their male partners and that 1.8 million were severely assaulted. "The figure of 1.8 million seriously assaulted women each year has been used in many legislative hearings and countless feminist publications to indicate the prevalence of the problem," he wrote. "If that estimate had to be replaced by 188,000, it would understate the extent of the problem and could handicap efforts to educate the public and secure funding." Straus tried to devise a way out of the dilemma, arguing that both the higher and lower estimates were right "because they highlight different aspects of the problem."

As Straus suggests, statistics on marital violence are not merely the concern of academic researchers. They have fundamentally shaped the national debate on how widespread spouse abuse is and how it should be dealt with. They have also contributed to the widespread perception that women in abusive relationships are almost always passive victims. In certain instances, that perception is manifestly correct, but a more accurate portrait of battered mates would be more complex, indicating that women sometimes are assailants, sometimes victims, and often both. It would show, in short, that some women in violent households simultaneously accept and perpetrate violence—presumably because they either feel they deserve to be hit, feel that hitting will get them what they want, or are wrongly convinced that their own violence has no harmful consequences.

Straus's numbers, of course, are not the only ones that have figured in the public dialogue. A host of agencies and nonprofit groups have attempted to define the problem. The National Institute of Mental Health, for instance, put out a fact sheet that reports that an estimated 2 million to 4 million women "will be seriously assaulted by domestic partners every year." The fact sheet further asserts that one in six couples will experience "physical aggression." Although NIMH notes that women are as likely to engage in aggression as men, it explains the finding with the remark that "much of the female to male aggression is defensive or retaliatory."

The National Crime Victimization Survey, put out by the Justice Department, is another source of statistics on battered spouses. Its figures on marital violence are considerably lower than those obtained from several other sources. In a critique of that survey, Straus commented that since both partners were present at the interviews, the participants were naturally reluctant to report abuse. In addition, because the survey was designed to gather information on crimes, many of the acts considered assaults by other surveys were not reported. Straus also speculated that since men are less likely to consider a woman's attack on them an illegal act, they are not inclined to report such assaults.

The 1994 National Crime Victimization Report, for instance, found that between 1987 and 1991, women were violently victimized by husbands, lovers, and exes at an annual rate of 5.4 per thousand, whereas men were reportedly victimized at a rate of .5 per thousand. These rates amount to 572,000 assaulted women and just under 49,000 assaulted men a year.

To arrive at the more impressive figure of 2.6 million abused women, advocacy groups add up the numbers for violent victimization from all sources. The bulk of such assaults, however, as reported earlier, are not perpetrated by spouses. Nor, if the broader grouping is used, are women more likely to be victimized than men. Indeed, the comparable figure for assaults on men is just short of 4 million.

Another widely cited source of statistics is the *Journal of the American Medical Association*. In August 1990, *JAMA* reported, "Several studies have shown that 22% to 35% of women who visit emergency rooms are there for symptoms related to ongoing abuse, either because of an injury or as a manifestation of the stress of living in an abusive relationship."

The source of the 22 percent figure is apparently an article published in *JAMA* by Wendy Goldberg and Michael Tomlanovich in June 1984, based on their study of one hospital's emergency room. The investigators did not, in fact, ascertain whether people were in the emergency rooms for symptoms related to ongoing abuse. They simply handed out a survey that asked whether "at some time my boyfriend/husband or girlfriend/wife has pushed me around, hit me, kicked me, or hurt me."

Some 22 percent of the respondents, of whom 56 percent were females and 44 percent were males, answered yes to that question. When the researchers specifically asked about the incidence of abuse, 16 percent said they were no longer being abused, and 31 percent said they had been hurt only once. Fifty-three percent of those who were mistreated did report repeated abusive episodes. Even if we assume that all patients reporting repeated abuse had come to the emergency room because of ongoing abuse (as opposed to coming for some other reason and then mentioning the abuse), the proportion the *JAMA* article should have cited is not 22 percent but 11 percent. The writer of the 1990 article should also have made clear that the percentage referred not just to women, but to women and men. There is no indication in the study, however, that all the patients included in that 11 percent were at the hospital specifically because of spousal abuse. Nor, given the population surveyed, which was overwhelmingly poor and urban, with an unemployment rate of 60 percent, is it clear that the results can be generalized to emergency room patients in more affluent areas or nonurban areas.

In the 1990 issue that reported the 22-percent figure, *JAMA* provided "conservative estimates" of the amount of marital violence in the nation. It cited a 1981 national survey of married couples by Straus and reported that "26% of respondents admitted there had been violence in the previous year. Up to 60% had experienced violence at some time, with either wives beating husbands or husbands beating wives."

When I had my research assistant call Straus to corroborate the figures, Straus pointed out that he had not even conducted a survey in 1981, but that the statistics apparently were a misrepresentation of his 1975 findings. He had never, he said, reported that 26 percent of the respondents admitted to violence. The real proportion was 16 percent. Nor, he added, had he said that 60 percent of the wives and husbands had, at some point, beat their spouses. He had said that 30 percent admitted to some form of violence, most of it shoving and slapping, as opposed to "beating," and, since not everyone in a survey tells the truth, he had guessed that the actual figure might be twice as high.

In the blizzard of statistics, people rarely ask what the numbers truly mean. The problem is that the numbers often do not mean what they seem to. And therein lies the making of a paradox. For though the surveys no doubt underestimate the incidence of aggression, the most frequently quoted ones probably overstate the incidence of spousal beating. The reason for underreporting is obvious. Many people prefer to conceal or perhaps to forget about the violent behavior the surveys are attempting to measure. Even if the question is asked using nonjudgmental, neutral language, people are likely to clam up. When critics say that the surveys are hampered by underreporting, they are undoubtedly correct. When they argue that the real battery rate is therefore much higher than the survey numbers say, they may very well be wrong. The flaw is not with the reasoning but with the terms. The surveys the activists rely on are generally not measuring just battery, but a much broader range of behaviors.

When people are told that 6 million or (as the *JAMA* writer seems to believe) upward of 60 million spouses are annually beating their mates, they generally aren't informed that the numbers reflect acts ranging from pushing and grabbing to assault with a deadly weapon. The reporters and advocates who disseminate the statistics may not understand it themselves. Or they may believe that explaining the numbers would undermine the impression they are striving to create—of millions upon millions of Americans battering their spouses. Battering implies pounding a victim repeatedly and in a rough-enough manner to cause injury. That is not usually an accurate description of pushing or grabbing—which is not to say that pushing and grabbing are inoffensive acts. They can be hurtful, even dangerous, especially when done in anger, and they should neither be condoned nor tolerated. But lumping such behavior with criminal assault and calling it all battery can create a host of problems, including undermining the credibility of those who are circulating the statistics.

The practice may also undermine efforts to educate the public about the true nature of family violence. By calling all aggressive spousal behavior "battery" or "beating," advocates risk minimizing the seriousness of less vicious assaults. In other words, since most people don't think of a slap or a push as battering, and since it is battering that is being condemned, they may conclude that it is perfectly all right to slap or grab their mates. By the same token, since much of the dialogue on marital violence focuses on battery and "beating," it's not surprising that so many people reject the notion that women are assaulting men. For the kind of assault that most of the women are committing simply doesn't rise to the level of husband *beating*.

When I asked Straus what he thought of the statistics being tossed around, he wryly replied, "People who want to show women are evil cite just the fact that the assault rate is about the same. People who want to show women are angels and men are devils point to the fact that women are injured about seven times more."

When I asked him how large he thought the problem of spousal abuse was, he observed that defensible numbers "don't make magazine or newspaper stories that anyone would want to read." Numbers ranging as high as 6 million, he noted, would not necessarily be wrong. "It depends on your criteria," he said. "But when you look at what we could consider wife beating," he added, "the number is more likely [to be] two hundred thousand." At times, he said, he became frustrated with the exaggeration of the statistics and had to remind himself "that this is what advocacy groups are about."

Murder statistics are perhaps the one set of figures that are not easily subject to distortion and manipulation. For that reason alone they are worth examining. In 1992, out of a total of 22,549 murders, 1,296, less than 6 percent, were of spouses, according to the FBI; an additional 759 were of boyfriends or girlfriends. Spouses and lovers, in others words, accounted for just over 9 percent of those who were murdered. Women were more than twice as likely to be murdered by their mates as were men. Overall, men were more than three-and-a-half times as likely to be killed as women—mostly by other men. The 1993 numbers were in the same ballpark, with spouses and lovers again making up 9 percent of those who were killed.

One encouraging development illuminated by the data is that family violence seems to be diminishing, even as overall violence goes up. In 1965, murders within families accounted for 31 percent of the total homicides; in 1992, the figure was 12 percent. In 1976, the first year for which the FBI compiled statistics on murders of spouses and lovers, such murders accounted for 15 percent of the total. Of the 2,529 spouses and lovers who were killed, 55 percent were men and 45 percent were women. FBI statisticians could not explain why the ratio of husbands to wives killed had gone down in recent years.

In a special analysis published with its 1993 crime statistics, FBI experts noted, "While murder has traditionally been called a crime of passion resulting from romantic triangles and lovers' quarrels, recent statistics reveal that these types of murders have been declining as a percentage of total homicides. . . . The fastest growing murder circumstance is juvenile gang killings."

In 1994, the Bureau of Justice Statistics tried to get beyond the bare-bones information in the FBI data by taking a close look at 8,000 homicides disposed of in 1988 in a representative sample of large urban areas. The bureau found that 16 percent of the murders were committed by family members of the victims, and in four in ten of those cases, the killer was a spouse.

Among whites, six out of ten of the victims were women. Among blacks, the ratio was more even: 47 percent of the victims were men and 53 percent were women. Although men were more likely than women to kill their spouses, women were more likely to kill their children. Fifty-five percent of the parents who killed their offspring were female, and women were almost twice as likely to kill a son as a daughter.

Alcohol played a major role in spousal killings: More than half the assailants had been drinking. The effect of other drugs was not assessed. Unemployment and mental illness were important factors as well: One-fourth of the killers were unemployed, 12 percent had a history of mental illness, and more than half had criminal records.

Gender weighed heavily in the resolution of the cases. Women were less likely than men to stand trial, less likely to be convicted if they were tried, less likely to be convicted of serious charges, and less likely to spend time in jail if they were convicted. Prosecutors rejected or diverted from the justice system 9 percent of the cases with a female assailant, compared to 4.5 percent with a male assailant. Of the men charged with killing their wives, 86.6 percent were convicted of something, compared to 69.8 of the women accused of killing their husbands.

Of those spouses convicted of the most serious charges— murder or nonnegligent manslaughter—16 percent of the women got straight probation, compared to 1.6 percent of the men. And women who were convicted of any crime in connection with murder were three times more likely to get probation than were men. If they did serve time, women served much less time: an average of 6 years compared to 16.5 for men. In short, at every point in the criminal justice system, women who were accused of murder were treated much more leniently than were men.

What the gender differences mean is not clear. The Bureau of Justice Statistics provided no gender breakdown on prior criminal records or on the circumstances surrounding the murders, so it is impossible to say whether the characteristics of female murderers in the study matched those of the male murderers. The research cited by Straus indicates that the characteristics are likely to be similar. But even if they are not, there is no obvious reason why men and women who are charged with precisely the same crime should be treated so differently at every step in the process. One reason may be that judges, juries, and prosecutors, just like the general public, have a hard time taking female violence seriously. That attitude has ramifications not only for murder defendants, but for anyone who cares about coming to grips with family violence.

One reason that society may have a hard time accepting the possibility of violence from women is that we tend to think of females as dainty, fragile creatures. How could such a small, delicate woman, many people are liable to say, hurt a big, strong man? And, up to a point, that attitude may make a certain amount of sense.

Obviously, most men are stronger than most women. Clearly, men, in most cases, exact more damage than do women when the two sexes collide. But to conclude, for that reason, that female violence should be sanctioned or excused is a bit like saying that it's OK for motorcyclists to run into cars, since cars do more damage than motorcycles. If the objective is to protect women, such an approach will not accomplish it. And if the objective is to keep spouses from violently colliding in the first place, focusing on one is surely not enough.

Moreover, if violently abusive adults are, in large measure, the end product of improper upbringing, focusing only on violent men will not prevent the next generation of wife beaters from developing. In other words, if mothers and fathers who beat or otherwise abuse their children are planting seeds that eventually turn those children into violent adults, the problem of spousal abuse becomes inseparable from that of child abuse. To take the long view is to recognize that preventing girls from turning into battered women means creating a healthy environment in the households in which those girls grow up—as well as in the households of the boys who, unless taught to reject violence, may turn out to be battered or battering men.

When Ronnie Weiss, of the National Coalition Against Domestic Violence, angrily rejects the "tacit assumption that the same women who have been addressing the issue of violence against women should solve this one [of battered men] too," her point is well taken. It would be criminal to use the issue of battered men to excuse the battering of women or to minimize the anguish, stress, and suffering that battered women go through.

The fact is that the phenomena of battered women and battered men are linked. To work effectively on one also implies that the other be honestly addressed. It demands as well that one recognize that wife beating takes place within the context of a larger problem—the problem of family violence; and family violence is neither perpetrated nor sustained solely by members of one sex. Whatever one believes about the specific numbers generated by the various spousal assault surveys, the evidence that violence is frequently mutual is too persuasive to ignore. By focusing primarily on one aspect of the problem—men who abuse women—Americans have clearly made some important strides. At the least, an increasing number of men have learned the lesson that it is wrong, regardless of the provocation, to brutalize their spouses. Important as that lesson is—and it is extremely important—mastering it should not obscure a larger truth: that violence against people, whatever their gender or kinship, is reprehensible. Many people of both sexes still need help to realize that savage behavior is neither a justifiable means to get one's way, an indication of profound love, or a suitable means of punishment.

If we cling to the belief that women are incapable of violence or that only the men in abusive relationships are troubled, we will not see the problem for what it is, and we will find it difficult to give many of the men and women who are ensnared in violent unions the kind of help they need. By the same token, if we persist in swallowing the claim that spouse batterers are ubiquitous, that millions of normal, seemingly well-adjusted American men routinely go home and whack their wives, we may ultimately lose sight of the fact that brutally beating one's spouse is aberrant and pathological behavior, not a gender characteristic, and that batterers are not troops in some grand war between the sexes, but sick and tormented human beings.

Chapter 11

IN PURSUIT OF
GENDER RECONCILIATION

In late September 1994, I spent most of a weekend attending a seminar held in Arlington, Virginia, billed as "the first international gender reconciliation conference." During their time together, the two hundred or so participants engaged in such "soul work" as putting red dots on their "wounds," dancing with their "shadows"—meaning the part of themselves "hidden away, cast away, or denied"—and learning to create "safe space" in which to express their feelings. They also heard some of America's premier gender guides spread a message of peace and goodwill between the sexes.

Susan Jeffers, a psychologist and author of *Feel the Fear and Do It Anyway*, observed, "It's not because of men that women are trapped in their unwanted roles. And it's not because of women that men are trapped in unwanted roles. What's it because of? It's because of our anxiety about separating ourselves from the known."

The comfortable roles of tradition, she suggested, had trapped men and women alike, leaving members of both sexes feeling powerless and victimized. But instead of taking control of their lives, many had simply become combative; they had embraced their anger "like a mantle of virtue." Instead of summoning the strength to walk out of destructive relationships, some were wallowing in self-righteous dependence. "Anger, coming from a place of the victim, is not virtuous. It's very disempowering," she declared.

Jeffers addressed the concept of "psychological numbing." "Whenever there is a war, any kind of a war, people become numb," she said. "You can drop the bomb on an enemy. It's very hard to drop a bomb on women, children and men. So people like dropping bombs from planes. They don't see a person. Well, I suggest that women and men who are angry are also psychologically numb." She exhorted the group to reject such sentiments as those imprinted on a button reading, The Best Man Is a Dead Man, and to embrace self-empowerment and cooperation.

Warren Farrell, author of *The Myth of Male Power,* also lectured on empowerment, but from a masculine perspective. The women's movement of the past twenty-five years, he said, had created new options for women, but "no one has really yet freed men from our stereotype sex roles." To make matters worse, since men do not talk about their problems but women do, it seems that only women are being exploited. That perception, he suggested, had led to a deep anger against men—even though men are just as abused as women.

Imagine what would happen, Farrell said, if President Clinton were to announce that because over a million men had died in American wars, until an equivalent number of women were killed, "we will be ... registering only women for the draft." Such a statement, he noted, would torpedo any chances Clinton might have for reelection. Clinton "would intuitively know that ... women are smart enough to not want that part of equality as an obligation. [They] would want the possibility, the option of registering for the draft. But when President Clinton signs a reinstatement of draft legislation so that only men can register for the draft do we complain ... ? *No.* Did men protest it? *No.* Did legislators protest it? Did judges protest it? Did traditionalists protest it? Nobody protested. Did Rush Limbaugh protest it? No matter which side of the political or economic or social or psychological spectrum you were on, it was just taken as a given—that when registering for death occurred men will not only do it, but we will call it power.

"Now think about that for a moment. Imagine that . . . President Clinton said, 'As of tomorrow, I will be introducing legislation in which only Jews will have to register for the draft.' Feel the feeling that we would feel. What is the political leader that would come most readily to mind? Hitler? Suppose he said, 'I made a mistake.' Then he said, 'What I meant to say was, *As of tomorrow, we will be drafting only blacks.*'" If the president "were to single out only blacks or only Jews or only women to register for the draft—based on their characteristics at birth as a woman, as a Jew, as a black—women, Jews and blacks would all be intelligent enough to call that singling out of them genocide. . . . It's only one group of people who have learned to call that which any other group would call genocide or racism or sexism . . . power. That . . . is a group of people called males."

He went on for nearly an hour, tossing out one example of role reversal after another. What if women always had to risk the rejection of asking for dates? What if they were expected to pay for men's company? What if teenage girls were told that they had to go out on football fields and risk spinal cord injuries and broken noses to get love and attention from boys? Instead of addressing such questions and allowing men and women to break gender barriers together, "we have rather politicized this experience . . . and said that men have all the power and that women don't." In fact, he said, neither sex has power; both have "roles."

Instead of seeing men as the oppressors, said Farrell, "we have the opportunity to have women and men love each other in a way that we never had a chance to love each other before." For the first time ever, he added, "we have the opportunity to select a different type of man into our lives: a man who is able to listen to women. A man who is able to be connected to children. A man who is able ... to be in touch with his musical loving side."

During her conference wrap-up, Riki Robbins Jones, cofounder of the Network for Empowering Women, provided some insight into the defensive tone of some of the speakers. Men and women, she said, need to get beyond the present "conversation," which could be summed up with: "Whatever is happening is all your fault. If only we didn't have men, if only we didn't have the patriarchy, the world would be fine." Men, in other words, are being unfairly pilloried, and she and the other conference organizers were out to remedy that situation.

I left the "gender-reconciliation" conference unconvinced that the organizers had come up with a program for the masses. I couldn't imagine that the number of people eager to "dance with their shadows" was large. Anyone who was not already a veteran of group therapy would probably find the whole experience more than a little hokey—not to mention embarrassing. I was persuaded, however, that the gender-reconciliation people were sincerely addressing an important issue: the effect of the modern-day war between the sexes on male-female relations and on the struggle for equality.

Several months earlier, in response to Lance Morrow's essay, "Are Men Really that Awful?" in *Time,* Jones wrote a letter published in the magazine asserting, "It's true that today's women are putting down, bashing and hating men. But this is only half the story. The emerging 'pro-men' women's movement, spearheaded by the Network for Empowering Women (NEW instead of NOW), is the antidote to the radical feminists' poison. . . . Cheer up, beleaguered men—there is hope!"

The letter ran alongside one from Warren Farrell stating that he was "well aware that up to now this has been not a battle between the sexes but a war in which just one side has shown up: only women have contributed their tone to the monologue on gender. Men must contribute their views before we are ready for a synthesis." Gloria Steinem offered the contrary view, denouncing the Morrow article for its "hostility, distortion and defensiveness that usually stem from guilt." Steinem also defended feminist antipornography crusaders Andrea Dworkin and Catharine MacKinnon. "If, as Morrow claims, some feminists are nervously edging away from them, it is likely to be because essays like his try to isolate them," she wrote.

How real is the war that the conference and many of the letter writers were trying to address? Dworkin seems to believe it is horrifyingly real. In her book, *Letters from a War Zone,* published in 1993, Dworkin delivers what amounts to a pep talk to the troops:

"Sisters: I don't know who you are, or how many, but I will tell you what happened to us. We were brave and we were fools; some of us collaborated; I don't know the outcome. It is late 1986 now, and we are losing. The war is men against women; the country is the United States. Here, a woman is beaten every eighteen seconds: by her husband or the man she lives with, not by a psychotic stranger in an alley." Dworkin then hurls out a series of assertions and statistics in support of her thesis. "Women-beating, the intimate kind, is the most commonly committed violent crime in the country, according to the FBI, not feminists. A woman is raped every three minutes, nearly half the rapes committed by someone the woman knows. Forty-four percent of the adult women in the United States have been raped at least once. Forty-one percent (in some studies seventy-one percent) of all rapes are committed by two or more men. . . . There are an estimated 16000 new cases of father-daughter incest each year; and in the current generation of children, thirty-eight percent of girls are sexually molested. Here, now, less than eight percent of women have not had some form of unwanted sex (from assault to obscene harassment) forced on them.

"We keep calling this war normal life," Dworkin declared. When she focuses on pornography, Dworkin gets even more apocalyptic. "The bad news is that we are in trouble. There is much violence against us, pornography-inspired. They make us, our bodies, pornography in their magazines, and tell the normal men to get us good." Dworkin ends the essay with an appeal for support, a defiant promise of resistance, and a swipe at her less enlightened sisters: "Our most privileged sisters prefer not to take sides. It's a nasty fight, all right. Feminism is dying here because so many woman who say they are feminists are collaborators or cowards."

If the situation were as bad as Dworkin portrays it, her call to arms might well be justified. If 90-plus percent of women were forced to have sex and more than a third of men were molesting their daughters and if woman-beating was, in fact, the "most commonly committed violent crime in the country," women might be well advised either to flee from or shoot men on sight. Dworkin, however, is a remarkably unreliable reporter.

The FBI does not claim that wife beating is America's most commonly committed violent crime. Assault, as Dworkin suggests, is indeed the most commonly committed violent crime. People are assaulted nearly twice as frequently as they are robbed and nearly fifty times as often as they are murdered, according to the FBI. Most of those assaults do not appear to be wife beatings, however. The majority are assaults against men.

The U.S. Department of Justice's National Crime Victimization Survey estimates that men are more than twice as likely to be victims of aggravated assault and more than 40 percent more likely to suffer simple assault than are women. "Except for rape, females were significantly less likely than males to experience all forms of violent crime during 1987–91," states the Justice Department's summation of its survey. The report does conclude (as discussed in Chapter 10) that wives are much more likely than husbands to be victimized by their spouses, but that is a much more limited claim than Dworkin apparently is interested in making.

Accurate rape statistics, as noted previously, are impossible to come by. Dworkin gives her readers a choice of several. All are shocking. They are also much higher than any well-regarded surveys (including those of the Justice Department) have come up with. The National Health and Social Life Survey attempted to measure the number of American women who had been coerced into having sex. Not wanting to limit responses by using a restrictive or legal definition of rape or sexual abuse, the University of Chicago-based NHSLS researchers asked the respondents whether they had been forced "to do anything sexually" they did not wish to do. Just under 22 percent of the female respondents said they had been forced into sexual activities. That is a disturbingly high proportion, and one that points to a serious problem—especially if one believes that it may reflect some underreporting. But it depicts a very different picture from the one Dworkin painted.

The NHSLS statistics on child abuse are also alarming, but—no surprise—they are much lower than Dworkin's. Roughly 17 percent of the women and 12 percent of the men said they had been "touched" sexually by an older person before the age of puberty. The NHSLS investigators also discovered that girls were touched more often by males, but that boys were touched more often by females. They concluded, in short, that childhood sexual molestation is not just a crime of men against girls, but of teenagers and adults against children. "The risk to girls is greatest from adult men, followed by adolescent men. The risk to boys is greatest from adolescent women, followed by adolescent and then older men," they reported.

Effectively combating the real problem of child sexual abuse, as opposed to Dworkin's simplistic version of the problem, would mean dealing with more than just the behavior of supposedly "normal" men. It would require dealing with the behavior of people—male *and* female—who are deviant or irresponsible. That truth does not advance the gender war, so Dworkin apparently prefers not to acknowledge it. Reality, in this case, simply does not fit within her political frame.

Several years ago, in testimony before the congressional body investigating the Iran-Contra debacle, Fawn Hall, Oliver North's former secretary, defended her shredding and altering of National Security Council documents by asserting, "Sometimes you have to go above the written law." Her point was that actions that are considered wrong, and, in this case, perhaps illegal, are proper if they are done in the service of a higher principle. A similar attitude apparently prevails among certain self-styled gender warriors, who have about as much respect for facts as Hall did for the law. In such hands, statistics are not tools to get at the truth, but grenades valued for their explosive effect. Any harm caused by their misuse is supposedly done in the service of a greater good.

The shocking statistics do, in fact, serve an important purpose. They garner support from (and engender righteous indignation among) decent women and men who are astounded at the magnitude of the evil perpetrated against women. I don't doubt that the people who are disseminating the distorted statistics generally have the best intentions. Many, obviously, believe the data to be justified exaggerations. Some, knowing that virtually all statistics related to sexual abuse are nothing but educated guesses, doubtlessly figure that their dismal assumptions are as valid as anyone else's, and they proceed to generate numbers based on the most frightening scenarios. Others, with little idea of how the numbers were produced, accept them for (and put them forth as) the true facts that they are said to be.

These statistics end up fueling the perception that the war between the sexes (and certainly the "war" against women) is a great deal more vicious than it actually is. But given that many of the more appalling numbers tend to be grounded either in fantasy or in questionable assumptions, they don't reflect the experiences of most normal people—especially people who, left to their own devices, have little interest in making war on the other sex. Most people, in other words, don't live in a world where a majority of men beat their wives, molest their daughters, and rape any woman unfortunate enough to cross their path. Consequently, people have begun to question the numbers.

In a 1994 article in the *Washington Post*, journalist Armin A. Brott took a close look at the statistics on battered wives. "By now, everyone knows about Nicole Brown Simpson and Ronald Goldman, whose brutal murders have kept millions of Americans close to their television sets," he wrote. "But there's a third victim of these killings: the truth about the prevalence of domestic violence and female victimization—a truth maimed almost beyond recognition by the irresponsible use of statistics."

Brott noted that the National Coalition Against Domestic Violence estimated that a majority of married women (more than 27 million) will experience violence during their marriages and that more than one-third were repeatedly battered every year. "But when I asked Rita Smith, coordinator of the NCADV, where these figures came from," Brott related, "she conceded that they were only 'estimates.' From where? 'Based on what we hear out there.' Out where? In battered women's shelters and from other advocacy groups. Common sense suggests that asking women at a shelter whether they've been hit would be like asking patrons at McDonald's whether they ever eat fast food. Obviously such answers cannot be extrapolated to the country as a whole." Brott also cited a radio talk show host's estimate that the number of battered women, after adjusting for underreporting, added up to 60 million—a higher number, as Brott put it, than "all the women in America who are currently in relationships with a man." Brott apparently meant to say who are currently "living" with men; the number of married women plus unmarried women cohabiting with men adds up to just under 58 million.

Such "facts," Brott argued, "fuel the claims that there's an 'epidemic of domestic violence' and a 'war against women,' but might ultimately be counterproductive: If advocates had confined themselves to the truth, domestic violence might have continued to be regarded as a serious, yet curable, problem. But if 19 or 50 or even 100 percent of women are 'brutalized,' a much more sweeping conclusion is suggested: that all men are dangerous and that all women need to be protected."

Foreigners can find America's gender war and its angry rhetoric a bit difficult to comprehend. In early 1994, following Lorena Bobbitt's acquittal for cutting off her husband's penis, a Canadian publication, *Maclean's*, attempted to place the verdict in context. Writer Mary Nemeth quoted gender warriors from both sides. Men's advocates, she noted, thought the verdict to be a tragedy, and women's spokespersons felt it to be a triumph. Meanwhile, she reported, Lorena Bobbitt had issued a statement expressing hope that her case would help other battered women—moving Nemeth to observe:

"It was a noble sentiment. But despite all the attention the case has attracted, despite all the potent gender-political fury it has provoked, Lorena and John Bobbitt's story is essentially a personal tragedy. In his closing arguments, defence attorney Howard called the severing of John Bobbitt's penis 'probably one of the most bizarre acts that has happened in this country in a long, long time.' Only slightly more bizarre is the way the case has captured the American psyche."

In an interview published in *Le Nouvel Observateur*, the French feminist and author Elisabeth Badinter also commented on the strange fascination that Americans seemed to have with the Bobbitts. "One is entitled to wonder why Lorena Bobbitt was taken so seriously by American women," she said. "I find a women's severing her husband's penis because he abused her to be a pathological response to a pathological behavior. The acquittal of this guilty woman, with no mention whatsoever that castration is a crime, means that castration is valued as self-defense."

Badinter said she was stunned to read Barbara Ehrenreich's analysis of the case in *Time* magazine. "I admire the male body and prefer to find the penis attached to it rather than having to root around in vacant lots with Ziploc bag in hand," Ehrenreich wrote. "But I'm not willing to wait another decade or two for gender peace to prevail. And if a fellow insists on using his penis as a weapon, I say that, one way or another, he ought to be swiftly disarmed." Badinter saw Ehrenreich's sentiments as a natural reflection of the traces left in the American psyche by feminists "who associate sexual penetration with rape." To the French, she said, such an interaction "means, first and foremost, an exchange of pleasure."

She attributed much of the American attitude to the frustrations that American women had met in their struggle for equality: "Because American feminists feel they have been unable to change men, they are erecting more and more barriers between women and men. That's the case with both sexual harassment law and political correctness. Since they have obtained close to nothing, American feminists have imposed social, professional and intellectual relationships based on equality and on the protection of second-class citizens. But these measures are superficial sets of behavior which society has not assimilated. Artificially adopting such measures leads women to excesses that we can neither envision nor comprehend." French women, she said, "don't want separatism between the sexes. Separatism is neither what will make us happy nor what we're about." American activists, however, she believed, were crying for "distance" in male-female relation-ships and calling for "a morality close to that of the most totali-tarian puritanism."

Badinter, I suspect, overstates the intensity of the war in America, but the perception that American men and women are trying to flee each other is easy to understand. The overheated, belligerent rhetoric that so often accompanies discussions of gender issues not only fuels that perception but contributes to an atmosphere in which men and women are suspicious and fearful of each other—creating what the woman in Chapter 6 described as a "walking on eggshells kind of feeling."

Some of the rhetoric, though presented as serious analysis, is so absurd as to be comical. Psychologist June Stephenson, in a book titled *Men Are Not Cost-effective*, argues that men are a "criminal gender." For those who object to the characterization, she presents the following argument:

Most men, she concedes, would claim, "*I don't rape women, don't participate in drive-by shootings, don't murder, don't drive drunk, don't commit arson, don't bilk people out of their life savings, and I'm not responsible for men who do.*" Stephenson's response: "*Maybe you don't batter women, but your brothers do. Even if you don't commit serial or mass murder, your brothers do. Maybe you're not a drunk driver, but your brothers are. Your brothers are murder-ers, stock market manipulators, gang rapists, robbers, arsonists, lit-terers, polluters and child-abusers. Your brothers are killing us.*" (Emphasis in the original.)

Stephenson goes on to rage about the 4 million women who are battered annually, 1 million of whom she claims need hospitalization. She also kisses off the notion of battered men ("A battered *men's* shelter is not even imaginable") and rails against the Republican "Poppa" party. She concludes that nothing short of making "men pay for being men" will curtail men's vicious behavior. The form of payment she proposes is taxes—or, to be more precise, a state and federal income tax deduction limited to women. The proposal, she claims, "would provide gender equity in taxation for crime, and it would so antagonize men as to make them take a second look at their responsibility."

It is more likely to cause them to take a second look at nutty psychologists who believe that only men would be "antagonized" by a change in the tax code that would concern just about every woman who has a father, husband, or son.

The polarizing rhetoric that Stephenson spouts has little room for fine distinctions—such as those between a male humanitarian and a male mass murderer. The simple fact that men are men links them in an unholy brotherhood whose bonds are deemed to be stronger than those that link a man to his spouse or daughter. Buying into such rhetoric also often means buying into an assumption about the power relationship between the sexes—that men have it all and women have none—which seems little more than a prescription for female helplessness. As Elizabeth Heron noted in *Gender War, Gender Peace* (coauthored with Aaron Kipnis), "When we believe that men have all the power and cause all the problems, then we believe things will change only when men change."

If the men I talked to are at all typical, the average Joe is not convinced that he does have all the power or that being a man these days is necessarily easier than being a woman. Some of those who do concede that men have more power than women question whether it means that men are getting the better end of the deal.

Social theorist Victor Seidler spoke for many such men in *Rediscovering Masculinity* when he wrote, "If we live in a 'man's world,' it is not a world that has been built upon the needs and nourishment of men. Rather, it is a social world of power and subordination in which men have been forced to compete if they are to benefit from their inherited masculinity."

Los Angeles psychologist Carl Faber argues that men may

be protesting too much. "I understand that men feel that they're giving up a lot," he says. And what they are having to give up, in his eyes, are "the irrational advantages of privilege." Faber believes men should respond to their confusion not by denying their privileged status but by letting their sense of privilege be "scalded away by women's pain." That does not mean that men should "get castrated and crawl up on the cross with [women]," but that they should make a supreme effort to understand the agony that women go through.

Faber admits that few men are likely to adopt his radical prescription. Most are too busy struggling with their own problems to immerse themselves willingly in anyone else's misery. And even those who acknowledge that life is far from great for many women don't generally hold themselves totally responsible for that situation. Nor do they see much point in buying into a thesis that considers all men tyrants or worse. Such a view strikes many thinking people as no less idiotic than one that would make all men into sex toys or all women into shrews. Whatever the reality of the patriarchy once was, the relationship between men and women is changing. And confusing though the period of change may be, no interest is served by trying to force people into one-dimensional stereotypes, especially if those stereotypes are rooted in anger.

Happily, most Americans don't seem to be swallowing the notion that men and women must be in a constant state of war. That is not to say, however, that most men and women are serenely at peace. Some serious conflicts exist. The NHSLS finding, for instance, that 22 percent of the female respondents had been forced to do something sexual is unsettling and disturbing, all the more so in light of the corollary finding that less than 3 percent of the male respondents acknowledged that they had ever forced a woman sexually.

There are at least three different explanations for the wide disparity in responses. One is that a few depraved men are preying on a large number of women. The second is that many of the respondents are lying. The third is that both men and women are telling the truth as they perceive it, but that a huge misunderstanding exists between the sexes about what constitutes forced sex and about how consent is expressed. Since the majority of women reported their assailants to be their husbands or loved ones and few reported their assailants to be strangers, the researchers rejected the first explanation. They were also convinced (rightly or wrongly) that their interviewers managed to get most people to tell the truth. Most of the discrepancy, they concluded, must be a function of differing perceptions—especially since so few men, roughly 3 percent in the survey, admitted finding the prospect of forced sex at all appealing.

Perceptions could vary along any number of points. Was the sex forced if both parties were drunk? Or if no protest was offered? What about if a woman felt psychologically pressured but not in physical danger? What if consent was given, but grudgingly?—or purely out of a sense of duty? What if sex was agreed to but a specific act was not? Or what if men are defining forced "to do anything sexually" as only applying to intercourse, while women are interpreting the phrase much more broadly? Different people will obviously disagree about what specific behavior constitutes coercion, but the fact that so many men and women seem to interpret the same situation so differently underscores the existence of a huge communications problem.

It may be true, as the bachelor in Chapter 6 argued, that the vast majority of times men know if they are "not welcome," but many men clearly have no idea when their sexual attentions are not desired—at least some of the time. And many women seem totally unaware of how to get the message across. If the researchers are to be believed, that the problem is most acute between parties who are most intimate—that is, when husbands and loved ones are the aggressors.

Assuming, as I do, that men are not naturally brutes, the statistics constitute a powerful argument for men and women to become much better than we are at reading each other's signals. We need to cultivate more empathy for each other and to become better at saying what we mean and describing what we feel. We need, in short, to become much better at precisely those things that gender polarization and its warlike rhetoric make difficult. For whatever points male bashing like Stephenson's may score, it tends to provoke one of four reactions: dismissal, defensiveness, disdain, or anger—none of which is conducive to trust, cooperation, or mutual understanding. It may also make one wonder how good a psychologist she could be if her approach to getting men to change their behavior is to call them names and blame them for crimes they did not commit.

In 1994, Canadian journalist Brian Johnson set out to explore man's changing role in society. His conclusion, reported in *Maclean's*, was that men are confused and in crisis. "For a while, men found it fashionable to accommodate feminism, at least in spirit," he wrote. "In some cases, they happily acquiesced, becoming respectful colleagues, nurturing fathers and equal-opportunity lovers. But in the 1990s, as women continue to push for equality at the office and at home, men seem to be losing their patience. Yes, they still rule the working world. But it's not as much fun. And sensitivity can be such a chore. No matter how sensitive they are, they complain, they are still men—tarred by the broad brush of gender guilt. And the new etiquette around flirting, dating and seduction turns out to be about as complicated as constitutional law. . . . As men get in touch with their feelings, they are discovering that one of them is anger—at women."

Faber also believes that he has detected some anger in the air. "What I see . . . is a wave of what I call misogyny. . . . There's a backlash against the women's movement, a backlash against the bitter hate that's out there too against men. There's a backlash against it; and a reassertion of the old deal. And . . . this will never be a popular position, but to me the old deal is [Warren] Farrell and company saying, 'Fuck you; they're abusing us; stop all of this shit.'"

I'm far from convinced that any significant number of men are as angry as Johnson and Faber seem to assume. I do believe, however, that many men resent being assigned the villain's role in a script they find just as bewildering as women do.

Ron Henry, the lawyer who works with the Washington-based Men's Health Network, describes that sense of bewilderment as "a struggle in the minds of many men to figure out where they're going, what they're doing, what their place is, and how best to move ahead." "I think, though," Henry quickly adds, "that there's a great risk of that being overblown. A lot of the psychoanalysis we do of ourselves and of one another loses sight of the fact that most guys are functioning just fine. . . . Dad's doing his dad thing; and he's functioning with comfort and with ease and great enjoyment in his role as a father. And he's not staying awake at night worrying whether Doctor Spock is pleased or Robert Bly is pleased. He's just going on doing the best he can."

Yet even those men who are largely unfazed by the gender role transition are having to adjust to it. And part of that adjustment is dealing with questions that have a way of becoming more complicated than they initially seem. How should men go about sharing power with women? What does sexual equality mean? Women are struggling with such questions no less so than are men.

After running a losing race for the New York State Senate in 1990, Sherrye Henry was unable to get one question out of her mind: "Why hadn't more women voters supported my candidacy, and those of the other women challengers through the state?" Henry's curiosity eventually led her (with the support of the Women's Campaign Fund) to commission a national poll of women and a series of focus groups across the country.

By the time she published the results of her research in 1994, Henry had reached a sobering conclusion. "Two commonly held assumptions about women today are that they understand what equality is, and they are determined to achieve it. Once I held those assumptions, too, but now I know they are wrong, " she reported in her book, *The Deep Divide.*

Henry discovered, among other things, that even though nine out of ten women said equality was important to them, only one in four was very concerned about increasing it. Why, she asked, did only 25 percent of women care enough about equality to "work hard" to achieve it? "Because women aren't really sure what equality is. Because some who *think* they know—and are mistaken—don't want it. And because women believe they have *some* equality, somewhere, they therefore don't feel victimized by the system."

A mirror image of the ambivalence Henry identified among women exists among men—who recognize that the age of unchallenged male privilege is passing and who, to some extent, welcome its demise. These men recognize that the privilege has always come with a substantial burden and look forward to having someone with whom to share its stress-inducing load, but they are also fearful of losing their place in the world. So they are unsure whether to give up the privilege or how to let it go. And women are equally uncertain of whether they want to accept the burdens that men once kept for themselves. As Jeffers observed, there is "anxiety about separating ourselves from the known." And all the weird rhetoric notwithstanding, that anxiety is not limited to or solely caused by the members of one sex.

It therefore makes little sense to see the world as comprised merely of perpetrators and victims, of bad boys and good girls. Surely most of us are somewhat more sophisticated than we were when we learned that boys are made of "frogs and snails and puppy dogs' tails" and girls of "sugar and spice and all that's nice."

Not only are such beliefs juvenile and insulting to both males and females, but they are limiting in virtually every respect. At the least we need a broader perspective—one that acknowledges that some real problems and differences between the sexes still exist and that the political and economic battle for equality is far from won, but that recognizes as well that both genders are struggling against centuries of conditioning, that neither can be successful without the support of the other, and that it is not fair or even useful to pretend that either sex holds all the cards or suffers all the pain.

In the midst of writing this book, I took time to have brunch with a longtime friend—a woman who has an undergraduate degree from a prestigious university and two graduate degrees, including an MBA from one of America's top schools. She is successful in her chosen field and has a husband who is proud of her achievements. She also has a young son. When I asked whether she had ever wished for a girl, she confided that she had always hoped for a boy. "It seemed that boys just have an easier time of it," she said. Her own parents, she noted, had always favored her brother over the two girls. Yet strangely enough, she added, he seemed less settled and less content with his life than his sisters were with theirs.

Her comments moved me to reflect on the fact that so many people favor boys in so many ways. We fill them with ambitions and audacious expectations that we generally don't lavish on girls. Yet, even as we dote on them, we also imprison them in illusions. We tell them, though not necessarily directly, that they are smarter and more emotionally stable than girls, that they can handle power and pain so much better. And because these things are not true, boys learn early to pretend, to hide their inadequacies behind a mask. Or, worse, they take the premise of superiority as a fact and endeavor to personify it—even if it kills them, as it sometimes does.

In *Iron John*, Robert Bly asserts, "The grief in men has been increasing steadily since the start of the Industrial Revolution and the grief has reached a depth now that cannot be ignored." Clearly, Bly is on to something—though I suspect that what he senses is not so much grief as confusion and, in some cases, resentment. I also doubt that the complete cure lies in what Carl Faber calls "retribalising with other men." There is only so much interest in ancient myths, rituals, and connecting with the Wild Man. Even those who eagerly pursue initiation with men must eventually come to terms with women.

Shortly after the aforementioned brunch, I spoke with another successful professional woman who shared her frustration with the situation in her office. It seems that during lunch or other free periods, the men were in the habit of getting together in one male supervisor's office. His quarters became essentially a men's lounge. Women rarely entered the sanctum, and they didn't feel particularly welcome when they did. The male camaraderie affected working relationships; the men tended to support each other's efforts and often ignored the women. Things came to a head one day when the supervisor criticized a woman for not being a team player. How could she be expected to play on a team, she asked, that had never allowed her to be a member? The suddenly sheepish supervisor had no satisfactory answer.

Male groups already exist in abundance, and more are forming all the time, not only in the workplace, but in homes, meeting rooms, and therapists' offices. They have an obvious value—especially for those men who feel isolated, unsupported, and unfulfilled. All in all, I suspect, men are a bit less confused about how they ought to relate to one another than about how they ought to relate to women.

Being a man is probably no harder today than it has ever been, but it is a great deal more bewildering than in times past. And women (as Sherrye Henry suggests) are every bit as befuddled as are men.

The confounding questions can be posed facetiously: Do women want the dashing, debonair, sexist or the nurturing, egalitarian wimp? The hard-charging careerist? Or the modest Mr. Mom? The warrior? Or the pacifist?

Or they can be posed more seriously: How can we free men and women from roles that confine us both, without embracing an androgyny that no one seems to want? How do we revise the language of romance so that men and women will understand the same words and gestures to mean the same things? How can we free fathers to be more involved with their children? How can we ensure that even fatherless children are "fathered"? How can we demilitarize divorce so that children don't become collateral casualties? How do we get people to understand that violence is not a way of showing love? How can we keep workplaces from splitting into warring camps, with one set of rules for men and another set for women, as they warily regard each other across the chasm? Is it possible to teach men and women to stop blaming each other for not being everything they themselves are not?

Some answers, of course, are easier to come by than others. But the quest for solutions begins with acceptance of the fact that bewilderment is not necessarily a curse but often a natural condition. Communication—especially across genders—is fraught with potentials for misunderstandings and confusion, and the antidote lies neither in unrelenting hostility or in exasperated resignation, but in doing the hard work of getting beyond sexual stereotypes and striving to see people for who and what they are.

Unfortunately, there is no enchanted path to enlightenment. The best attitude may well be one that approaches the present era as an exciting transitional period in which, as Faber suggests, "nobody has any answers," but in which men and women are freer than at any time in American history to stretch the bounds of tradition. What that means, however, is that even within the context of their personal relationships, people can no longer assume what their roles will be, and therefore they will need to negotiate—in ways that may be uncomfortably explicit—if they are to find fulfillment.

As I write this, a newsletter sits on my desk from a San Anselmo, California-based group that calls itself the National Men's Resource Center. The publication lists a number of topics—addiction, aging, divorce, parenting, isolation, relationships, unemployment, and more—and concludes with this declaration: "These are men's issues and can't be ignored any longer!" One can quibble with whether they really are "men's" issues or simply human issues, but they clearly are important issues and beg some complicated questions about things that once seemed settled but no longer seem resolved.

The answers to these questions obviously do not lie in the woods or in ancient myths or in mind-numbing cant that masquerades as masculinist or feminist thought. They lie in us, if we are honest and wise enough to find them. And if we have the will to try.